The Business of Being Social

The Business of Being Social

Second edition

A practical guide to harnessing the power of Facebook, Twitter, LinkedIn, YouTube and other social media networks for all businesses

Michelle Carvill and
David Taylor

crimson

The Business of Being Social

This second edition first published in Great Britain in 2015 by Crimson Publishing Ltd
19-21C Charles Street
Bath BA1 1HX

First edition published by Crimson Publishing in 2013.

© Michelle Carvill and David Taylor, 2015

The rights of Michelle Carvill and David Taylor to be identified as the authors of this work have been asserted by them in accordance with the Copyright, Designs and Patents Act 1988.

Every possible effort has been made to ensure that the information contained in this book is accurate at the time of going to press, and the publishers and authors cannot accept responsibility for any errors or omissions, however caused. LinkedIn, Facebook, Twitter and YouTube have kindly granted permission for the use of their logos on the cover, but these organisations would like to clearly state that use of such logos does not constitute an endorsement of the book or its contents.

British Library Cataloguing in Publication Data
A catalogue record for this book is available from the British Library.

ISBN 978 1 78059 145 2

Typeset by IDSUK (DataConnection) Ltd
Printed and bound in Malta by Gutenberg Press Ltd

Praise for the first edition of *The Business of Being Social*

'As social media becomes ever more complex, and increases in importance for every business, it is essential to have access to reliable information. *The Business of Being Social* has proved to be an excellent reference tool for me, written as it is by two authors who are professionals in this field, and can speak from solid experience.'

***Shireen Smith, Founder, Azrights – Lawyers for a digital world; Best Selling Author of* Legally Branded.**

'Covered the first edition with my highlighter pen. Immensely practical.'

John Dodds, Global Director, Brand and Marketing Communications Excellence – Air Products

'*The Business of Being Social* has been a fantastic guide for us while building up our social media presence. Its easy to read style and practical advice on using the various social media platforms to their unique strengths makes it a great reference book which we turn to frequently. It also showed us how social media should be used with other channels to create an integrated marketing strategy.'

Nathan Bray, Co-founder and Chief Marketing Officer, ConnectMyApps

'A lot of business books are a good read and give great case studies, but then you wonder how to apply the learnings to your business. That's not the case with *The Business of Being Social* – there are great case studies and examples, which can be implemented in most businesses almost immediately. And it's a book which you can keep dipping in and out of – not one which you read and then gathers dust on the shelves. And, importantly, Michelle and David have worked in real businesses – they are not academics who have not been at the coal-face of business.'

Andrew Dobson, General Manager, We Are Tea

'Michelle and David have the unique ability to "make simple" social media. Their knowledge of business and the importance of having a social media strategy has been invaluable in helping me and my clients understand how social media can deliver results to the all important bottom line.'

Tricia Topping, Managing Director, Carlyle Consultants

Contents

Contents

About the authors

Michelle Carvill is a director of digital agency Carvill Creative, covering social media, web, online and digital marketing. She is also Marketing Director at MadeSimple Group. Over her 25-year career she has gained a wealth of experience in marketing, communications and the digital arena, and she regularly speaks, consults and trains in social media, digital and modern marketing.

David Taylor is a digital management consultant with almost 25 years' experience in journalism, media relations, public relations, marketing communications and social media consultancy. He works nationally and internationally with both small and large enterprises, helping them to make sense of the new digital landscape and adapt to meet the challenges posed by the always-on consumer.

Acknowledgements

Michelle gives thanks to: my wonderful family, Kevin, Josephine and Eliza, for love, patience and encouragement; Howard Graham and the great team at MadeSimple Group – without Business Training MadeSimple, David and I would never have trained together, and the idea to pen *The Business of Being Social* would never have been ignited; and last but certainly not least, the fabulously creative and supportive team at Carvill Creative. Oh – and of course, not to forget David – a great friend and a great laugh to work and write with – our Twitter DM conversations kept me on track and smiling.

David gives thanks to: my wife, Jenny, plus my two boys, Felix and Jack, for supporting me and keeping me sane; my parents for giving me years of unconditional love and assistance; Charles McLachlan for being a wonderful business adviser and teaching me about the corporate world; my many consultancy and training clients who have inspired me and encouraged me over the years; my friends for helping me to stay social; Howard Graham for giving me my first break in social media training; and of course Michelle, who has been a mentor, friend and co-trainer for the past four years.

Introduction

Welcome to the age of the social business, an age in which no organisation in the world can truly afford to ignore social media entirely. New generations of consumers and employees, as well as a profusion of communications channels, mean that companies must have some form of digital strategy to move their business forward and thrive.

From their emergence in the last decade, social networks have grown from being niche communications tools for early adopters and the young into fully fledged multimedia channels with billions of users worldwide.

So much has changed since the first edition of this book was published in May 2013. As authors, we have been staggered at how much we have had to alter. Therefore, instead of a simple update, we have ended up adding two completely new chapters, introducing social business and social advertising, and we have rewritten a high proportion of the original text, effectively making this second edition a completely new book.

Of the key social networks, Facebook has become a highly sophisticated targeted ad platform for companies, LinkedIn has evolved into a multi-faceted business-to-business communication tool and Twitter has also adopted a more corporate approach thanks to its initial public offering (IPO) in November 2013. Google+, while continuing to assist companies' search rankings, is increasingly being adopted as a specialist social network as well as an internal communications tool.

Then there's the steady growth in social messaging sites such as Whats-App, Snapchat, Keek and Kik. Used initially by the under-25s, these are now becoming a fixture of the media landscape.

Video, as we guessed, has also become huge. YouTube continues to dominate, but there are now other key channels used by millions such as Vine, Periscope and Instagram.

From teenagers using Snapchat or Vine to swap videos with their friends right up to chief executives of large corporations blogging on LinkedIn Pulse to grow their industry presence, or artisans using Facebook advertising to reach previously out-of-reach audiences, social media has now moved into the mainstream.

For those in business, it has also moved out of the marketing silo. As you will read in this book, there is barely an area of corporate life that hasn't been impacted upon by digital technology and the new 'sharing economy'.

The result is a massive shift in the ways in which all organisations, no matter what size they are, do business. From recruitment to public relations and from customer service to research and development, companies are having to find new ways to communicate, both externally and internally.

As authors and professional trainers, our job in *The Business of Being Social* is to guide you through this new digital and social landscape, explain how you can evolve to become a more social business and help you decide exactly how you are going to use these channels to your advantage.

Whether you are someone who is just starting out in business, the managing director of an SME or the marketing manager of an international law firm, or the CEO, commercial or marketing director of a large corporate, we give a step-by-step approach to maximising the effectiveness of social media channels.

Starting with basic business, marketing and communications principles, we move on to digital change management, becoming a social business, content creation and planning before diving in to explore all the key social media sites including Facebook, Twitter, LinkedIn, YouTube, Google+, Instagram, Pinterest, Snapchat, Ello and WhatsApp.

We believe that by taking this approach, *The Business of Being Social* will be of value to a wide range of people as it covers the many different subject areas affected by social networks.

So, whether you simply want to understand how to get the most use out of leveraging hashtags (#), want to explore how to use Facebook pay-per-click advertising or need ideas about creating a social media culture within your organisation, you will find plenty of practical tips and tactics within this book.

As with all our training courses, at the end of every chapter we include a Social Media Marketing Action Plan with some simple tips on what you should think about doing. There is also a glossary at the end of the book with explanations for many of the most commonly used terms in social media.

For many readers, this should be seen as only the start of the journey into making best use of social media. The trick now is to keep on learning, put into practice the information from this book and, most important, constantly stay abreast of new developments.

It's all about adopting a social or digital 'mindset' within your organisation. Doing nothing is no longer an option, as both the platforms and the audiences are constantly changing. Neither is hoping for the best and assuming that what has worked in the past will continue to do so ad infinitum. Remember Einstein's definition of insanity: *'Doing the same thing over and over again and expecting different results.'*

We recognise that the world of social media is constantly evolving, so we've created a blog to run alongside the book (www.thebusinessofbeingsocial.co.uk), as well as a Twitter account (@BOBSthebook).

That way we can keep you informed about what is happening in social media, plus we can make sure the book stays as up to date as possible – important in a world where even a week can be a long time!

Enjoy the book – and be sure to share your feedback and questions with us via Twitter on @michellecarvill and @savvysocialDT. After all – this book is all about being social.

Best wishes
Michelle Carvill and David Taylor

1 | Welcome to the social media age

What you will learn from this chapter:

- Background to the social networks
- How social media has become part of our daily lives
- Statistics showing that social media is a truly global phenomenon
- Importance of using social media to deliver on your business objectives
- How to integrate social media into your overall marketing plans
- Blending traditional and social media
- Instigating continuous conversations rather than start-stop campaigns

History can be seen as a series of events that, taken together, make the world what it is today. Technological innovation has played a major role in history, from the invention of the telephone in 1876, radio in 1896, television in 1925, the first computer in 1926 and the World Wide Web in 1990.

Here are four more dates that we could add to this list:

- 5 May 2003 – LinkedIn
- 4 February 2004 – Facebook
- 23 April 2005 – YouTube
- 21 March 2006 – Twitter.

Along with the launch of Apple's iPhone in 2007, which heralded the dawn of the smartphone age, these platforms have totally transformed the way in which we communicate, interact as a society and of course do business.

In the space of just one decade, these four key social networks, plus a vast number of other significant sites such as Google+, Pinterest and Instagram along with a profusion of social messaging sites such as WhatsApp and Snapchat, have achieved a level of global reach that other media could only dream about.

At the time of writing, Facebook now has over 1.4 billion active users, Twitter over 280 million, LinkedIn over 340 million, YouTube over 1 billion and Google+ around 300 million. These are staggering figures and they illustrate the enormous penetration that these sites have had in a comparatively short space of time. More details here: http://bit.ly/1nioAZC

A report by Statista shows that as of 2015, almost 2 billion people around the world will access social networks, rising to an estimated 2.44 billion by 2018. This rise is attributed to the emergence of the smartphone making it cheap and easy even for people living in the Third World and Emerging Nations to be connected.

Let's break these statistics down into the six current key social networks: Facebook, Twitter, LinkedIn, YouTube, Google+ and Instagram.

Facebook

Set up as a way for friends to communicate easily with each other online and with the mission statement, 'to give people the power to share and make the world more open and connected', Facebook has grown into a global media giant.

Floated on the Nasdaq in May 2012, the company now counts half of the global online population as users of the site.

Since then, Facebook has acquired companies they believe will secure their long term viability and deliver advertising revenues. These include Instagram (more on this later), WhatsApp and Oculus Rift, an augmented reality device.

At the tail end of 2014, Facebook founder and CEO Mark Zuckerberg set out his long terms plans for the site. These included growing its suite of products to 1 billion users, connecting everyone on the planet using these sites and offering more ways of reaching audiences using targeted advertising.

What's interesting is that in many parts of the Western world, particularly in urban areas with good 3G and 4G connectivity, many under 25s have stopped using the site and have turned to alternatives such as Facebook's own Instagram, Snapchat or WhatsApp. At the same time, the median age for those using the site is in the 35–50-year-old age group, ie: those with disposable incomes who are not put off by adverts.

Globally, over 70% of people who access Facebook do so from a mobile device – smartphone, tablet, games console or smart TV. This is up from 50% in 2012 and, according to eMarketer, this figure is expected to grow to 75% by 2018.

For more information on Facebook, check out eMarketer's recent report which looks at global trends around the site: www.adweek.com/

socialtimes/emarketer-1b-users-facebook-mobile-phones-monthly-2015/613205.

Twitter

Originally set up as a 'microblogging' site and a sort of more advanced way of texting one to many, Twitter limits users to just 140 characters in which to tell people what they are doing. The site's current mission statement is 'To instantly connect people everywhere to what's most important to them.'

Since its launch, Twitter has morphed into one of the most sophisticated marketing and communication tools that has ever existed. Indeed, the idea of real-time news was invented by Twitter. With hundreds of applications designed around accessing Twitter via PCs and mobile devices, this social network is now an important part of many organisations' marketing and communication strategies.

Over 280 million people around the world now access the site, the vast majority from their mobile devices. Not surprising as, unlike Facebook, Twitter was always designed primarily to be used on a phone.

In terms of countries, according to Northeastern University, the top 10 in terms of users are the USA, UK, Canada, Australia, Brazil, Germany, Netherlands, France, India and South Africa.

Interesting to note that China does not allow Twitter but Sina Weibo, their rough equivalent, has millions of users.

Since its flotation in November 2013, Twitter has followed Facebook's lead in offering advertising to large and small organisations and everything in between. It has also introduced more visual content such as photos and videos.

Now, the vast majority of journalists, publications, bloggers and other influencers are on this site, making it the premier 21st century public relations tool.

LinkedIn

Originally set up as a recruitment resource, LinkedIn can now be classed as the Facebook of the business world with over 340 million active users. In fact one in three professionals on the planet now has a profile on the site. (http://linkd.in/16LYU2o). Its mission statement reads, 'Connecting the world's professionals to make them more productive and successful.'

LinkedIn is increasingly being used not only as a brand-building device for individuals but also as the first port of call for researchers looking for information about companies. For many business to business (B2B) firms, and increasingly for consumer-facing organisations, their LinkedIn Company profile can often be as important as their website because it contains information about their most valuable commodity – their staff. Just as with Facebook, LinkedIn now offer a suite of products including Showcase Pages, targeted advertising, Pulse, multiple apps and Sales Navigator, to make the site invaluable for both individuals and brands.

As a result, many companies are now putting together bespoke Linked-In strategies which cover not only their marketing and sales teams but also the C-suite, human resources and PR departments along with their regular staff.

According to October 2014 figures produced by www.statista.com/ statistics/272783/linkedins-membership-worldwide-by-country) the top five countries in terms of members are:

USA	107 million
India	28 million
Brazil	19 million
UK	17 million
Canada	10 million.

And overall, LinkedIn had more than 80 million members in European countries.

In terms of usage, here are some interesting facts about the site:

- 17 minutes – average time a user spends on the site daily
- 35% users access the site daily
- There are 4 million business pages and 1.5 million groups
- More than one billion endorsements have been given
- 41% users access the site from a mobile device
- 39% of users pay for LinkedIn
- 25 million profiles are viewed every day.

Click here for more details – http://wersm.com/top-linkedin-facts-and-stats-infographic.

YouTube

With over 80% of all content viewed online now video based (according to Cisco Systems) – YouTube, Vimeo, Vine, Periscope, Snapchat, iPlayer, Instagram etc. – the importance of video in marketing and communications has grown immensely. At the heart of this is the Google-owned YouTube.

Originally set up as a video-sharing site, this is now the third most visited website and the second most used search engine in the world.

According to YouTube's own statistics (www.youtube.com/yt/press/en-GB/statistics.html) the site has over 1 billion users. Other useful information includes the following:

- The number of hours people are watching on YouTube each month is up 50% year on year
- 300 hours of video are uploaded to YouTube every minute
- Around 60% of a creator's views come from outside their home country
- YouTube is localised in 75 countries and available in 61 languages
- Half of YouTube views are on mobile devices
- Mobile revenue on YouTube is up over 100% year on year.

Combined with Google's other suite of products including Google+ (more on this below), Google AdWords and Google Analytics, YouTube can become an important part of any organisation's sales and lead generation strategy.

Google+

Launched in June 2011 (much later than the other social networks), Google+ now has around 300 million regular users globally.

Built around the traditional social networking platform of a central news feed, what differentiates Google+ is the option to segment your network of contacts into Circles. Through its Hangouts feature, the site also offers the option to include video conferencing among users, great for building advocacy, engaging with your customers and improving your internal communications. In addition, in the context of an overall search engine optimisation strategy, content posted on to Google+ has been shown to assist an organisation's ranking on Google.

In terms of users, according to Statista, the site is most popular in Indonesia, India, Vietnam, the Philippines and Thailand where almost 80% of the online population are on the site. This contrasts with just 39% in the UK and 47% in the US.

Instagram

Begun in 2010, this photo and video-sharing social network was only available initially for use on mobile devices via an app but can now be accessed through a PC. Acquired by Facebook in 2012, the site now boasts a global audience of over 300 million active users.

Instagram supports hashtags, allows people to create videos of 3–15 seconds and includes photo editing software.

Many under 25s who may have stopped using Facebook on a regular basis are very much active on this site. Indeed, unlike Facebook, the vast majority of users are under 34 making it an excellent tool to communicate with Millennials (more on this in Chapter 3).

According to Instagram's own statistics, 30 billion images have been shared, there have been 2.5 billion likes and an average of 70 million photos are uploaded to the site every day.

How social and mobile media have changed the way we communicate

People and organisations have always had to rely on third parties to be able to communicate with mass audiences.

Advertising in flyers, pamphlets, newspapers, magazines, radio and TV, or undertaking public relations campaigns, were the only realistic ways to get visibility for your brand.

The ability to get your voice heard changed with the advent of the internet, and more recently has become even easier via smartphones and mobile-enabled social networks. Very simply, there has been a complete democratisation in the way we communicate. With just a phone and internet access, anyone in the world can be a publisher, broadcaster or editor.

This shift is extremely powerful and has deep ramifications not just for marketing divisions but for all aspects of an organisation: sales, human resources, recruitment, public relations, brand protection, customer services and internal communications. It even has an impact on how organisations are structured.

Giving staff, clients, customers and stakeholders a voice can offer up a range of opportunities as well as major challenges for organisations. As a result, we are moving into the age of the social business, in which all aspects of an organisation are influenced by social media.

Indeed, since the end of 2013 more people have been using mobile devices than computers to go online, heralding the start of the true mobile internet age. So millions of people aren't just *ON* social networks, they are *IN* them. The truly connected consumer has moved away from 'linear conversations'.

Most businesses, at some point in their life, will have professed to want to *truly understand* customer needs. For decades marketers and customer service departments have run customer surveys or focus groups in an attempt to get closer to their customers and to enable them to fully understand their customers' needs.

Why? In a nutshell, because as markets have become more and more crowded, customer service has become an important differentiator, and the service delivery 'bar' has been well and truly raised, along with customer expectation. It's now commonplace for organisations' strategic plans to include the aim of being seen to be 'listening to the customer'.

Over the years, the mechanisms for researching and delivering customer needs have been vast and varied, and many organisations have created whole new departments to deal with the important subject.

Technology has enabled the systemisation of data and information capture, so that, as customers, we're continuously and seamlessly able to share our *views and needs* with the organisation. We can have a continuous conversation with the people we're buying products and services from. But it's not always a seamless process.

Now, through social networking platforms, not only are we able to share our views directly with the organisation, but at the same time we're also able to share our views with anyone else who is willing to listen too – our friends, family, strangers, other prospective purchasers – whoever.

'Social media' are exactly what the phrase implies:

- **Media:** content of some form. It could be promotional or advisory; it could be a blog about a new product release, or a story about a dreadful customer experience. It can be delivered in a range of formats – the written word, video, still images, etc.
- **Social:** rather than a linear, one-way conversation (e.g. a brand broadcasting a message to its audience) it's a shared or *networked conversation*. Others can share it, pass it on, comment and consume.

What this means for businesses is that a great or dreadful customer experience, product or promotion can be shared. It can go viral and reach untold numbers of people at the touch of a button.

A continuous conversation

The floodgates to conversation marketing are well and truly open . . . and that conversation is 'continuous'.

One-to-one, one-to-many, many-to-many conversations

We have moved away from a traditional 'linear' conversation, in which the brand or organisation would promote their message or offering and people could merely consume it if they liked it, or not consume it if they didn't; and perhaps they might talk offline about it.

Instead we now have a truly 'networked' conversation where people can not only talk with their peers, friends and strangers, but also have direct conversations with the brands and businesses too.

Businesses that pay lip service to wanting to understand customer needs can no longer hide behind the annual customer survey. Consumers are beginning to expect to have a direct dialogue with a brand, product or service.

For many large monolithic organisations that are embroiled in red tape and make policies and decisions by committee, getting to grips with such an open dialogue is terrifying.

To be a social business means implementing genuine and transparent channels of communication. It's about opening the doors to listen to what customers have to say and, where necessary, creating a new set of policies for safeguarding and managing 'social media marketing' responsibility.

There's no getting away from 'listening to what customers really want' because there are conversations happening all the time – conversations that businesses can choose to ignore (at their peril) or embrace.

We're now living in an 'always on' society

Given the pace at which social media are being embraced by all sectors of society, and the ever-growing pace of technology, businesses that don't 'get' social media are seriously likely to get left behind.

We love the statement regularly shared by strategist and author (and probably one of the people talking the most sense about social media strategy), Brian Solis (@briansolis): 'We are in the age of digital Darwinism – organisations need to adapt or die.'

If your business isn't part of the conversation, you might ask yourself, in the words of the Socialnomics team, 'The ROI [return on investment] of social media is, will your business still be around in five years?'

Think before you dive in

If we view social media platforms as far-reaching communication channels, that poses the question of *how* organisations can leverage these channels to deliver on business objectives.

The remit of any marketing strategy is to deliver on the business objectives – ultimately driving activity to achieve results that make sense for the business. Social media isn't something an organisation does just for the sake of doing social media (because everyone else is!) but, rather, something you do to deliver on specific business objectives, as part of a well-defined marketing strategy.

Business owners, CEOs and marketing directors should be thinking *how* they can plug social media into what they currently do to leverage what the platforms offer (and, remember, each platform offers something different) and ultimately deliver on their objectives.

However, probably as a result of eagerness to get onto the channels, businesses often dive into social media without any real thinking or planning. This simple model (adapted from the brilliant book by Olivier Blanchard, *Social Media ROI*) outlines in a very simple way a strategic approach to social media.

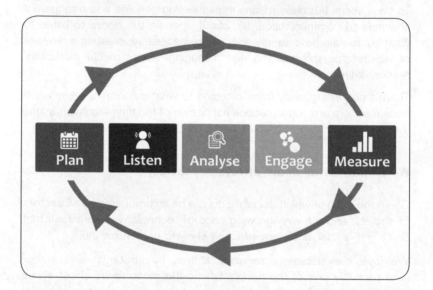

As marketing and communication strategists, we have spent a significant number of years developing communication and marketing strategies for clients. To date, we're both unaware of any other marketing or communication activity where a business would just dive in without any thinking, planning or research.

Far too often, both in our training and in our consulting lives, when we ask business people the question, 'So, you're on Twitter – what's the objective of the channel?', we're met with blank faces, or answers such as, 'Well, we saw that our competitors were on Twitter so we thought we'd better get on it too.'

In our view, these far-reaching communication channels require even more planning and thinking than usual, and that's because they are resource-hungry channels.

Hungry channels need regular feeding

There are few things more pointless than approaching a Twitter channel thinking, 'I'm not sure what we should be tweeting about.' This is where taking a strategic approach comes in. With any other strategic project, you would always embark on some research to learn about your audiences. The same goes for social audiences.

Understanding your business objectives and how each channel works is absolutely key – and there are seven (if not more) reasons why.

1. If you have clear objectives, you know what you are listening for.
2. You know who you are looking to target.
3. You can research effectively – which channels are your target audience using?
4. You can understand who is influential and who you need to be befriending.
5. You know who to listen to and what they are saying (and you should listen more than you talk – more on that later).
6. Having listened, you will have gained useful insights into consumer needs.
7. You're better able to direct and create useful content/conversations.

As Michael Gerber says in his book *The E-Myth*:

Those that aim for nothing, hit it with remarkable accuracy.

So you need to be sure that you have set specific objectives and that you have a very clear understanding of the purpose of your social media activity (and indeed any other activity).

It is easy to understand why businesses dive in and start engaging. The channels have deliberately been made very user friendly and therefore setting up accounts is simple. No expert or coding knowledge is required; all you need to do is fill out a few simple fields and you're away.

And, of course, all the social platforms are currently free to set up and create (though this may change down the line). You can set up a Facebook Page, a Google+ page, a Twitter, LinkedIn or YouTube account for absolutely no cost. Anyone can do it. And so they do.

However, the key is to ensure that you are (as the sub-title of this book describes) *harnessing the power* of these channels – optimising them to deliver on your specific objectives.

As any good craftsperson will tell you, you can make your life simpler if you use the right tools for the job. However, it is what you do with the tools that matters. Remember, anyone can use the tools, anyone can engage with them, so standing out from the crowd and ensuring you're using them effectively is absolutely vital. The channels are merely the platforms that enable mass communication. What you do with them is the all-important element.

When getting started, a basic plan is better than no plan. So, following the simple five step framework – Plan, Listen, Analyse, Engage, Measure – will at least enable you to follow a process of thinking, listening and learning – before you engage.

Blending social media into your marketing mix

Social media don't just impact on the promotional side of your business. Day to day they are leveraged in customer services, HR (human resources) and other areas of your business. Too often it is 'siloed' off into marketing instead of being wholly integrated by the organisation. Unsurprisingly then, a common objective of delegates on our training courses is, 'We want to learn how to integrate social media into our marketing activities.'

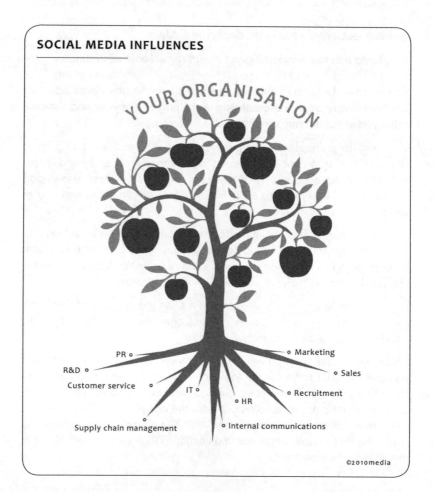

SOCIAL MEDIA INFLUENCES

YOUR ORGANISATION

PR ○
R&D ○
Customer service ○
IT ○
Supply chain management ○
HR ○
Internal communications ○
Marketing
Sales
Recruitment

©2010media

Traditional and social: a complementary model

As we have discussed, social media marketing is gathering momentum, but traditional marketing channels still very much have their place. Rather than seeing the two as different disciplines, you should view them as complementary to one another.

For example, television is a traditional vehicle, and methods of engaging and interacting with viewers of a television programme might involve an invitation to 'Call us on 0800 . . .' or 'Email us on . . .'. Now it's commonplace for television programmes (think ITV News, for example) to invite their audience to tweet them pictures or questions. Some of the rawest footage is filmed not by stealthy cameramen, but by Joe or Jane Public, who just happened to get a dramatic or newsworthy picture on their iPhone.

Similarly, hashtags (#) are promoted both at the beginning of and during programmes. The hashtag (which we'll discuss in more detail later) enables people to engage with a potentially global audience all talking about what's happening on the programme.

Watch most Channel 4 programmes and you'll see a # (hashtag) promoted at the start and end of the programme as well as during the ads breaks. Even Question Time displays live tweets via the Red Button. In fact some programmes even show tweets from viewers during the ads breaks. Each time these hashtags are aired, activity around them sets Twitter buzzing. This is a perfect example of a traditional channel blending social media to leverage activity and further amplify the message.

Reality TV shows such as The Voice, XFactor and Britain's Got Talent are some of the UK's most tweeted-about programmes. That's largely because as it airs the stars of the show, also go on to Twitter and engage with fans. This takes engaging the user to a whole new dimension. The user has to watch the programme *when it airs* (not later via on-demand TV such as iPlayer and TiVo) so that they can join the real-time conversation on Twitter. Remember, the programme isn't live, but the tweeting is.

So whatever your activity is – television show, trade press advertisement, station billboard, direct mail piece, email, newsletter or door drop – consider how you can plug in to social media to keep the conversation going.

Here's another business to business (B2B) example.

An event was held in Birmingham by the Federation of Small Businesses. Their 2015 National Conference had its own hashtag, #FSBconf, and, as you would expect from an organisation of 200,000 members, it served as a great way for people to network online as well as offline.

Acting as a virtual conversation, #FSBconf enabled people, both at the conference and in the wider world, to network before, during and after the event.

It was even possible to measure the effectiveness of the hashtag using a tool such as Tweetreach (www.tweetreach.com) (see Chapter 5).

Planning

Start with the end in mind

Our advice for people who are undertaking strategic planning is to start with the end in mind. When you know what you want to achieve, you can plan effectively.

From a practical perspective, typical questions you could ask at the planning stage include:

- What are our objectives? (The *why*.)
- What is the key message?
- Who are the target audience?
- What is market research telling us?
- What's our USP? (Unique selling proposition.)
- What are our competitors doing?
- What are our tactics? (The *what*.)
- Which channels are we going to use? (Direct mail, billboard, PR, etc.)
- Where shall we send people? (Website, call centre, landing page.)
- How do we incentivise them?
- Are we resourced effectively?
- What's our tone of voice?
- What are we going to share?
- What's our compelling content?
- What are our keywords? (More on the importance of these later.)

Planning template

Our advice at the planning stage is that when you get to the 'tactical' element of what you are actually going to do, you need to be thinking, 'How do we plug social media channels into these activities?'

And, of course, the social channels broaden the scope of your planning. We can look at some of the typical traditional questions in another way.

1 What is the goal?

This remains the dominant feature of planning. The goal (as mentioned before) is the *business goal* rather than the communications goal.

2 Who is the audience?

You can get really very 'human' in your exploration here. Go beyond the typical demographics that focus on age and location, and instead ask yourself: 'What does our audience look like? What's their frame of mind right now? Who are they influenced by?'

3 Where is the audience?

Which social channels are they using? Mostly one particular channel, or many different ones? Where are they based – UK or overseas? Therefore, what time does your social activity need to be scheduled for?

4 How do we connect in a compelling way?

This isn't just about getting people to Like your Facebook Page. It's more about thinking creatively about what you know about the audience and what is going to engage them – and, hopefully, compel them to share your content and posts and get others engaged.

5 How do we keep the conversation continuous?

It's not just about getting that Twitter follower or running a promotion to get people to Like your page. As we'll see in the Facebook chapter, the Like is the equivalent of getting someone to walk through the door. Getting them to linger, buy, and become advocates of what you do is another thing. So you need to be thinking about a longer-term engagement.

6 How do we get our audience to recommend us to others?

I'm sure you'll agree that 'word of mouth' is a powerful source of new business generation. With social media, the virality potential of the channels and the ease with which one person can share content with another (and another, and another . . .), thereby quickly amplifying the message, is something that should be thoroughly considered. It isn't even identified in many marketing plans we've seen!

Putting in the right effort at the start pays off

Most projects or initiatives tend to be front-loaded, and social media activity is no different. The analogy we make in our social media training or consulting sessions is that of a plane taking off.

The more thinking and planning you do with your social media platforms at the outset the more effective they will become.

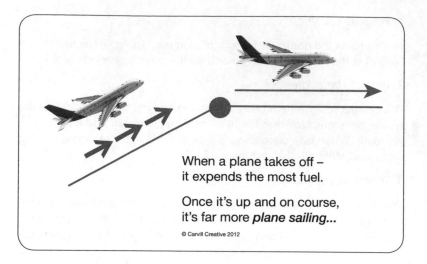

When a plane takes off –
it expends the most fuel.

Once it's up and on course,
it's far more *plane sailing...*

© Carvill Creative 2012

Taking a targeted approach

If you take some time to research who are the key influencers in your space and make the effort to target them, connect with them and nurture them so that they become advocates, that's likely to be far more productive than what we refer to as 'machine gun social media' – following anyone and everyone in the hope that someone will be right.

Building a network of influencers and an audience that is targeted to deliver on your business objectives will get you to the circle on the aeroplane diagram – and that's what we refer to as the 'sweet point' of your activity.

At that point, your social activity tends to create a life of its own. Of course you will have to remain focused on your objectives, but the nature of what you are creating and the engagement level of those you engage with will have created some advocates. Those advocates then start to share on your behalf and bring others to you. Effort becomes shared.

The way you get to that sweet point will be different for each platform and each business. Down the line someone will develop a formula that relates methodology and time to outcome. But for now, when these channels are still very fertile territory, we can't share with you any magic timescales or numbers – just a robust methodology that we've been utilising with our clients over the past few years.

Continuous conversations versus stop-start marketing

Many marketing campaigns have a kind of stop-start element to them. Think about your marketing plans or activity plans and you'll see that the schedule usually goes something like this.

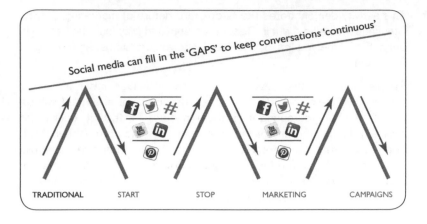

To demonstrate the point, let's say we're marketing an annual conference for all the members who read this book and sign up to the blog. The event – the Business of Being Social, or BOBS for short – is scheduled for September 2016 and all BOBS readers will be invited to attend. The planning will start months in advance, some teaser activity will take place a good few months before, and there will be a strong push of marketing activity approximately six to eight weeks before the event itself.

Let's take a look at how this could play out.

BOBS conference planning

Event date: 17 September 2016.

Some teaser introductory activity before the hard marketing push:

- **December 2015:** 'save the date' message included in Christmas cards sent to all members.
- **April, May, June:** members' newsletter includes a reminder of the Annual Conference and showcases where, when, what, who, etc.
- **1 June:** campaign starts in earnest. Three rounds of emails, sent two weeks apart, encourage users to book online and include various early bird promotions. This activity runs to mid-July.
- **Late July:** telesales activity commences, sweeping up those members who have been invited, haven't declined and haven't booked. This activity runs through to mid-August.
- **Mid- to late August:** last push campaign. Email and telesales to encourage as many members as possible to come to the event.

This activity demonstrates the 'stop-start' nature of marketing activity. Messages were sent out in December, April and May, and then some in June. Each time you 'push' out an activity, you are almost starting again from scratch.

People who read the 'save the date' cards in December but didn't respond will have forgotten all about the communication and will be reminded when you spring it on them in April. Those that receive the May email reminder may or may not remember the promotion in April. The hope is that the more you push a continuous message, the more 'share of mind' you are building. But there are gaps in the middle. As consumers, we are bombarded by messages all the time. Research shows that we don't remember all of them.

Continuous conversations

Now let's look at some ideas about how you can leverage your communications by including social media to make a conversation continuous.

Making the conversation continuous

- Let's say that in the December communication you showcase a hashtag for the event – #annualconfBOBS (there's more on demystifying hashtags in Chapter 5).
- You encourage all your members who are already on Twitter to follow the hashtag for updates and special insights – perhaps even incentivising engagement via competitions and offers.
- Further, to build awareness of the event and BOBS, you encourage your members to share the hashtag and you use the hashtag to promote the great content you're providing.
- Over on Facebook, you get each of the conference participants to come online to answer marketing, digital or social media questions. You promote these 'live chats' both on Twitter and in your newsletters to encourage as much traction as possible.
- The hashtag for the event is included on all marketing promotional materials, in your newsletters, on your email footers, on any press ads, etc., so that you can build awareness generally and continuously encourage people to join the conversation.
- If people advise that they can't make the event you can still encourage them to join the event 'virtually' by simply tuning into the event on the day via the #annualconfBOBS hashtag.
- After the event the hashtag lives on. People can still converse and share. Ideally, you should track all uses of the hashtag and save all those people who joined that hashtag conversation into a Twitter list (more on Twitter Lists in Chapter 5).

- Make sure that you 'followed' them and encouraged them to come and ask questions on your Facebook Page.
- Watch the conversations around the hashtag and the questions raised to provide you with a steer for creating new and relevant content.
- Address any positive or negative elements – listening to what people say will give you useful insights into what you could do better next time.
- Endeavour to continue the conversation. Having engaged people in relation to the event in the first year, try to keep that conversation going so that by year two you will have built some advocates.
- Continue to create content that is useful and purposeful, encourage people to download it from your website and capture their email addresses. This helps build your database in a targeted and purposeful way.

This simple example demonstrates the difference between a stilted, stop-start approach and one in which blending traditional and social media creates a more joined-up and continuous approach.

Traditional and social media are truly complementary. Indeed, where traditional is becoming more challenging, getting creative and blending in social elements can be a powerful tactic when applied effectively. The thinking and planning still has to be very 'joined up'.

Social media marketing action plan

- Plan effectively.
- Establish the purpose of each marketing channel.
- Decide on your tone of voice.
- Reflect the correct image for your brand.
- Take a targeted approach.
- Think about content. You are what you share – is what you're sharing doing you justice?
- Traditional versus social. A complementary model makes sense.

2| The many uses of social media

What you will learn from this chapter:

- Why it is important to have objectives for social media
- How flexible social media can be
- The different ways to use social media for business
- Understanding how to apply these to your organisation

As we've mentioned, many organisations dive into social media without any real thinking or planning. Time and time again in our training courses, we come across people who have been told to attend the training by their boss or manager so that they can 'do' Twitter or 'do' Facebook, yet without really understanding why.

Similarly, over the past six or seven years, thousands of organisations have jumped on the social media bandwagon either because their competitors have or because they've felt pressured into doing it to keep abreast of the times. They often have very little understanding about why they should be embarking on a social media strategy, which channels they should be employing or, indeed, how it will benefit them as an organisation.

We have set out the importance of having a targeted approach and meeting specific business objectives using social media. Now we need to look at the ways in which social media can be used to achieve these targets.

Unfortunately, people make assumptions about social media. It is often seen as a cure-all to solve all marketing problems or a quick fix to increase customer engagement. It can even be used as yet another 'outbound' or broadcast marketing tool to spam potential customers.

Clearly, like any other form of technology, social media can be used in a variety of different ways – for good or ill – and there will often be occasions when organisations use the same social networks for entirely different purposes.

But it is vital for any brand to have a properly delineated strategy for using social media so that it doesn't waste time or money just doing it for the sake of doing it. Without this in place, the results will be disappointing and could even be harmful.

In this chapter, we identify a number of key ways that organisations can use social networks to meet specific objectives. These vary from customer service to lead generation and from news distribution to product promotion. There are also case studies of how platforms have been successfully employed.

In Chapter 1 we saw how social media affects so much more than just marketing and sales. What will become even more evident in this chapter is how the many other areas of business including customer service, media relations, HR, R&D (research and development), IT, internal communications and CSR (corporate and social responsibility) are impacted by the digital channels.

Customer support and service

In the past, if a customer had an issue about a product or service, they would have had to write in or speak to a complaints department. In recent years, customers with queries or complaints have been diverted to a call centre in another country, often further infuriating them and providing inadequate levels of customer support.

With the advent of social networks, customers can now bypass these traditional channels and communicate directly with brands via sites like Facebook or Twitter. This can be done in two different ways, each of which requires a different approach. People either access a brand's online social media presence and start a conversation or they use their own social media profiles to voice their concerns or complaints.

Brands like Vodafone (www.facebook.com/vodafoneuk) and Delta Airlines (@deltaAssist) use social channels as specific customer service tools. Individual, and in many cases named, customer support staff answer queries online, and most of these queries remain in the public domain.

However, it is also possible to have private conversations on both Facebook and Twitter. On Twitter you need to get the person to follow you before you can send them a direct (i.e. private) message. On Facebook, you need to go to your Page's admin settings and tick the box that says Allow people to contact my Page privately by showing the Message button. This enables any Facebook user – whether or not they Like your Page – to send the Page a direct (private) message. You can then respond to this message. (Note: you cannot initiate private conversations with people from your Facebook Page.)

Clearly, if your objective is to use social media as a customer support channel, you need to ensure that you have the policies and procedures in place to do it properly. These may include:

- round-the-clock monitoring of your site(s). This means ensuring all appointed admins have the applicable app on their phones or tablets
- dedicated and correctly trained staff to deal with complaints
- close collaboration between internal departments to ensure a joined-up approach.

Here is a fascinating blog from eConsultancy which looks at how some of the top 20 retailers in the UK respond to requests on social media. https://econsultancy.com/blog/65478-how-20-top-uk-retailers-handle-social-customer-service.

What's clear is that all the applicable social media channels are now being closely watched by the large corporations. Brand reputation is clearly being managed very closely online, with the remit to capture any negativity before it spirals out of control and does real damage.

Let's hope that more and more businesses start to use Twitter not only as a means of responding to customer queries but also as a way to add real value. Most customers would much rather deal with a ten-minute response than a 90-minute one. That would speak volumes for a brand – the fact that they are actually giving a service to their customers, rather than simply aiming to preserve their brand reputation. The two are interlinked.

Being responsive in the social media arena can't just be about apologies – it's got to be about servicing the consumer. So take heed, any organisations who are simply jumping on the Twitter bandwagon. Don't just pay lip service and make your presence all about managing your brand reputation. Get a proper customer support service running via Twitter and really make your presence count!

Brand reputation management

While it is important that you manage your own online presence, it is also vital that you monitor what is being said about you elsewhere online, whether in blogs, forums or social media sites.

Just as media relations is about protecting your brand in the public domain, so social media relations is about ensuring that you are on top of what is being said about you online – and dealing with it in a profes-sional and well-thought-through manner. The consequences of remain-ing completely in the dark could be pretty serious.

Monitoring what is being said – both positive and negative – online about your brand can be done in a number of ways which we will touch on here but expand further in Chapter 11.

Regularly putting your organisation's name into the search bars of the key social networking sites or setting up alerts – simple ones via Google

Alert (www.google.com/alerts) and tools like www.socialmention.com – enables you to stay on top of any issues and react swiftly if you need to. (More tools are discussed in Chapter 11.)

Speed of response is the key. Traditionally, when a negative story broke in the press, organisations would be forewarned and would be able to prepare some form of response or rebuttal. Experienced press officers will know all about this. For large customer-facing organisations with a high-profile media presence, 'lines to take' have to be prepared, as do crisis communication strategies. In addition, press officers need to be on an on-call rota to ensure 24-hour media relations cover.

In the social media age, when people can post on Facebook pages or on Twitter 24 hours a day, the same discipline needs to be applied, but you have far less time to defend your brand. As a result, community managers working for organisations that serve the public out of normal office hours – restaurants, bars, clubs, transport companies, etc. – need to monitor sites 24/7 to ensure that damaging comments are dealt with and queries are not left unanswered.

Social story

This real-life story is a great example of how some top-end brands aren't monitoring what is being said about them online.

One of our friends bought a coat from a luxury retailer for £300, and was assured that she could return the coat within 14 days of purchase. When she got it home she discovered that her boyfriend had bought the exact same coat for her for Christmas. Touched by this unusual display of attentiveness from her partner, she took one of the coats back to the shop in order to get a refund.

Unfortunately, they explained, they didn't offer refunds unless the item was faulty and she was only entitled to a £300 gift voucher or exchange! (Apparently the small print on the receipt explained this.) Tearful and distressed, she had no choice but to leave the shop with the coat, in the hope that the retailer's higher powers would view this situation as very unfortunate and see it as an opportunity to offer a high standard of customer service out of good will.

They did completely the opposite. Not only did they refuse any form of refund, two emails she sent to two separate people were completely ignored. Being ignored not only annoyed her but also encouraged her to take further action – she decided to use social media to get her voice heard. She wrote a blog post about her experience, and naturally shared it via Twitter. She also searched for the brand in the hope that they too were on Twitter and that she could share the blog post with them and get some customer service joy via the channel.

When she did her search for the brand, she discovered not only that they didn't appear to have any formal presence on Twitter but also that many others in a similar situation to her were also talking about the brand, and about their grievances with the 'no refunds' policy.

She also found that tweeters were sharing tried and tested tips and tactics for how to damage the garments – because if the product was deemed faulty, a full refund was permissible.

At this point she decided to inform the brand of both her blog post and indeed all the comments she had found on Twitter. They had not been listening. They did not know this was going on.

Eventually the company did offer her a full refund and apologised for not responding promptly to her emails. They also thanked her for sharing what she had found on Twitter and promised to act on the negative comments. But how much damage had already been done to their brand, let alone their garments?

Interestingly, this brand is now firmly on Twitter, but not, in our view, doing a great job of it. They've taken to the channel in the only way they know how – 'broadcast media' – and are pushing traditional-style messaging into a conversational channel. (More on this in Chapter 5.)

Lead generation

Many organisations incorrectly see social media as purely a lead generation tool. While there are many ways in which it is possible to drive sales leads – using both organic and paid-for methods – very often, social may not be as effective as, say, using pay-per-click on Google, email or even a PR campaign.

Much will rest on the nature of your organisation, your target audience and how you use the social channels to engage with audiences.

One of the key things to bear in mind when using social networks for lead generation is that on social media, you rarely sell directly. This would be seen as spamming and is likely to alienate your fans or followers. Instead, you create the conditions under which people will naturally want to do business with you. Remember, these are social networks. Networking takes time and effort. You need to get people to know you, like you, trust you – and ultimately to do business with you.

To build this trust and awareness we come back to the need for engaging, targeted content as well as specific calls to action and decent landing or splash pages.

In order to respond to leads, you've also got to be 'listening' in rather than simply using the channels as 'broadcast' platforms. Far better to respond to a need than simply to push out irrelevant noise.

Facebook, Twitter and LinkedIn can all be used successfully to build databases, get email sign-ups, attract new audiences and encourage engagement with targeted customers. Here is an excellent article from Social Media Examiner that looks at some tips for lead generation. www.socialmediaexaminer.com/social-media-lead-generation

However, in order to make any campaign work, you need to have the following:

- interesting, engaging and relevant content on all your applicable channels and throughout the 'customer journey'. (More on this in chapters 3 & 4.)
- a thorough understanding of your target audience(s).
- a defined call to action
- online and offline channels that can easily capture the leads
- a joined-up approach within your marketing strategy to lead generation.

Lead conversion

Following on from lead generation and an area often overlooked by marketers is lead conversion. Today's consumers often 'touch' brands on many different channels – website, traditional, social networks, social messaging – and it may be a combination of these that helps people make buying decisions about your company, brand, product or service.

Particularly when you are trying to sell to Millennials (more on this in the next chapter), it is important to build your story across a number of channels. For example, many big brands will now start a conversation on TV or in magazines, move them onto a social channel (Facebook, Instagram, Twitter) then perhaps to a website and finally perhaps to a sign-up or booking engine.

As with lead generation, it is the quality of your content that will ultimately make the difference between a hot lead going cold and making a sale.

News distribution and public relations

The PR profession has been quick to understand how social media can be adapted to suit their needs. Which is just as well because now virtually every person of influence in the world has a presence on social media.

We're now very much in an age of 'influencer' rather than public relations, where companies need not only to reach out to journalists but increasingly to influential bloggers, thought leaders and industry professionals too.

For decades, PR professionals and company press offices have issued press releases first by post, then via email. Now sites like Twitter, Google+ and Tumblr (www.tumblr.com) are perfectly placed as channels to get your message across to a wide audience. In conjunction with a news feed, they are very quick, easy and cost-effective ways to broadcast information.

It's simply a case of filling in a short, catchy headline, then adding a shortened link to the URL where the press release is uploaded. The added advantage of issuing a release via Twitter is that it can be reposted several times, using slightly different wording, to ensure that the message resonates – something that might traditionally be regarded as overkill.

More and more press offices as well as PR agencies are now migrating their press release distribution onto social media, either directly or using third party companies such as Cision (http://us.cision.com/press-release-distribution/social-media-distribution.asp).

Air France (www.airfrance.info) has a dedicated bilingual Twitter feed (@AFNewsroom), which it uses as its news distribution channel, as distinct from its customer service Twitter account, @airfrancefr.

As well as a news distribution platform, social media are also a very effective way to communicate messages about brands.

Journalists are very active on social media, particularly on Twitter, and will be monitoring what is being distributed online, looking for stories and case studies.

Company press offices and PR agencies now have specific methods of reaching out to these journalists, many of whom rarely respond to emails or phone calls any more.

As we'll see in Chapter 5, there are a number of ways to engage with journalists, build your network and work on fostering online relationships.

Case study: Greater Manchester Police

A great example of using social media as a PR tool was by Greater Manchester Police. Faced with budget cuts approved by the government, the force wanted to communicate to politicians and the media how much work they were having to deal with. Police officers posted updates on three different Greater Manchester Police Twitter feeds (@gmp24_1, @gmp24_2, @gmp24_3) for 24 hours.

Over this period, the police Twitter page (@gmpolice), which was also being displayed on the force's website, was updated with 3,205 tweets.

This one-day campaign attracted extensive interest from both print and broadcast media, leading to a debate in the press, all of which served to raise the profile of the force and highlight the difficulties they would face if their budget was cut – and helping to raise brand awareness about Greater Manchester Police in the process.

Brand awareness and establishment

Social media is the perfect arena in which to build or establish a brand. Until the advent of social networking sites, the only way companies could communicate their brand online was via their website – a one-dimensional tool that might be little more than a corporate e-brochure. In addition, reaching a mass audience required huge advertising budgets which were beyond the reach of all but the largest corporations.

Now, in conjunction with their website (or, for a few consumer-facing businesses, without a website), organisations can create a much more varied and multi-dimensional presence.

As we've seen already in this chapter, it is important to move away from thinking about a single online presence for our company and start looking at multiple sites, as you can never be sure how you can reach the maximum possible audience. Using one or more of the social media channels

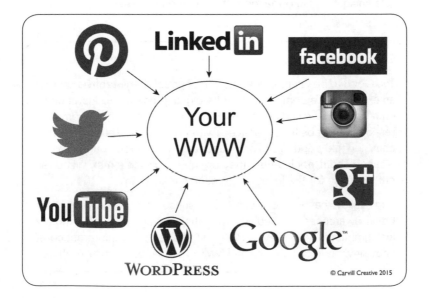

© Carvill Creative 2015

enables companies to reach the widest number of people. And in some cases, if the content they are posting strikes a chord, there is always the possibility of it going viral – and potentially reaching millions of people.

Armed with good-quality content, a comprehensive engagement strategy and an understanding of your target markets, it is possible to punch way above your weight.

Clearly global corporations such as Coca-Cola, Starbucks, Benetton, Mercedes-Benz and Amazon automatically have a high profile on social media, simply because they are established brands offline. However, they still use sites like Facebook and YouTube to reinforce their brands, engage with their communities and reach out to potentially new audiences. At the same time, they save millions of dollars in TV advertising by using their own channels, giving rise to the expression 'social TV' (see this article from Mashable – http://mashable.com/2014/09/02/social-tv-brandspeak).

However, SMEs, firms and charities could equally be using social media to build their brands and get their messages across. There are now a huge range of artists, musicians, start-ups and businesses that have achieved prominence through the use of social media. Whether you are Ed Sheeran, a charity like the Clatterbridge Cancer Charity or Westbury Chartered Accountants, you can really start to build your brand with people who are actually interested in what you do.

At the same time, visual organisations such as designers, artists, jewellers and architects can really benefit from using sites like YouTube, Facebook, Pinterest and Instagram as a way of showcasing what they do, while professional service-orientated brands can use Twitter, Google+ and LinkedIn, as well as blogs, as a fantastic way of providing regular insight and information to their customer base.

Case studies

Too Good to be Gluten Free (http://toogoodtobeglutenfree.com) is an example of a company using its digital presence to increase its brand awareness and effectively punch above its weight. From their responsive website to active Twitter presence (https://twitter.com/nog_uk) and regularly updated Facebook page (www.facebook.com/noglutenuk) they are able to reach a maximised target audience for the least investment in marketing.

Yeo Valley have also been very successful at growing their brand awareness, particularly with their Instagram Page (https://instagram.com/yeovalley), Pinterest Page (www.pinterest.com/yeovalley) and YouTube channel (www.youtube.com/user/Yeotube).

Product promotion and launch

It is a fallacy that you cannot sell on social media. You can, but you have to employ methods that are more reflective of inbound marketing than traditional methods of selling. In addition, with paid-for advertising methods on social media – whether sponsored tweets, pay-per-click on Facebook or promoted content on LinkedIn Showcase Pages (more on these in Chapter 10) – it is possible to get your product or service right in front of your target audience.

The key is to engage with your target audience and slowly build momentum around your brand using a variety of social networks and high-quality content.

As authors, we are well aware of the power of social media to promote this book and indeed are using @BOBSthebook on Twitter to drive traffic to our book's website, www.thebusinessofbeingsocial.co.uk.

Launches can also be made far more exciting using the full array of social media sites. Twitter hashtags, live tweets, streamed videos on YouTube and updates on Facebook give much greater depth to events.

An excellent example of this is Jaguar Cars who last year launched their new model the Jaguar XE. They chose the hashtag #FEELXE (https://twitter.com/hashtag/feelxe) then used a combination of newspaper advertising, TV ads, Twitter and YouTube to promote the car. Instead of pushing the vehicle itself, they were keen to encourage conversation around the car. They also understand, as we saw in Chapter 1, that traditional media and social media play very well together.

A similar example was the #Youdrive campaign for Mercedes which they used to launch their new A-class to a younger audience for whom the word Mercedes was more synonymous with a character in *Glee* rather than a car! More on this here: https://vimeo.com/58619777.

Gathering support for a cause

No one can have missed the Ice Bucket Challenge in 2014. Starting in the USA with celebrities, by the end of the year millions of people around the globe had thrown a bucket of ice water (or in fact rubble in Syria) over their heads to raise the profile of Motor Neurone Disease.

Similarly, the No Make-Up Selfies which appeared all over social media in 2014, raised millions for Cancer Research UK and were there to highlight cancer awareness.

Both these relied on two key things – (1) user generated content (more on this in the next chapter) and (2) a cause or issue that thousands of people could relate to.

Charities can make full use of social media to build their presence and gather support, just as businesses can. The key difference here is that they can use their audience to spread the message and act as 'digital' volunteers.

For example, World Child Cancer (www.worldchildcancer.org) are using all the social media channels (both consumer and business facing ones) to magnify the work of their marketing team and to reach out to communities around the UK and the rest of the world.

Clearly, it has always been possible to ask for signatures on a petition to gather support, but the use of social media has transformed the way in which charities and not-for-profit organisations can get their messages across and help build momentum.

We are now in an age when everyone has a voice and every charity fundraising participant can promote themselves and their Just Giving (www.justgiving.com) page via social networks.

Indeed, social networking channels can provide many charities and non-governmental organisations (NGOs) with the publicity they may otherwise be unable to afford. Mobilising teams of volunteers to act as 'buzz marketers' (marketing through word of mouth) can dramatically amplify the effectiveness of any campaign. Spreading messages virally through the social networks, as happened in the Middle East in 2010 and beyond, has a powerful effect – it just needs to be harnessed properly.

Making your brand more 'human': P2P

Everyone is familiar with the terms B2B (business to business) and B2C (business to consumer). Now we're in a *P2P* – people to people – age. From the dawn of civilisation, people have always dealt with people. The only thing that has changed over time is the technology and how it is used.

Ironically, many brands have moved away from the person-to-person human element with their online presences. Faceless websites that don't include members of staff, promotional materials that don't mention the human beings behind the brand and bland mission statements only serve to alienate potential customers.

In a society where customers have a voice to praise or harm your brand using social media, it is important that we return to old-fashioned customer service values.

At the same time, future customers want to know who they are doing business with – they are more interested in the human beings who are serving them than they are in your brand.

Search for any service on Google and you will get a host of websites offering much the same thing, with very little to differentiate them. A key unique selling point (USP) for organisations must be the people who work there. So why not showcase them using LinkedIn profiles, blogs and videos?

Remember, any organisation is the sum of the people who work there, so why not play on this? For example, by listing the LinkedIn profiles of employees in your organisation, you are providing a more illuminating snapshot than any corporate brochure or website.

Case study: Innocent

Innocent put a real emphasis on portraying themselves as a company run by humans for humans. From their website (www.innocentdrinks.co.uk) to their array of social media sites, they highlight the people who work at the company, explain what they do and provide insights into their job as well as their daily lives. All of which helps to build the overall brand of an organisation.

Networking

Using Twitter is like attending the ultimate business conference that runs 24/7, 365 days a year, with millions of people having thousands of different conversations. LinkedIn, on the other hand, is like the ultimate business reunion where everyone you have ever met in your professional life – who you like (!) – is in one room.

According to the *Oxford English Dictionary*, networking in the business sense is defined as 'interacting with others to exchange information and develop professional or social contacts'. Social media provide the perfect conditions for doing this.

As well as LinkedIn, Facebook and Twitter, other social networks such as Google+, Tumblr (www.tumblr.com) and Quora (www.quora.com) plus, of course, blogging sites such as WordPress (www.wordpress.com) and Blogger (www.blogger.com), all provide an environment where people can communicate with each other online.

However, the two most popular sites for business networking are Twitter and LinkedIn. It is possible to use these channels to strengthen existing relationships as well as building brand new ones.

Ivan Misner, the founder of Business Networking International (www.bni.com) came up with the VCP model: **V**isibility + **C**redibility = **P**rofitability. This is as true of online networking as it is of face-to-face networking.

The more visible you are, the more credible you become. The more credible you become, the more likely it is that people will want to do business with you.

On LinkedIn, 'groups' act almost like micro social networks where specialists can engage with each other. Whether you want groups about retail management, cat grooming, molecular biology or independent restaurant owners, it is possible to 'meet' like-minded people who work in the same field as you or could connect you to your chosen target audience. Google+'s circles are a similar way of communicating with and staying visible within specific networks of people. And on Twitter, by creating lists of suppliers or introducers it is possible to stay informed about what these people and/or businesses are doing.

As in normal face-to-face networking, it is important to establish who you wish to talk to/communicate with and to understand the rules of engagement and what content you wish to provide to these target audiences.

Business intelligence

Understanding your target audiences and gaining valuable business intelligence has never been simpler for organisations. There is a huge wealth of information online, whether posted by companies themselves or comments that others have posted in blogs, tweets or updates.

Indeed some organisations are now diverting their research and development budgets into social media so they can develop the products and services their customers may want in the future.

With Twitter, it is possible to capture conversations about key brands and products. At the same time, by putting all competitors into private lists, companies can gain valuable market understanding about those organisations.

After corporate websites, company profiles and Showcase Pages on LinkedIn are often the first port of call to find information on organisations. Indeed, recruiters, competitors, journalists and students can often elicit more valuable data than they would from other sources.

From recruiters using Facebook to get background information on candidates to potential suppliers checking out branded YouTube channels for corporations in order to understand how to communicate more effectively with them, social media can provide a huge amount of data.

There is also now a huge range of software products on the market that will help you drill down even further to extract the information you need. More on this in the next chapter.

Thought leadership

Blogs and social media provide a great medium for people to build their personal brands. Authors, artists, industry leaders and politicians all use a combination of channels to raise their profiles.

Acting as a metaphorical soap box, these channels give individuals the opportunity to raise their credibility, improve their visibility and communicate with their audience, in much the same way as companies do.

Celebrities have appropriated the power of the social networks to reach their fans across the world: indeed, in their own field, they are aiming to become 'thought leaders', whether in music, art, film or fashion. And increasingly, their fans wish to have a conduit through which they can communicate with their heroes.

In the corporate world, it is also becoming increasingly important for CEOs and leading people in professions to have some form of online 'voice'. Customers, clients and stakeholders are interested to hear their thoughts, in much the same way that journalists seek out opinion formers when writing about certain subjects in the traditional media.

Using social media channels in conjunction with blogs effectively enables individuals to reach audiences they would otherwise not have had access to.

From political bloggers such as Guido Fawkes (@GuidoFawkes) to business commentator Jack Welch (@jack_welch), and from leading environmental activists like Al Gore (@algore) to thought leaders such as Jack Dorsey (@jack), Twitter is a quick and easy way to get your message across.

On LinkedIn, there are a number of ways to increase your personal profile. You can Share an Update, write a post to go up on LinkedIn Pulse or you can contribute to Groups.

YouTube channels can provide much more of a human element to your personal brand through video blogs, video newsletters and even showreels. Here is a clip of the authors speaking at the 2014 Oxford Farming Conference – www.ofc.org.uk/videos/2014/david-taylor-and-michelle-carvill.

Social media marketing action plan

- Think about your own organisation's business objectives.
- Then work out how you can use the social networks to meet those objectives.

- You may well be able to use one social network for a variety of purposes: for example, Facebook could be used for customer service and corporate and social responsibility; or you may need two separate Facebook Pages.
- Compile a grid showing the different social media channels on one axis and the various ways they can be used on the other axis. This will help you to see where they fit in your own organisation.
- Start small. You might consider using social media for one thing only. Get this right before expanding into other channels or trying to meet a plethora of different objectives.
- Keep updated with the latest developments in social media to stay ahead of the game. A great way to do this may be via the blog at www.thebusinessofbeingsocial.co.uk.

3 | Becoming an adaptive, social business

What you will learn from this chapter:

- Having a proper strategy in your business
- How different generations communicate
- Creating the right culture for social media to thrive
- Thinking like an editor to create, collate and curate content
- Managing your channels, sometimes on a 24/7 basis
- The role of social advertising
- Using big data to achieve your business goals

As we saw in Chapter 1, it is vital that proper planning is done in your organisation before you embark on any social media campaign. However, what's becoming increasingly clear is that the social networks – whether external ones or internal ones, such as Yammer, SharePoint or Jostle – are now changing the way we communicate as organisations.

Most people still view social media as being the preserve of the marketing department or press office, when in reality many areas of the business – including research and development, customer service, supply chain management, IT, internal communications, human resources, recruitment and sales – are impacted by social media.

Whether you are a small or medium enterprise, microbusiness, public body or large corporation, you clearly need to have the right approach to embracing digital technology if you are going to achieve your business objectives. This means becoming a truly **adaptive** organisation that is ready to meet the challenges and opportunities posed by today's 'always connected' customer.

Case study

A dairy making specialist cheeses embarked on a social media campaign, using Facebook and an e-commerce website, to drive online sales. The campaign was so successful that demand massively exceeded supply and many customers' orders were not processed. To make matters worse, the management team did not understand social media so instead of sorting out the supply chain, they asked the marketing manager to, in effect, stop marketing using their digital channels! This wasn't great for brand or business.

To ensure that, as an organisation, you embrace social media activity effectively across different functions, we have developed a simple six-step plan that will help you reorganise your business and help you ultimately to achieve three key objectives:

1. increase your profits
2. lower your costs
3. ensure a long-term future for your business.

Dnasix™

CREATING THE MODERN, SOCIAL BUSINESS

BUSINESS GOALS

BIG DATA 6

SOCIAL ADVERTISING 5

COMMUNITY MANAGEMENT 4

CONTENT CREATION 3

CORPORATE CULTURE 2

STRATEGY 1

©2010media

Get your business strategy right

The first step on the path to creating a modern, 'social' business is to have a proper strategy in place: not a social strategy, or even a marketing strategy, but an overarching business strategy that will help you guide your organisation into the future. As we saw in Chapter 1, it is important to Plan, Listen, Analyse **before** you Engage. This takes the planning process a level deeper – right to the very heart of your company.

Why is this important? Aside from the fact that every organisation, from the smallest sole trader to the largest international body, needs to have a cohesive strategy in place, in the new social age it is harder to 'wing it' and muddle along. As we've seen, social media now affects so many parts of an organisation. Failure to plan at the outset could result in your business stagnating or even failing altogether.

While most firms will have a one- or two-year plan, few have a long-term vision for their business – which is important when technological advances mean that the world is changing so rapidly. Sole traders may want to think about their exit strategy; medium-sized enterprises may be eyeing expansion; while large corporations will be thinking about shareholder returns.

Next comes an understanding of your target audience(s). In the past, when there were only a handful of ways to communicate with customers, this was fairly simple. However, now that there are so many channels to communicate with – traditional, online, social networks, social messaging sites, forums – it is imperative that you have a plan for reaching people in the way in which they prefer to be communicated with.

How different generations communicate

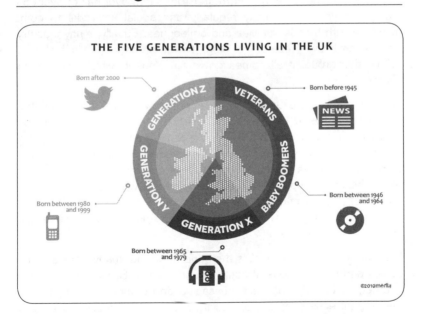

As you can see from this diagram, there are now five separate generations living in the UK. Each of them communicates in entirely different ways and each requires their own strategy.

Note: While there is a general consensus that we have five generations, there are several different interpretations of when each generation begins and ends. There are many papers and online studies that discuss in detail each of these generations.

Speaking generally – of course, there are always exceptions! – the oldest people in the country, the so-called Veterans, use traditional channels. They will take a paid-for newspaper daily, listen to the wireless and watch terrestrial television. They may even happily accept cold calls and take time to read printed material sent to them through the post. However, a sizeable proportion of these people are starting to use social media.

Next up are the Baby Boomers, aged between 50 and 70. Most of the leaders in the country – whether in politics, education or business – fall into this age group and they split neatly into those who prefer the old ways of doing business (they think more like Veterans) and those who understand the old Darwinian 'adapt or die' principle.

This is where issues can start to arise in companies: while the 'old guard' refuse to change their marketing and communications strategies, instead relying on tried and trusted methods, younger executives and marketing professionals become increasingly frustrated as they try to sell their new ideas to people who just don't want to listen. However, a recent survey by Forrester found that over half of over-65s are on Facebook and many regularly use social networks to communicate with friends, families and colleagues. Equally, many industry leaders are now prepared to blog, tweet or network via LinkedIn. Within this group, it all comes down to mindset, which we'll cover shortly.

We then come to the Generation Xers, people who, like the co-authors, were born between 1964 and 1979. This group is the last generation ever to read paid-for newspapers on a regular basis; we make up the median age group on Facebook; we've adapted quickly to new ways of working; and we've used email for most of our working lives. Yet even within this age group there are still many people who yearn for the pre-BlackBerry days when work was limited to an eight-hour day and you knew where you stood with communications. And many of these people are now senior managers!

Millennials, or Generation Y, is the generation that many brands, companies and organisations struggle to understand. Brought up with the internet, mobile phones, text messaging and computers, these were the original early adopters of social media. As a consequence, they are also the first to migrate away from sites like Facebook, which they feel are too commercialised and populated by their parents. Generally speaking, Millennials don't like being marketed or sold to, which makes the job of communicating with them much more difficult than with the other generations. This group like short-form content (images, videos, infographics) which are easily digestible and convey interesting, informative and relevant messaging about brands.

In fact, it's not only Millennials who like this content. Just look at any newspaper or magazine and compare them to ones from 20 or even 10 years ago. There are far more pictures, charts, content lists and images, simply because we don't have time to digest information any more.

The youngest group here in the UK is Generation Z. These under-16s have grown up with smartphones, tablets, multi-channel communications, video, social messaging and the mobile internet. The jury is still out on how these consumers of the future will wish to communicate, but there is evidence to suggest that they want to connect instantly to sites via their phone, they love video content, are very tech savvy and are more inclined than the Millennials to seek privacy online.

Creating the right culture for social media to thrive

While having a decent business strategy is vital for social media to work, the corporate culture is equally important. Does it support social media or actively fight against it? In many of our training courses we see communications professionals, whether in-house or from agencies, who get little or no support from within organisations when it comes to social media. And very often the problem starts at the very top with the management team.

As we've already observed, most managers are either younger Baby Boomers or late Generation Xers who simply don't understand and don't want to understand the digitally engaged workplace.

In our experience, the best environments for social media to thrive are in organisations where there is a corporate 'growth mindset'. Here, everyone from the CEO, the board or MD down to the office junior is open to change and wants to embrace new ways of working. A great example of this is a company like Innocent Drinks, where the corporate environment is geared naturally to being social; and the management structure is considerably 'flatter'.

Even in companies of just one or two people, there has to be a willingness to embrace social media – even if this means creating interesting content to post on your website or monitoring what your competitors are doing.

The better the culture, the more likely it is that social media will succeed, as good communications start from within. In an ideal scenario, as well as a desire to embrace change, social media goals should be made clear to everyone in the company, management should lead from the front with a strong vision for the business, internal communications should be good and everyone – particularly those not in marketing – should be willing to come up with ideas which could be posted on the corporate social media channels.

We know of plenty of companies where staff are incentivised to share ideas internally and where even the CEO is willing to tweet. In fact, many companies are abandoning internal emails and using Google Hangouts or bespoke internal social networks instead.

With small companies or charities, it's about having a positive mental attitude, thinking about all the people who could work with you on a voluntary basis (volunteers, interns, apprentices, students on work experience) and creating 'ambassadors' for your brand to help you punch above your marketing weight.

Thinking like an editor to create, collate and curate content

As we will discover in Chapter 4, content is still very much king, particularly when there are now so many different communications channels. We'll be looking at what content is and how it is created. However, building on the first two steps of our diagram, we need to think carefully about where the content is likely to come from, where it will be used and how to manage it.

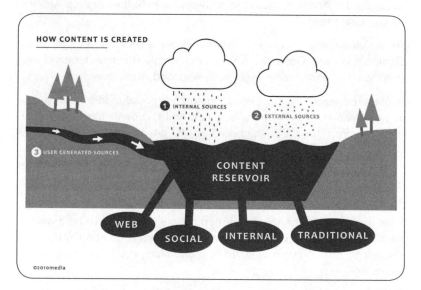

Try and imagine a content 'reservoir'. This needs to 'feed' your marketing channels – website, social networks, internal communications and, of course, your traditional media such as PR, newsletters, presentations, advertising, etc. Like a real-life reservoir, it must be large, stay reasonably full and should contain plenty of fresh and engaging content. Clearly, the larger your organisation, the larger your reservoir needs to be. Likewise, the more channels you have, the more content you'll need.

Note: If you are struggling to come up with material to post on your own website, be very wary about diving into social media activity without having thought about where you are going to procure and generate content. Many companies fall into the trap of simply not having the right amount of content to make their digital strategies work.

The key complaint we hear time and time again, from both small and large businesses, is that they simply don't have enough content to post. This is where you just have to be a little canny about where you get your content from.

There are three main sources. The first is from inside your organisation, which is why it is important to have good internal communications and colleagues/volunteers (in the case of charities) who are willing to supply you with information. Even if you are a sole trader, you still have business associates, suppliers and friends who can help you come up with ideas. The second source is external. There are so many places where you can source content – traditional media, social media, websites, blogs, conferences, networking events. This is where Lists and Favorites on Twitter (more on this in Chapter 5), LinkedIn Pulse and Groups (see Chapter 7) and also Liking other Pages on Facebook (Chapter 6) can be so valuable. There is a wealth of information out there. It's a case of collating and curating this content into something that you can use.

Handy hint: You can use Pinterest (Chapter 9) as a great way of 'pinning' all the content you have collected onto one or several boards. This will then help you to visualise your stories and plan how you are going to use them.

The final source, and one which, despite being increasingly important (particularly among the Millennials), is almost totally overlooked, is user-generated content (UGC). Here, your customers, clients, stakeholders or guests create their own content that they can post on your social media channels. This might be by using your hashtag, tagging you on Facebook, mentioning you on Twitter, commenting about your company on LinkedIn or writing you a LinkedIn recommendation.

UGC, because it is created not by you but your customers, is perceived to have the highest value of any content; and the best thing about it is that it's free. The trick is to think about your audience – remember that nearly everyone these days has a smartphone with a camera and video at their fingertips – your job is to work out how you can incentivise them to take pictures, check in or comment.

Handy hint: Some hotels and restaurants have so-called selfie sticks to make it easier for people to take pictures of themselves. Others direct people to picturesque features or landmarks in order to get the best pictures. And don't forget to ask people to mention you on social media!

Managing your channels

Posting content on social media is one thing; managing the channels is something quite different. Social media is just that, a 'social' activity, which entails being willing to have conversations with people online. Time and time again, the co-authors come across companies who proudly trumpet the fact that they are 'on social media' but in reality are creating the online equivalent of a monologue, like someone on a blind date talking at the other person for the whole time and then leaving. Customers, particularly Millennials, want to communicate with the brands they like and increasingly, customer service is something done via social networks, as we saw in Chapter 2. People want and expect a response from brands.

Actual 'community management', the act of looking after social media, involves listening, analysing, engaging, reporting and measuring – all of which can be time-consuming.

Therefore, the role of the community manager is vital in maximising the effectiveness of your social networks and digital channels. This job could include customer service, having conversations with journalists/

bloggers/influencers/customers, 'attending' conferences via monitoring hashtags and building viable networks of followers.

In addition, community management may need to be something that is done on the move via a smartphone or tablet and is managed 24/7, particularly if you are customer-facing. Why? Because people don't just comment on social media during office hours and they may expect someone to respond to them in a matter of minutes.

Community management also involves listening, something that very few companies are able or willing to do successfully. Almost half the people on Twitter do not tweet, while many professionals use social networks simply to upskill and gain valuable insights.

We often find that people who attend our training courses have to do community management over and above their usual role, making it nigh-on impossible to run accounts successfully. Or they have to spend much of their free time managing social sites unpaid.

However, if you have a proper social media strategy, a positive digital mindset and colleagues happy to supply you with ideas and content, the role becomes a whole lot easier.

A note of caution: Think carefully about who you appoint as community manager(s), whether they are in-house or external. Do they have proper social media guidelines? A contract? What level of admin do they have? Who has access to the passwords? What happens in a crisis or emergency? There are scores of examples of what can happen when community management goes wrong.

The role of social advertising

Every single major social network now offers some form of paid-for advertising, as you will discover in Chapter 10. Facebook has nine different ways of promoting yourself or your products. This shouldn't really come as a surprise to anyone who has worked in sales or marketing. Social media is simply copying the traditional channels by offering a chance for you to create interesting content, allocate a budget, select an audience and run an ad campaign – just as you would with print, TV or even Google advertising.

Most companies we train and work with still haven't used social advertising, probably, we suspect, because they don't have the confidence or understanding of the sites. However, in many cases, the only way for you to achieve your strategic business objectives is through a certain amount of targeted advertising. This means allocating a budget, identifying your precise target audiences and making sure that the rest of your marketing is up to the job in order to maximise the return from your investment.

Using big data to achieve your business goals

The final step in the model is to think about how you can use the vast amount of data available online to benefit your company. Corporate strategy, content creation, product development, competitor analysis, media relations and business intelligence all depend on you being able to make sense of this data.

Fortunately there is a vast array of 'social listening' tools that can help you extract the information you need. These range from free features within the social networks and sites like Hootsuite and TweetDeck (more on these in Chapter 12) to software that can cost from just a few pounds a month up to several thousands.

Clearly you need to have a proper strategy, an understanding of your target audiences and precise objectives or you'll just be faced with a mass of useless data. Just as with Google Analytics, mailing lists or databases, you need to know what you are looking for. Get the right data, though, and you'll be able to feed this back into your strategy, your content creation strategy and your social advertising.

Social media marketing action plan

- Arrange an away-day for the key decision-makers in your business to work on your medium- and long-term business strategy.
- Think about your audience(s). Who exactly are they? How do they communicate? What content do they want? What are the best channels to reach them?
- Identify social media champions within your business and use them to help you communicate your social media plans and strategy.
- Draw up social media guidelines for staff, consultants and interns to ensure that everyone knows what they can and can't do online.
- Think about your content. Where does it come from, who manages it and is it of a sufficient quality?
- Who manages your social media channels? Think carefully about appointing specific community managers. Ideally, they need to be naturally 'social' people!
- Put aside a budget for advertising on social media. Plan campaigns carefully and measure the results.
- Extract the data you need to make your business succeed. Use software to cut down on the 'noise' and listen in to what is important. More on this later in the book!

4| Content is king

> What you will learn from this chapter:
>
> - You are what you share
> - Content marketing is marketing
> - Creating a content strategy
> - Content vehicles
> - Blogging tips
> - The importance of keywords
> - Unlocking the content potential in your business

You are what you share

The social media marketing channels we explore in this book, such as Twitter, Facebook, LinkedIn, Blogs, YouTube and the others covered in Chapter 9, present you with opportunities to share your content and get your messages across. However, now more than ever, *what* you share has never been more important. These channels have the potential to be far-reaching, extending beyond your usual 'databases', as they present opportunities for advocacy. If people love what they've read, seen or heard, they can share the content on their networks too, helping a wide audience to get to know about you, like you, trust you, share your messages and ultimately, even do business with you. And, of course, this isn't an onerous task; it's simply a case of hitting a button – like, share or retweet.

Given how potentially far-reaching the social media platforms can be, you need to ensure that you are not wasting the opportunity these channels provide by talking about the cheese sandwich you've just eaten. (Unless, of course, you're Pret A Manger and it's a tactic you've employed to showcase a new product!)

Businesses of all shapes and sizes need to get their 'content house' in order.

Ask yourself . . .

- Have you got a strategy for regularly creating fresh and acceptable content that meets specific business objectives?

- Have you got a blog that you regularly update for your business?
- Do you regularly create videos for your business – how-to videos, sharing FAQs, customer testimonials, new product and service features?
- Have you got any research information that others would be interested in? Could it be turned into an ebook and provide potential for data capture?
- Are you a leading authority in a specific area? Can you create thought leadership articles, 'white papers' or industry reports?
- Do you have interesting infographics that capture a subject perfectly?

Content is all around you, from your websites to service standards, internal training, product demos, new products, etc., so you need to ensure that you have a mechanism for collating the content in your business so that you can leverage it effectively.

Reasons why content is king

Fresh and compelling content is key for a number of reasons.

- **It helps you get found online.** Regular, fresh content is great for SEO (search engine optimisation) purposes. The more fresh and relevant content you provide, the more the search 'spiders' (so named because of 'the web') know that they can come to you and they will find updated, keyword-enabled content.
- **It keeps your online presence fresh.** Do you have any old news articles on your site? What's the date of your latest blog post – January 2011? Or even 2010? If so, how does that look to those reading your blog or visiting your website? Keeping your content fresh shares a really positive message about your business. And in an age where people search out products and services online and make decisions in just a few seconds, it's important that you appear up to date.
- **It grows trust and authority.** The content you create gives you something credible to shout about. The offline networking model VCP (outlined in Chapter 2) also fits with how people get to know you online. If you regularly share relevant and compelling content, you will grow a positive reputation. If you regularly share a load of spam links and promotional guff, ask yourself just how engaging or compelling that appears.
- **It grows brand awareness and reach.** As we mentioned at the start of the chapter, social media marketing channels can be far reaching – you just don't know where your content will end up and who will end up reading it. It may get picked up and shared in a

very 'viral' way, growing awareness in ways that traditional media simply can't compete with.

- **It showcases the expertise and personality of the business.** Whether you are formally leveraging content in this way for thought leadership, or want to show a more human side of the business, what you communicate to the outside world creates an impression.

Of course, if you have a content strategy in place, there's also the opportunity of safeguarding what others are saying in your business. You can clearly set boundaries as to what is and what is not shared. Of course, content is best when it's authentic and transparent. However, you certainly don't want to be sharing content that is potentially damaging to your brand!

Why content matters so much

Once upon a time all an organisation had to worry about was its website presence.

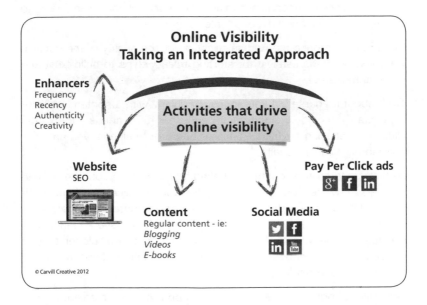

You need to ensure that your website content is regularly updated and refreshed – to maximise SEO efforts – but if you choose to participate on Facebook, Twitter, LinkedIn, YouTube, Pinterest, Google+ (and any vertical or social networks of the many that exist – more on that in Chapter 9), you need to be aware that these channels are all very content hungry.

Content Marketing 'is' Marketing

In an age where consumers are wary of being bombarded with irrelevant communications – business, brands and organisations of all shapes and sizes are having to think how they connect with people.

Taking advantage of the technologies we as consumers keep close to us everyday–such as our smartphones, which enable us to seek and find resources to educate, entertain and compel, 24/7 on the move, at the touch of a button – can play a key part in modern marketing techniques.

The Content Marketing Institute (www.contentmarketinginstitute.com) put it pretty simply:

> 'Content marketing is a strategic marketing approach focused on creating and distributing valuable, relevant, and consistent content to attract and retain a clearly-defined audience – and, ultimately, to drive profitable customer action.'

Social network interactions, whilst limited in characters, invariably share 'links' – signposting us to a relevant article, blog post, video or infographic, to satisfy our enquiring minds. The social channels enable us to effectively signpost and direct people to 'content'.

Content is all around us. And as consumers, the quality of the content we consume is the catalyst for starting relationships to build trust and share of mind.

Think about it yourself, if you engage regularly with a content provider – because you enjoy their content, because it fulfils needs – then even without purchasing anything from that brand or business, you are subconsciously building loyalty.

Recent research into content marketing taking place in both the UK and US – again by the Content Marketing Institute – indicates that customers that first engage with a brand or business via content are likely to go on to buy, and when they do buy they are likely to have a higher than average lifetime value – having subconsciously grown closer to that brand or business and built a level of trust through the consumption of relevant and purposeful content.

Let's take a look at some of the most popular social media channels from a content perspective.

1. **Twitter:** You are what you tweet. Whether you are retweeting someone else's content or showcasing your own, you need to have clear objectives and policies and to ensure that the content is on message. In addition, the frequency is high: Twitter is a fast and fluid platform, so you could be posting ten or more updates a day. So what are you going to talk about? And remember on Twitter, you

can add images and videos, directly into the platform feed now too. You can even add some words on those images to create images that share a message.

2. **Facebook:** You are what you share. Whether you are advocating someone else's content or sharing your own, it needs to compel others to engage with it – to like, to share, to comment. One or two status updates a day still seem to gain more engagement than posting four to seven posts a day on Facebook (see Facebook chapter for statistics). However, you still need to be thinking about the content that engages this audience. Two updates a day is still 14 a week. (And, yes, weekends count.)

3. **YouTube:** You are looking for people to watch, rate, like and share your video content. You may have the resources to create regular video content or you may be using apps like Animoto to turn presentations and images into video. YouTube is potentially the most resource-hungry medium of them all. If you plan out your video content, film 14 videos in one day and push out one a week, you will be filming three months' worth of content in one session. And doing that quarterly.

4. **LinkedIn:** You want to share status updates with your connections that compel them to share and engage with you. You may be able to leverage some of the content you share to Twitter and Facebook here. However, it may be that the content you are pushing to Facebook and Twitter isn't relevant for your professional connections. Again, you need to think about which content you serve to which audience. As you'll read in the LinkedIn chapter (Chapter 7), through LinkedIn Pulse, if relevant, you can effectively have your own blog/ publishing platform – where you can share authentic content to assist with growing your reputation as a thought leader in a specific area.

5. **Pinterest** – As you'll see in Chapter 9, Pinterest enables you to capture, curate and share visual content very easily and is a wonderful resource for driving traffic to a website. And if you think about content that people love to engage with – pictures and images are right up there. From a visual content perspective, if you have a product which lends itself to being visually compelling (take a look at Ikea's Pinterest account for example), Pinterest is the perfect vehicle. However, even if your content isn't that visually driven – let's say you're a management consultancy – don't write visual content off. Most of the blogs you create, research reports, customer case studies, etc. – will have visual aspects. You can simply add the engaging image to Pinterest – which then drives people back to the core article.

6. **Instagram** – Again, in Chapter 9 we cover Instagram quite extensively. Another visually driven application, enabling you to share images and video content (limited to 15 seconds). Again, for businesses that have a visual product, Instagram is a no-brainer. Fill

your feed with wonderful compelling content that may be as simple as photographing your latest product line, or new collection, applying the magnitude of helpful filters and #tagging the post with as many relevant hashtags as possible to aid reach. But again, don't be too distraught if you don't have a direct visual product – if you're an event organisation, travel agent, property agent – think about the places you're marketing and people you meet when you're out and about. Take inspiration from others. We love the Instagram activity for the charity 'CharityWater' who are using Instagram images and video to inspire people to give.

We often find that 'traditional marketing messages' are pushed into these conversational channels: 'The content for traditional campaigns is already being created – so let's just push it across to our social channels too.' If the content fits and is relevant to the channel, this practice is perfectly acceptable. However, many traditional campaigns lead with a much more promotional element, so it may be that your messaging needs to be repositioned into a more conversational tone for the social platforms.

Developing a content road map

A couple of things we often hear when consulting or working with clients are, 'What do we talk about?' and 'We've run out of things to say.' Our response is that magical but simple mantra, 'Plan, Listen, Analyse – before you Engage.' If you've done all the planning and listening before you engage, you will either have a whole suite of content ready to roll, or you will have built a process of consistently developing content to feed the hungry channels in a targeted and purposeful way.

Let's take a look at some of the ingredients you could build into a content road map for your organisation.

1 Content audit

What content do you already have, and what content are you missing? Do some 'listening' to figure out what information gaps there are that you can fill. Customer pain points and problems are often a good starting point as you can then create useful content around purposeful solutions. Do the research and build up a list of topics around which to create content. Run a survey; listen to what people are saying (Twitter is a great resource for this); watch your analytics and see which pages people visit on your site; find out the questions customers most often ask your customer service team, chat services or online enquiries.

Watch what competitors are doing and, which is important, watch the engagement levels of the information you are sharing. Very quickly you will start to pick up which topics resonate.

2 Content topics

Focus on business objectives to decide on key content themes and messages. Create a topic list, ideally focused on audience need. It could be that there are seasonal elements to the topic you wish to create. For example, an accountancy firm could consider tax seasons and certain business accounting deadlines throughout the year. So think about seasonality, if relevant, when creating your topics – just as a features editor would when putting together a year's content schedule for a magazine or journal.

3 Content collation

Now you know what you need, and you have a list of potential content topics, it's time to start pulling your content together. If relevant, work with different departments in the organisation to procure relevant content, and get them involved in regularly sharing information that can be leveraged for useful content and insights. Sharing your expertise is likely to be compelling content. And if you don't have the content in house, or the ability to create the content (e.g. if you think you require a professional team to create video content or infographics or blogs), consider whether you need to outsource or bring in resources to help you create it.

4 Content tone of voice and policies

As you are creating content, it's important to determine clear guidelines about what can and can't be communicated. Is it okay to mention competitors' or clients' names? What style or tone of voice do you adopt? A casual conversational tone works really well on blogs and Facebook, but if you're creating a white paper or research analysis, you may need to use a more formal business tone. Ensure that these elements are clear so that those creating and sharing the content have clear guidelines to work within.

5 Publishing schedule

With content creation in place, and tone of voice clearly understood, you now need to decide what and when you publish. Creating a timeline (e.g. weekly, monthly, annually) of when to publish your content is a useful exercise and you can make it as detailed as you wish.

You might want to create publishing schedules for different networks (a publishing matrix), focusing on frequency for each platform, for example:

- Twitter: 5–8 posts a day
- Facebook: 2–3 posts a day
- LinkedIn: 1–2 posts a week
- YouTube: 1 video a week
- Pinterest: 5 pins a day
- Google+: 3 posts a day.

You could even take the matrix further by including specific topics for each medium to focus on each week.

If you are dealing with audiences overseas, you may also want to consider the hour of day you publish your content to ensure optimum visibility during overseas business hours. Of course, your own platform analysis will start to advise you on the best times to post each day – so you can consider the times when engagement is higher and build that into your publishing schedule too.

Keep your content interesting

Think about traditional media – magazines and newspapers – and the type of content they include. And, of course, think about news websites such as the BBC, Bloomberg or Mashable. A common theme is that they are a blend of media:

- videos
- articles
- images
- stories
- blogs
- FAQs
- expert advice
- tips and tactics
- webinars
- podcasts
- case studies
- Q&A sessions
- interviews
- polls and surveys.

When developing your content road map, think about these different media and what you could create, and how you can leverage each medium.

For example, you might take ten FAQs and create ten blogs or ten videos around these subjects. You could then create a podcast or a video blog. Or indeed a case study-style story to get a key point across. You could then tweet the blogs and video links and include relevant images, stories and videos on your Facebook Page; or ask questions and gauge audience feedback by running a poll or survey around the topic and, if relevant, push this poll across to your LinkedIn connections too.

You can see how you can 're-use' and recycle the same content in different ways, targeting it slightly differently according to the medium.

The power of blogging

Blogging is probably one of the simplest and most common methods organisations regularly use to communicate a more 'human' side of their business. A blog is a perfect mouthpiece for sharing a variety of content. Whether it's a video, an article, a case study or a story, a blog enables multimedia to be communicated in a regular and consistent way.

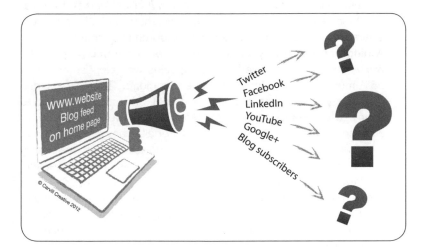

So, given that a blog is the most common form of content creation for organisations, let's take a good look at blogging. Before we get started, let's cover some essential blogging terminology.

- **Blog:** short for 'web log', a blog is a personal or company online journal. Others can participate – comment or share – one to many.
- **Post:** an article that has been published on a blog. You post a blog post, just as you would post a letter.
- **Category:** a blog category is simply a way of grouping posts that share a common theme. You can categorise posts into relevant sectors, e.g. social media, marketing, content management, online advertising, etc.

- **Blogging platform:** there are a number of platforms, some self-created, that form part of a website's content management system. Open source platforms such as WordPress, Blogger or Typepad (and there are many others) are more commonly used.

Now we've covered the terminology, let's get into the details of blogging.

Why blog?

- **Blogging enables you to say more.** It's a freer communication tool – and far more conversational – than many of the traditional media. Very often businesses find it difficult to share their brand message continuously or personally through visual advertising and traditional media, so blogging provides more insight into what that person, business or brand stands for, effectively sharing a more human voice of the business.
- **You can share authentic content on social platforms.** As we explored earlier in the chapter, you are what you share. Therefore, it's important that, as a business or brand, you have a good pot of authentic content to share with others. What better way to advocate what you do than to blog about it and share with others to grow awareness and opinion from those who potentially matter?
- **A blog embedded in your website generates traffic.** A study by www.hubspot.com showed that companies who blogged achieved 55% more website traffic than those that didn't. This makes sense because you are sharing something that drives people back to your site to read it. A blog embedded in your website gives your audience something to engage with. After all, many websites aren't designed as two-way communication portals; they are usually quite passive. So a blog (and indeed other social networks) enable a two-way conversation.
- **Blogs help grow brand and personal authority.** A blog enables you to share expertise about what you do, growing advocacy, awareness and authority for your brand or business as a thought leader in a particular area.
- **They entertain and grow 'fans'.** If people enjoy what you write, they will in time grow fond of your musings. Keep them entertained and they will share with others and ultimately you will develop a following. The more 'fans' you create, the more opportunity you have for advocacy and broadening your reach. Your readers effectively become your marketers.

These are some great reasons for blogging, so let's now look at some tactical and practical blogging tips.

1. **Keep your blogs brief** (ideally about 400–700 words). But you can mix it up. Have a look at Seth Godin's blog (www.sethgodin.com).

Some of his posts are literally two sentences. Others are two pages. But remember, you have to keep the audience engaged, and concise is usually best. And if you have got a lot to say then create a 'series' – we often break our blogs down into Part 1 and Part 2 – so that a) the blog isn't too long and b) there's a reason for the reader to stay tuned for more.

2. **Vary the topic.**
   o *Factual* – could focus around a recent change in legislation and implications, or a highly topical theme.
   o *Useful and practical* – ten tips, five steps to understanding ABC. People tend to enjoy 'quick tip'-style blog posts. But don't write every post in that style.
   o *Entertaining* – light and humorous so that the user understands that while you know your stuff, you're not taking life too seriously (if that fits with your overall tone of voice, of course).
   o *Opinion-driven* – asking for viewpoints from your audience. This is our view – what's yours? Do you agree, disagree?

3. **Watch yor splling and grammer.** Errors can really hinder credibility. Be sure to take advantage of spell-checking tools and brush up on your grammar. (*The Elements of Style* by William Strunk is a well-thumbed tome on the subject – and www.grammarly.com is the number 1 rated grammar checker).

4. **Use images** in a post to break up the text and add some relevant interest. Check out www.flickr.com, www.istockphoto.com or www.fotolia.co.uk for some low-cost yet good-quality shots. If you use images from Flickr, be sure to follow the guidelines and cite the reference in your posts.

5. **Consider video blogs.** You could consider turning your content into a 30- to 90-second video (short and to the point). Check out apps such as www.animoto.com, which is really useful for taking images and turning them into great video.

6. **Create attention-grabbing headings.** You should write the headline imagining that the user won't even see the article. So the headline has to grab attention and tell the story.

7. **Headline tips:**
   o *Question:* 'Would you let a marketer extract your teeth?' or 'Which test do you think got the most results?'
   o *How to:* 'How to get everyone to do what you want'
   o *Curiosity:* 'LinkedIn smarter than Facebook' (this piece was actually about photos on LinkedIn, where people were clearly more smartly dressed than in the more casual pictures on Facebook
   o *Command:* 'If you read one thing today – read this'
   o *Quantify:* 'Twenty reasons you should do X'; 'Eight essential blogging tips you can't live without'.

8. **Use keywords** where you can – both in headers and throughout the content of the article. For example, 'Tax Planning Tips to blow your mind'.

9. **Schedule.** Stick to a tight publishing schedule. Blogging pays off over time – it's a marathon rather than a sprint and it takes time to build up relevant and optimised content. Ideally, blog at least three times a week.

10. **Insert a 'call to action'**, such as subscribe to the blog or to a newsletter, download our free guide, or get in touch – are really useful to direct the user to do what you want them to do. Also be mindful that you want the user to read your blog – and ideally find out more about what it is that you do. Therefore, be sure to add relevant links throughout your blog content that signposts the reader back to resources, products or services on your website.

11. **Promote your blog.** Promote links to your blog on your website and in email footers, business cards and other relevant offline and online marketing materials.

12. **Share your blog on relevant news services.** Search other relevant blogs in your sector and see what scope there is for you to post your blogs on other portals. For example, www.businesszone.co.uk encourages bloggers to share their blogs. And there are many other portals that enable you to do so. Search out those that are relevant for your business and start sharing. On LinkedIn you now have LinkedIn Pulse (more in Chapter 7) where you can recycle your blog posts to showcase your own personal expertise.

13. **Share on social media.** Get your blog noticed by publishing links on social media vehicles such as Twitter, Facebook and LinkedIn (all social spaces relevant to your industry). And **make sharing simple**. Ensure that your blog has the 'sharing widgets' embedded.

14. **Write for the web.** Remember, people don't read online, they scan. Use short paragraphs. Short sentences. Bullet points. Clear headers. Links signposting readers to explore deeper into your website and services.

15. **Be useful.** Try to provide at least one piece of practical 'how to' advice in each blog post. That way the reader will learn that you are always going to provide something useful. In order to attract people to you – you've got to give them something of value.

16. **Don't push.** Don't focus your posts on selling your products or users will switch off (as they do in other conversational platforms like Twitter and Facebook). Instead, share advice, news and information that will prove useful to your readers (and grow your authority in the space).

17. **Be creative** in procuring your content. If you have published materials offline, 'blogify' them where relevant.

18. **Follow the leader.** If you find a respected and popular blogger/expert who focuses on areas you are interested in, your business area, subject, etc., write a post commenting on their post.

19. **Guest blog.** Ask others to guest blog on your blog and advise other blogs you respect that you'd be happy to do the same. You can make requests for guest blogging via Twitter using popular hashtags

#PRrequest or #journorequest – and you'll reach a whole load of bloggers.

20. **Create a blog boiler plate.** Create a succinct '60-second elevator pitch' that describes your business, the author and includes a link back to your site. Ensure this blog boiler plate is included at the end of every blog post you create (keyword enabled where possible).

21. **Link to other posts.** Refer to other posts you've written and include links so that you showcase other relevant and related content in your blog. (There are many plugins you can add to your blog that automate this process; for example on WordPress check out the 'Related Posts' plugin.)

Now you're armed with some tactical tips, you're ready to get started. So let's look at . . .

Types of blog posts to get you started

- **News articles.** These are the bread and butter of most companies' blogs. News articles could include industry news, company news, information for staff and anything new that is going on.
- **Case studies** make brilliant blog posts as they will help to sell your business. Case studies are the perfect story – start, middle and end. They will help visitors to your blog decide whether they want to do business with you and can lead to an increase in enquiries.
- **List posts.** People always like to read list posts, for example 'The top 10 reasons to avoid . . .' or 'The five best ways to . . .'
- **Stories.** People love a good story, especially if it's witty and they can relate to it. Think of any funny or poignant business stories you might have with a meaningful message. (There's more on stories later in this chapter.)
- **FAQ posts.** If you are constantly fielding questions on a particular subject, or want to help people find the answer to a question, FAQ posts are a very good idea. Think of the top five most-asked questions and start there.
- **Employee spotlight.** One way of engaging with and rewarding your employees is to spotlight one each month. You could interview them or praise them for work they have been carrying out via a blog article.

Whether you are setting off alone or creating a corporate blogging team – here's your checklist:

What now?

- Appoint an editor (that may just be you!).
- Create an editorial/features list.

- Brainstorm some headlines.
- Create an editorial process/content/images/style.
- Create a Content calendar.
- Allocate blog posts to relevant team to write – set targets.
- Set aside an hour to blog each week/month.
- Set alerts in Outlook or on your phone to ensure you hit your blogging targets.
- Be conversational and be yourself (don't be too formal).
- Keep at it.

Remember . . .

Blogging is a marathon, not a sprint. It's unlikely to be an overnight success, so give it time and keep at it. And remember, learn from what engages. If you see a spike in traffic or engagement – then think about why that is. Did someone retweet it, or was your subject highly topical. For example, '5 Things all Businesses Can Learn from *Game of Thrones'* posted on the eve of the next series may tap into a *Game of Thrones* audience.

The importance of keywords when planning content

As a consumer it's likely that when you are looking for a new product or service you turn to Google or another search engine (maybe even Twitter, Facebook and LinkedIn) and hit their search bars with some all important 'keywords' – or sometimes a 'key phrase'. For example:

- social media consultancy London
- Cat groomer Berkshire
- Tax advice Salford.

When people search online, they use just a few keywords to find what they are looking for. Therefore, if you want to be found by those seeking your products and services, it's important that you provide a consistent and optimised presence online across all the portals that you are represented on (website, Facebook, blog, Twitter, Google+, LinkedIn, Instagram, Pinterest, YouTube, etc.).

Keywords are the 'DNA' of your business. They are of paramount importance for:

- search engine optimisation
- online social platform profiles
- website content

- tweets
- Facebook Page updates
- tagging YouTube videos
- pay-per-click campaigns
- building communities on social media
- Business intelligence
- #Hashtags.

Throughout this book we emphasise the importance of using keywords to optimise your profiles and status updates. Discovering your keywords is key, so let's take a look at ways of exploring and determining your keywords.

Discovering your keywords

When you created your website, you will ideally have engaged an SEO (search engine optimisation) expert or team to ensure that your website platform would be as optimised as possible for web searches.

The SEO team would be fully conversant with keywords and would (usually) have undertaken a keyword exercise to identify your keywords in order for them to populate your website with relevant information.

Other less scientific methods you may wish to explore include the following.

- Ask your colleagues and business associates to list the top five words that apply to your business.
- Ask your customers to do the same (How did you find us? Which words did you type into a Google search to find us?). This could be a manual or automated process.
- Look at Google Analytics to see what keywords people use. If you have Google Analytics running on your site, you can review the keywords people have used to find you, following this route:
  - o   All traffic
  - o   Channels
  - o   Organic search.
- This will show you a list of the words, in order of relevance, that people have used to find your services. Undertake this process regularly to watch for any shifts in keyword trends.
- Use Google's Keyword Planner to find the most popular searches around your products or services. If you are stuck for ideas, Google's Keyword Planner offers you a free resource to explore. The tool provides you with traffic information related to specific keywords, so you might want to experiment with specific key-words to see if you gain more traction by optimising your content with high-traffic keywords that are relevant to your product or service.

Keep monitoring keyword activity via Analytics and keyword tools so that you are continually optimising.

You may want to optimise different facets of your business with different keywords, so explore and be consistent across your content in line with your specific objectives.

Make your communications count

Clearly, one way to make your communications count is to ensure that they are keyword optimised. However, while you want to optimise your content so that it's leveraged for search engines, first and foremost you are writing to engage people.

Experts agree that when you are promoting your services and writing your email, sales letter or website promotional material, Facebook update, etc., the key activity is to 'plan your writing'. Ninety per cent of the thinking should happen before those eager fingers start tapping at the keypad.

The focus of your communication is to grow 'share of mind', to get people to know you, like you, trust you – and, ultimately, do business with you. So let's take a look at some elements you need to consider when crafting your communications.

- **Focus on the objective.** What's the end game? Ask yourself the question, 'What do I want my communication to achieve?' Consider this and then work backwards, asking yourself key questions such as, 'How do we best communicate that?' Simply put, start with the end in mind.
- **Be yourself.** Personalise the communication as much as you can and demonstrate a sound knowledge of your audience's business dynamics and needs as well as a clear understanding of the obstacles they face. If the reader believes that you have empathy with their situation they are far more likely to continue reading. Be human!
- **Don't talk too much about yourself.** Readers are far more interested in what you can do for them than they are in what you do. Focus on the opportunities and benefits your products and services offer them.
- **Use the words 'you' and 'your'** as much as possible and minimise 'we' and 'us'. This will warm up your communications considerably. Avoid words such as difficult, fail, failure, hard, loss, obligation, try, sold, worry, cost, bad, fail, lose, sold, worry. (Consumer psychology research has tested communications littered with such words and found that they have a negative impact on your audience.) Use positive words – such as results, discover, approve, deserve, easy, proven, save, trust, truth, understand, value and vital – when you can.

- **Use sub-heads**, bullet points and highlighted or underlined text to convey key points. Be sure that your key messages don't get lost in a sea of text. And when writing online, be sure that things that look like they should be links are links. If you underline a sub-heading to make it stand out people will start clicking on it, expecting it to be a link.
- **Communicate a very clear proposition.** Have you seen the 'Dollar Shave' video? We love it for a number of reasons. It's humorous, it's simple; but, very cleverly, it gets the value proposition across very quickly. In the first sentence we hear 'I'm the founder of Dollar Shave Club and for a dollar a month we'll send your razors straight to your door' – a very simple proposition, said very succinctly. Whether your medium is video, written, visual or auditory – keep the proposition simple.
- **Make it easy for people to engage.** Have clear 'calls to action' and very clear instructions and signposts as to what you want people to do. If it's a video, include your website URL or Facebook Page address at the end of the video (depending on where you want to send your readers). If you want them to download an ebook or guide, make the instructions very clear and simple to follow. If you want them to share something, include social sharing icons in obvious places. The more instructions you provide, and the simpler and clearer you make the instructions, the better.

Content that engages

Providing engaging content isn't just about making it simple for people to engage with your content. In today's information-rich world, we need to stand out from the crowd and create content that resonates with our audiences and compels them to share.

Stories have always created a strong human connection. From stories told round a campfire to being tucked up in bed listening to our parents read us the dark wonders of Hans Christian Andersen and the brothers Grimm, the engagement of storytelling is timeless.

When considering how to create content that compels others to share your content, and therefore amplify your message, another element to think of in your blend of content is the stories you can create about experiences around your products and services.

Let's take a look at some storytelling ideas.

- **Educate others about the range of solutions you provide.** You may already have FAQs or user manuals/guides in place, but they may be pretty dry and unappealing. Challenge yourself and/or your team to think about how you could create an educational story about your products or services. You could perhaps create a character who has a specific problem; you could write in dialogue or use an 'agony aunt' style. Whatever style you use, creating a story provides a warmer and more compelling tale than a dry list of FAQs that run on for pages and pages.

- **Share real-life examples of what's working for others.** Case studies are actually perfect stories. In a case study you have the opportunity to use real-life experiences, from both your perspective and the client's point of view. If the information is sensitive and your client does not want their name revealed, you can simply use a generic term instead, e.g. 'Cosmetic Dentist in east London'. With a case study you can explain what was happening before your involvement, how you managed the project and the outcomes. A beginning, a middle and an end – the perfect structure for a successful story. You could also include a 'to be continued' element so that you can keep adding to the story as things progress further.
- **Share expertise and thought leadership.** Your opinion and viewpoint can be turned into a story. Let's say there's something really topical in the news or trending on social networks around which you can create a story. This enables you to share your personality and your viewpoint and showcase your experience and expertise in a specific area – thus growing your credibility as a thought leader.

You could interview someone, have a Q&A session or undertake a piece of research and build a story around that. These examples are just a few ways in which you can create compelling stories to share as part of your content strategy.

As well as the classic great authors throughout time who have told stories there are some wonderful digital classics to follow too. We've mentioned him before, and we'll mention him again – Seth Godin is a great storyteller, and his daily blog is always widely shared. Why? For the very reason that he's sharing compelling, thought-provoking and educational stories.

A key message here is to get creative with your content creation opportunities. Don't hold back on how you can leverage storytelling in your social media marketing and content strategy. After all, as we've said a few times, you are what you share, so be sure to make your content as compelling as possible.

This really useful matrix, kindly shared by @davechaffey and the team at Smart Insights (www.smartinsights.com) will assist you with your content planning – ensuring that you are striking a balance of content.

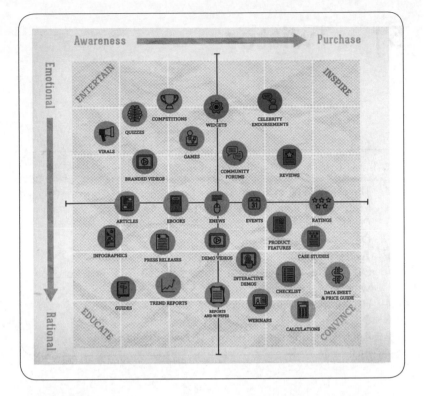

Social media marketing action plan

- You are what you share – consider how you weave content marketing into your marketing activity.
- Develop a content road map.
- Use a mix of media.
- Understand the power of blogging.
- Think about the importance of keywords when planning and sharing content.
- Create a publishing schedule for content.

5 | Twitter

> **What you will learn from this chapter:**
>
> - The many uses of Twitter
> - Practical set-up and getting started
> - Profile set-up
> - Day-to-day management
> - Twitter trivia
> - Dos and don'ts, etiquette, good practice, e.g. how to cope with being spammed
> - HR internal policies on Twitter
> - Disclaimers
> - Analytics (Tools; TweetReach, Google Analytics, etc.)

What is Twitter?

Twitter launched in March 2006 and at the time it was branded as a microblogging service (in other words, blogging with very few words). Back in the day, Twitter encouraged users to answer the simple question, *'What are you doing?'*

Over the years Twitter has evolved considerably. When one of the authors of this book attended a conference two years ago, Bruce Daisley – the seemingly ever connected and highly responsive UK MD – described the platform's function as *'connecting you with people and information that matters to you'*.

Today, twitter.com states: *'Connect with your friends – and other fascinating people. Get in-the-moment updates on the things that interest you. And watch events unfold, in real time, from every angle.'*

When we started using Twitter, around seven years ago, the tweets that people were sharing very much focused on answering the question, 'What are you doing?' Tweets like *'I'm eating a cheese sandwich'*, *'I'm just heading to the park to read a book'*, *'Meeting up with Suzie at 3pm – heading there now'* took up the majority of the Twitter airspace.

And even we, number one Twitter advocates, watched the world of Twitter roll by, thinking *'What's the point of that?'*

Those of you who have been tweeting for a few years now will have noticed a seismic shift away from largely mundane tweets towards more focused, information-rich, useful and compelling information. Many tweets now include live links and engaging imagery, directing people to articles, landing pages, offers, images, videos, websites and more, thereby becoming a fabulous tool for driving traffic and audiences to a specific event (whether that event is a blog post, a research paper, a picture or a video, etc.). As happens with most tech-nologies, they start off as one thing and evolve into something else. Why the shift? Well, the marketers woke up and realised that a shift in consumerism was upon us. Their customers, their target audiences, were happily chatting on Twitter for hours every day, and they realised that here was a potentially far-reaching communication channel that they could adopt.

While today some people do still use Twitter for personal use – to talk about cheese sandwiches to their genuine friends – the channel has also been appropriated by businesses, communication teams, brands, pressure groups, political parties, communities and marketers the world over leveraging the simplicity and scale of the platform in an often tar-geted and purposeful way. Eighty per cent of world leaders have a Twit-ter account, with Barack Obama ranked No. 1. There are some serious conversations taking place.

The current picture

By the time this edition of the book is published, these figures are likely to be out of date, but the numbers are highly unlikely to have decreased.

The appetite for Twitter continues to gather pace. The site has approxi-mately 15 million users in the UK, and around 288 million active users worldwide – and it continues to grow.

One of Twitter's greatest assets (and there are many, which we will explore in detail during this chapter) is the fact that each communication is short.

Messages, known as tweets, are limited to just 140 characters – so those of us who participate are having to become masters of saying more with less. In an age when we are saturated with information, the fact that messages are limited to such short snippets feeds our growing appetite to assimilate an abundance of information quickly. In effect, you can still listen to the noise, but in a condensed way, enabling you to take what you need and ignore anything surplus to requirements.

Twitter works wonderfully with mobile

At the beginning of this book we talked about the growth of mobile as well as how mobile browsing and purchasing via mobile is on the increase (and more recently has overtaken desktop browsing). Twitter works in harmony with mobile communications, as evidenced in the UK by the fact that it is now the fourth-largest country for Twitter users in the world, with 80% of users accessing Twitter via mobile phones.

Real time

Another key asset of Twitter is just how 'real time' the platform is. We often refer to Twitter as the Usain Bolt of the social networks. In contrast to Facebook and LinkedIn, Twitter updates don't stick around for all that long. The sheer volume of tweets (www.internetlivestats.com reports that around 6,000 tweets are tweeted every second, which corresponds to over 350,000 per minute, 500 million per day and around 200 billion per year!) means that what you see in your Twitter stream changes rapidly. Within seconds a stream is populated with new tweets.

It's reported that the average lifetime of a tweet is just 22 seconds. So this has a significant impact on how you manage your communications in this fast moving and real-time space.

The other key aspect of real-time publishing on Twitter is that unlike other platforms, such as Facebook, which use algorithms to determine who gets to see what, Twitter keeps it very simple. If you publish something to your news feed on Twitter, and you have 500 followers, that tweet hits every single one of your followers' news feeds.

Real-time feedback

Another positive element of real time is the fact that you can listen in to conversations in real time too. Research programs that previously might have taken weeks or months to pull together can be executed via Twitter, giving a real-time understanding of impact and feedback as things actually unfold.

For example, a few years ago the UK supermarket Waitrose ran a campaign on Twitter through which they wanted to engage their audience and find out why people love shopping at Waitrose. They posed the question: *'I love shopping at Waitrose because _____'* #WaitroseReasons.

Unfortunately, the campaign didn't go quite as they had expected. However, it did create a significant amount of free PR for the brand. (You can read more on this in an article published in the *Daily Mail*, www. dailymail.co.uk/news/article-2205975/Waitrose-Twitter-backlash-I-shop-Waitrose—I-dont-like-surrounded-poor-people.html?ito=feeds-newsxml.)

Perhaps it would have been better to have given some 'steer' to this question rather than leaving it so wide open. Had they said, *'We love shopping at Waitrose because the strawberries are super fresh and locally sourced – what do you love?'*, that would potentially have steered the feedback along a 'food quality' direction, rather than keeping the questioning so broad that people could take it anywhere.

On Twitter, people are talking online and in real time. With relevant tools and know-how you can engage with an audience to ask questions and get real-time responses (as Waitrose endeavoured to do) and indeed you can track keywords and be alerted to any specific conversations around those keywords or sentiments. This is useful to grow engagement and connect with relevant people or simply to learn about views. So real time presents some key opportunities.

44% of active Twitter accounts don't tweet

What's interesting is that a high number of Twitter users don't actually tweet via their account, but instead use Twitter as a targeted news feed. They tune in to the content creators, people, brands, businesses, advisory services, etc. they love. Whether it's for well-being, humour, traffic and travel updates, etc., the real-time aspect of Twitter and its adaptability gives you, the user, the opportunity to tune in and use Twitter exactly as you want to.

Uses of Twitter

Twitter is a hive of activity. It's one of the buzziest open networks, probably second only to WhatsApp, and its versatility makes it the must-have social media channel as it's a perfect vehicle for sharing, targeting, connecting and listening. Such versatility means that even if a business doesn't actually want to be engaging via Twitter and promoting a formal Twitter presence, it can still be used as a research channel – tracking conversations, brand mentions, sentiment and insights.

Let's take a look at some real world uses for Twitter.

Customer support and service

A number of organisations now leverage Twitter as a key resource for customer support. Take a look at First Great Western's Twitter feed,

@fgw. This travel update and travel support account regularly engages by tweeting tactics and tips in answer to questions. The account makes it clear that the support service is manned 24/7, and it explains what it does: providing service updates and answering questions.

Another support account to review is @XboxSupport. Its profile showcases that it is 'Guinness World Record Holder' for being the most responsive brand on Twitter. Again, the profile clearly indicates when the support account is staffed and the team who is involved in the support service.

If you use Twitter for customer support, just as we mentioned in Chapter 2, you need to cover a few elements.

1 Speed of response

If you are promoting a support service, you really have to deliver. Minutes can be too long a response time. So you have to be resourced effectively, both with tools to track the queries and with people ready and equipped to respond.

Profile summary ✕

@XboxSupport

Andrew	AC	Damen	AZ	Khoa	KN
Ben	BB	Evan	EB	Lee	LB
Berto	AA	Francis	AJ	Nate	NX
Bradly	BB	Garett	GC	Mike	ASK
Casey	AZL	James	AJD	Peter	APC
Chad	AC	Jens	AV	Phil	PS
Chris	HG	Jerey	A-P	PJ	MD
Chris	CB	Jesse	AJG	Rob	ARH
Chris	XCW	Jex	AJB	Ryan	AV
Chip	YCH	Jonny	XJN	Savannah	ASV
Dann	AZ	Josh	AXZ	Sharmon	ASB
Deno	AAD	Joshua	AJX		

| TWEETS | FOLLOWING | FOLLOWERS |
| 1.9M | 218K | 577K |

Xbox Support (1-5) ✅

@XboxSupport

Guinness World Record Holder: Most Responsive Brand on Twitter! /// Hours: Mon-Sun 6am-12am PT /// For News, follow @Xbox & @MajorNelson

> ### Social media story
>
> A member of our team needed a code to update a piece of antivirus software. It was a simple procedure, but they didn't have the code. They went to the Symantec website and at the time there were no signs of social media on their website, so the main point of contact for support queries was a phone number. A call was made and so began the button-pressing, navigating services and holding on, while being told how important they were. The problem was, they were held in the queue for about 40 minutes. Of course, they took to Twitter with the message, *'Arrgh Symantec – nightmare been on hold to support for 40 mins.'*
>
> It took just a few seconds for someone from @symantec to respond with, *'Hi – It's the support team here. How can we help?'* We quickly advised them of the challenge, they came back with a link to a website which opened a chat session and the issue was resolved in just a few minutes. Of course, the then happy customer went back on Twitter praising the company's customer service efforts: *'@symantec Excellent use of Twitter for customer support. 5 Stars'.*

Speed of response and having a mechanism and process in place to get the complainant off the live channel to resolve the issue can turn a negative experience into a very positive one – and one which is visible for all your followers to view too.

2 Get them off the platform

You really don't want someone ranting and raving on Twitter so that all your followers can see it. This can spark negative feedback from others and, before you know it, you have a barrage of insults to deal with. Therefore, be sure you have a mechanism in place, as in the Symantec example above. For example, are you going to send people off to a chat page, ask them to call you or get them to direct message you (a direct message is private from everyone else's view)? Do you have a website link or a chat facility to send them to, or even a support number for them to call?

3 Setting expectations

The accounts mentioned above, and many support accounts on Twitter, say clearly when the support account is staffed. If you say your support account is available 24/7, you've got to deliver. Setting expectations of when the account is staffed doesn't, however, always delight customers. A recent delegate from one of our Business Training MadeSimple training courses tweeted us to advise about poor customer service from @waitrose. She had tweeted them on a Saturday evening and had not had a response and had therefore had a moan at them. In fairness,

Waitrose's Twitter account clearly states, *'Follow us for all the latest news, recipes and offers from Waitrose. We're available on Twitter whenever our shops are open.'* And clearly their shops were closed at the time she tweeted them, hence no response.

Even though Waitrose had clearly laid out the terms of their engagement, the delegate was still disappointed. They continued to tweet them and then brought in competitor supermarket chain Sainsbury's who, unfortunately for Waitrose, were very responsive and engaged with the delegate regarding the question she had originally raised about freezing salmon.

This is clear evidence that consumers now expect to get a quick response via Twitter even when the company or brand has clearly tried to manage expectations – and further, that they will potentially switch allegiances to those that are listening and engaging.

4 Escalation and response policies

Always expect the best but plan for the worst. It's important that organisations at least plan some response measures for 'what happens if it all goes wrong'. Many of the #fails on Twitter (a hashtag commonly used when a person is sharing a gripe around a negative service issue) are largely down to the fact that effective planning and procedures haven't been put in place to deal effectively with complaints or unrest.

McDonald's ran a well-publicised campaign around the hashtag #McDStories. They promoted the tweet in Twitter streams, encouraging people to share their McDonald's stories. Like the #WaitroseReasons campaign, the call to action was much too broad, and of course it laid McDonald's wide open to receive feedback about all experiences with the brand, the majority of which were not positive. The PR team at McDonalds very quickly saw what was happening (that there was a bit of 'bashtagging' going on) and removed the promoted hashtag. It eventually took about a week for the noise to die down (and we're sure it hardly made a dent to the huge brand). However, with better planning they might have steered consumers down another path.

Many people were watching for Waitrose's response to the #WaitroseReasons campaign. Pretty quickly (within just a matter of hours) their PR team came out with their heads held high. They did the right thing. They very quickly thanked everyone for their responses, they were transparent and, in as many words, said, *'Well, that wasn't really what we were expecting – however, it's been a hugely illuminating exercise and one which we have learned a great deal from.'*

If you are using Twitter for customer service, be sure to get your escalation policies and procedures in place, just as you would in the offline world. In a highly connected and potentially viral world, the way you manage complaints and challenges is absolutely key. Remember, people aren't necessarily looking for the answer there and then. They often just want to know that their voice is being heard and that someone will look into things and get back to them. Ignoring social communications (or any service-focused communications for that matter) is not the right thing to do. So be sure that you have clear processes in place. Don't be stuck for words – be sure you have it all covered.

Brand reputation management

Many organisations we meet express this sentiment: *'I don't want our organisation to go onto Twitter because what if someone says something awful about us?'* The truth of the matter is, whether or not your organisation is on Twitter, people may still be talking about you – both positively and negatively. The question is, would you rather let them talk about you and have no idea what they are saying, and no means of talking back to them; or would you rather embrace what they are saying and potentially join the conversation?

In Chapter 2 we showcased the Fashion Brand No Refunds Policy case study, a classic example of missing out on what is being said around a brand. That case study shows that tracking your brand online can be most illuminating. (Chapter 11 on Listening will discuss a range of practical ways of listening out for and tracking brand mentions.)

Polling and product feedback

Because Twitter is so 'real time', it's a wonderful platform for gathering information quickly. You might, for example, want to run a poll on a specific topic or get some feedback on a product or service. A really neat and simple tool for running polls or surveys on Twitter is www. twtpoll.com. The great thing about Twtpoll (and, no, that isn't a typo – there isn't an i) is just how simple it is to use. In addition, it provides you with diagrams and pie charts showing the feedback and information about who said what. So it is a useful tool for engaging your followers and potentially reaching new audiences, and also for content creation. A good example of using Twtpoll was when a university lecturer polled his students to get their view on the order of their tutorials – they were voting on which modules they wanted to tackle first. But of course, the options are endless.

Listening in, capturing conversations and sales leads

We've already mentioned that Twitter is a fast and noisy place. Millions of tweets are being circulated at any one time. Cutting through the noise and tuning into what's important to you is therefore key, otherwise it all becomes overwhelming and pointless. If you just get on Twitter and start talking, using the same promotional marketing speak as you would apply to your traditional marketing messages, you just become part of the noise. It's not targeted, it's not purposeful and – guess what – it's unlikely that anyone's tuning in. Listening in and doing your research as to what's being said by the people you are keen to engage with is fundamental. (There's more on listening in Chapter 11.)

News distribution

Many businesses create regular newsletters or information to share with clients or prospective clients, helping them to stay in touch and keep up to date with what they're doing. Twitter provides a perfect vehicle for showcasing news and updates about recent business activity. Of course, you don't want to simply fill your Twitter activity with all your own news – that would become pretty boring. But it's certainly a useful platform for sharing relevant news as well as keeping clients and prospective clients in touch with your activities.

Traditional PR activities can be leveraged not only by going through to all your usual traditional contacts, but also by sharing with relevant influencers on Twitter. Most (if not all) credible journalists are on Twitter, so it's worth tracking down those journalists who are relevant to your sector, following them and sharing information with them via Twitter. Whatever news you have to share, whether you're promoting an event, launching a product, leveraging a PR activity or showcasing your monthly newsletter, think about how you can share the news in a relevant and targeted way on Twitter. For example, if you have a monthly newsletter which includes five articles, perhaps you could break up those articles into five different tweets rather than simply tweeting a link to the whole newsletter.

Brand awareness

Brands and businesses of all shapes and sizes are on Twitter and many of the larger brands, such as Coca-Cola and Innocent, are largely there to engage with their followers and for general brand building. Even though research shows that people are more likely to follow individuals on Twitter and that it's on Facebook where they are more likely to engage with a brand, Twitter is still relevant for brand building and awareness.

If you are using Twitter for brand building, you have to consider what that means.

- What content shall we create?
- How shall we engage our followers?

In the traditional world, brand building is largely about advertising spend and being as visible as possible. Of course, extraordinarily innovative creative campaigns and breathtaking cinema advertisements get people talking – those same 'buzz' principles apply to Twitter, albeit you only have 140 characters to orchestrate it. Twitter's promotional platform has of course evolved in line with its progress, and advertising has progressed from promoted accounts and tweets to include creativity beyond 140 characters. (We'll look at Twitter advertising in more detail in Chapter 10.)

Creative use of Twitter for a community charity

The UK Citizens Advice Bureau (CAB) ran a brand awareness campaign focused around changing perception of what the CAB actually does. Over the years, the CAB had found that they came up against the same awareness challenge – people's key perception being that the CAB largely provided advice around consumer complaints. However, the CAB, a charity organisation, provide a whole range of diverse advisory services, and it was clear to them that the general public were largely unaware of the diversity of advice and services available via their local CAB.

Working within tight budgets, as many charities and organisations have to, the charity wanted to grow awareness in the most cost-effective way. So they turned to Twitter. They launched a campaign and branded it with a hashtag #CABLive which they promoted in various ways, not only to the general public, but also to other CABs in their region, thus amplifying the message and reach. The campaign focus was around a week in March: they tweeted every incident they dealt with and, of course, included the #CABLive hashtag in every tweet. This activity illuminated to their many followers the diversity of advice on offer. The campaign was hugely successful and it is going to be repeated by both the regional branches involved and other branches. Engagement levels grew and awareness of additional services was enhanced.

Creative use of Twitter for awareness and viral aspect

An abstract artist who goes by the Twitter handle @streetartdrop has fans on Twitter closely watching his tweets for clues as to where they can get their hands on his free artwork. The artist has been going around Buckinghamshire, Berkshire and London leaving large canvas paintings on the streets for anyone to find and claim for themselves. He's using the power of Twitter to share clues with his followers as to the whereabouts of each of his paintings. And in the process his followers doubled in just a couple of days.

We started following him about a year ago, having found out about his activities chatting over the fence with a neighbour. But this chatter is spreading much wider – and that's definitely @streetartdrop's intention. His mission now is to take his art drops nationwide. After tweeting the name of the location he intends to visit, he leaves his artwork, usually by street signs, for others to find. Anyone who spots the colourful canvases can literally pick them up and take them home for free. It's becoming a race to the treasure.

We love how innovative this guy is – using Twitter as a vehicle to share clues to a wide audience – and in turn get everyone talking about him and tuning in. As we always say, content matters on social media – after all, the 'media' element of 'social media' is the core element that people are interested in. And @streetartdrop gets that. He's created a 'game' – a fun art treasure hunt – using Twitter as the vehicle to share clues with an ever-growing tribe of followers. Hats off to him!

So if you are looking for some free and interesting art which has a story to tell, follow @streetartdrop on Twitter and be sure to follow the clues for the next painting, which may be coming to a street near you sometime soon!

Gathering support for a cause

Many charities and causes use the power of Twitter to orchestrate a mass stance. For example, when police stations or services are being cut, people turn to Twitter to build awareness of the work they do. The online lobbying organisation 38 Degrees (www.38degrees.org.uk – 'People, Power, Change') brings millions of people together to use the power of the crowd. They use their @38_degrees account to extend the leverage of their online campaigns, amplify their messages and reach new audiences. They report their successes and keep their supporters engaged. And they encourage their supporters to share via Facebook and Twitter and get their friends involved too.

Another example is celebrity chef Hugh Fearnley-Whittingstall's campaign against overfishing. When a documentary about the overfishing issues was aired on Channel 4 in the UK, the hashtag #hughsfishfight was promoted throughout the programme. People were encouraged to join his campaign on Twitter and Facebook and to sign up to his website. In three years he had over 250,000 Likes on Facebook, over 50,000 followers on Twitter and over 850,000 people had signed up to his online overfishing petition. His tagline, 'You can't ignore [number of people signed up to his petition]' holds great sway. A great example of a socially integrated awareness campaign. While the number of Likes or sign-ups to his website may dwarf the number of followers he has on Twitter, the campaign uses the site very wisely. Whenever Hugh needs to bring attention to some parliamentary debate or put pressure on MPs who are debating key issues surrounding policy making, he reaches out on Twitter to his trusted fish fighters and asks them to tweet @MP_NAME to advise that the fish fighters are watching and to encourage the MP to do the right thing. This has generated 225,000 emails being sent to MEPs and 220,000 tweets to MEPs. On his website, www.fishfight.net, you will see that he has set up interactive Twitter handles for all the major supermarkets so that users can directly tweet their supermarket to ask them questions about their procurement and sustainable fishing policies.

The campaign continues to build a captive and targeted audience that Fearnley-Whittingstall can draw on when required. Offline, in our traditional world, this just couldn't happen. It would be far too difficult to orchestrate that many people to respond at a specific time. However, a quick tweet and a quick press of a button to retweet it (share it with your followers) takes very little effort and adds significant impact. How is an MEP going to feel if he or she receives 15,000 tweets advising them to do the right thing?

Humanising your brand

People do business with people, and Twitter is a perfect vehicle for showcasing the people behind the brand. As with some of the support accounts outlined previously, many accounts show pictures of a number of the team and their different Twitter handles (your Twitter name – @name – is referred to, in an old Citizens Band (CB) radio term, as your 'handle'). This is getting the people behind the organisation out there and talking.

The trust factor

Another key thing to consider is that we are now in an era in which searching for products and services via search engines is the norm. As a consumer it is highly likely that you now research on Google or other search engines what you are planning to purchase before you buy it. As consumers in this 'always on' society, instead of hitting the high street or shopping mall to find products and services, we now regularly check out our trusty mobile devices. Whether we're using a smartphone, tablet, laptop or desktop, we open a search engine (still largely Google) and search for products and services. When searching we insert the all-important **keywords** or a short **keyphrase** we're looking for – for example 'chartered accountant Edinburgh' – then await the results. When we then click on a relevant link, we're hoping that the end journey fits with what we're looking for. If it doesn't, it's no real problem, as there are lots of other choices we can click back to.

Example

Let's say you click on a link and find the following websites:

Site A

A rather outmoded-looking website. There is a blog feed on the home page, but the latest piece of news is dated November 2010. Other than that there are no signs of life. Do we trust we're going to get a great service or product from a site like this?

Site B

This is a fast-loading and polished-looking website. On the home page there are social media icons advising you that you can 'join the conversation'. Not only does the site you are looking at have a blog feed – and the latest blog post is just a couple of days old – they also have a Twitter feed pulled through, where you can see what they are sharing and talking about in real time – and that they are clearly very much alive, as their latest tweet was just a few minutes ago.

Which site would you feel more inclined to do business with, A or B? For sure – it's B.

Targeting

Twitter is essentially a huge database. You have the ability to interrogate that database to find everyone you would wish to partner, network or engage with. Whether you are researching who the key influencers are in your sector, a specific target audience, ideal new business partners, advisers or peers, Twitter is a rich and open resource.

Admittedly, researching and targeting takes a bit of effort and time, but it certainly beats 'list purchasing' from data houses and then making cold contact. With Twitter, you can target influencers or audiences and then develop relationships with them, following them, sharing information with them, directing conversations to them, getting them to know you, like you and trust you, and ultimately do business with you.

Cutting corners in your targeting on Twitter

There is a quicker way of finding targets or contacts you may already have. For example, if you have a database of contacts, or a list of journalists you regularly communicate with, you can export those contacts via a CSV into an email account you already have (e.g. Gmail or Outlook), then once those contacts have been added to your email list you can visit your Twitter profile, click on the #Discover tab in the top menu and it gives you the opportunity to Find Friends. You can then select the email account against which you want to check contacts and it will search Twitter to see which of your contacts have opened Twitter accounts (with the email address that you have for them). All this makes it easier to find people on Twitter.

Hot tip

You can find people on Twitter via their email address. Often people don't use their name as their Twitter handle – and so it's tricky to find people. But if you've met someone, got their business card and know their email address – then simply type the email address into the search box on Twitter and if they have an account via that email address, up it will pop.

Once you find a contact, you can review who they follow and who is following them. You can look at their Lists (how they've segmented their followers) and see any lists that other Twitter users have put them into. This is a particularly useful feature, as someone may already have compiled a list of the types of people you are looking to connect with. (There's more on Twitter Lists later in this chapter.)

Home | Notifications | Messages | # Discover | Search Tw

Tweets

Activity

Who to follow

Find friends

Popular accounts

Find friends

Search your address book for friends

Choosing a service will open a window for you to log in securely and import your contacts to Twitter. We won't email anyone without your consent, but we may use contact information to improve Who To Follow suggestions.

AOL   [Search contacts]

Gmail   [Search contacts]

Outlook   [Search contacts]

Yahoo   [Search contacts]

You can manage the contacts you uploaded from your address book at anytime.

Getting started with Twitter

Joining is really simple – visit www.twitter.com and register. But then we suggest you seriously pause for a while before you dive in . . .

The geniuses behind Twitter have made it as simple and user-friendly as possible to set up an account, but you need to do some all-important thinking before you get started.

Here's some key terminology that we'll be using throughout the rest of the chapter. (Do check out the Social Media Glossary at the end of this book as well.)

Twitter handle

Taken from the CB radio term 'handle', this is the @name which is your brand on Twitter. For example, @michellecarvill, @savvysocialDT and @carvillcreative are the authors' handles: these are effectively our brands on Twitter.

Retweet

Retweeting a tweet simply means forwarding it to all your followers. As you can see below, Twitter makes it easy for you to share something by retweeting it (often abbreviated to RT). You simply hit the Retweet link.

In the past, when retweeting something, you had to be mindful of the character restrictions, particularly if you wanted to add a comment; but Twitter recently introduced the 'retweet with comment' feature. This enables a user to retweet and add their own comment, without having to shorten the original tweet.

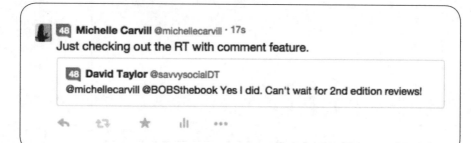

Michelle Carvill @michellecarvill · 17s
Just checking out the RT with comment feature.

> **David Taylor** @savvysocialDT
> @michellecarvill @BOBSthebook Yes I did. Can't wait for 2nd edition reviews!

Favorite

To Favorite (or favourite) a tweet is like bookmarking it. When you Favorite a tweet it is saved to your Favorites log, which can be found in your Profile settings.

Favorites can be really useful, for a number of reasons.

- To remind you of great articles you've found on Twitter.
- To keep positive testimonials about your brand, product or service, and showcase a link from your website saying *'See what people say about us on Twitter.'*
- To have a themed repository, for example: *'See all the tweets about our latest campaign.'*

How to Favorite or Unfavorite

To Favorite a tweet, you simply hit the Favorite link and you'll see an orange star appear in the right-hand corner or underneath the tweet. To Unfavorite something you simply click on the Favorite link again, and the highlight will disappear.

Following

If you follow someone, you see their tweets. Therefore, the more people you follow, the more tweets you see. But unless they are following you, they won't see your tweets.

If someone follows you, they see your tweets. And if you both follow each other you will both see each other's tweets.

Direct messaging

A bonus of two people following one another is that it gives you permission to take the conversation out of the public eye. The conversation stays on Twitter, but becomes one to one rather than one to many. You can send a direct message either by using the direct message function on Twitter – or by putting a **d** before the Twitter handle, e.g. 'd @michellecarvill' or just 'd michellecarvill' (both work) instead of @michellecarvill. (Note: you do need to leave a space after the d and before the handle.)

Following and unfollowing

When you find someone you want to follow, you click on the blue button on the right-hand side of their profile. When you click on that button it will switch to 'Following'. If you click the button again, it will switch to 'Unfollow'. Following or unfollowing someone is merely a matter of clicking a button.

Following and unfollowing is simple

When you find someone you want to follow, you will see that to the right hand side of their profile there is a blue button. When you click on that button it will switch to Following. If you want to unfollow, just click the Following button again. Following or unfollowing someone is merely a matter of clicking a button.

Hashtags

The # can be used to categorise your tweet to a particular topic. People who search Twitter for the topic that you are referring to will see your tweet. It's also used to promote an event or activity – TV programmes often use them to aggregate conversation around the specific programme or topic. Anyone can create a hashtag – it's simply a case of adding a # before any word or phrase: #hopethatmakessense! (We demystify Hashtags completely later in this chapter – see page 102.)

What next?

Now we've covered some common terminology, let's look in some more detail at getting started. While the platform is very simple to set up, what you do with it is the all-important factor; so **before** you get started, you really should decide what your objectives are and think about how you want to use Twitter – once you've started, it may be difficult to change tactics.

- Are you going to use it for general social interaction, or for business purposes?
- If the latter, what image do you want to portray?

Considering what you want to achieve from connecting on Twitter is vital to how you position yourself before you start.

Create a targeted profile

Once you've decided on your positioning you can set up your profile.

You can see from this profile overview that completing the fields is pretty simple. However, remember that your objectives steer exactly how you want to be positioned.

Let's say that you're an expert, award-winning cat groomer and your objectives on Twitter are:

1. to showcase your expertise, so that you become known as the 'go to' person about cat grooming issues

2. lead generation – listening in for people who may need your advice or your services, so that you can start networking with them, and encourage them to know you, like you, trust you and ultimately do business/engage with you.

When deciding on your Twitter @handle, would you therefore call yourself @marybloggs or @catgroomer? If you call yourself @catgroomer, the keyword in your handle gives you a good chance of being found when people are searching for cat groomers on Twitter. Also, your proposition is very clear. You don't have a cryptic brand that will be hard for someone to figure out what it is you do.

Changing your @handle

Your @handle can be changed at any time; you might start off with one @handle and decide to change it after a period of time. If you change your @handle, it doesn't mean that you lose all the Twitter followers who were following your previous @handle. You simply announce the change of @handle to your followers and your account remains intact in every other way.

Leverage your bio

The bio (biography) section (which is limited to 160 characters) allows you to showcase more about yourself or your organisation and it's probably one of the most important things people will check when they view your Twitter page. So optimising your bio is key. You can use keywords, signposts to URLs and even relevant #hashtags. However, first and foremost remember that you are writing your profile to appeal to people on Twitter rather than algorithms, so make sure your bio is very human.

Tips for effective bio writing

1. Keep it simple. You only have 160 characters to complete your bio, so be succinct. Get your proposition across as clearly as possible.
2. You may want to show your personality by adding a personal titbit about yourself.
3. Steer clear of politics, religion or sexuality (unless your objective is to focus specifically on any of these elements).
4. Include relevant @handles and web URLs to signpost people to other platforms.
5. You can include any relevant #hashtags – but only one or two.
6. Be sure that your bio is keyword optimised (but in an appealing way). For example, your bio would look pretty dull if it were just

---

a string of keywords – and it would come across as a bit 'spam-my' (e.g. *'Cat groomer – cat grooming – #cats – cat advice – cat expert'*). It's better to turn those keywords into a 'human-friendly' sentence: *'Award-winning **cat groomer** and founder of **@happycats**, sharing **cat grooming** advice, tips and tactics on how to keep your **#cats** happy and stress-free.'*

Clearly, the latter appeals, gets the proposition across – and also includes keywords, links and hashtags to better optimise your visibility on Twitter. (And it comes in at 146 characters, so it's well within the 160-character limit.)

A picture paints a thousand words

Your profile picture is one of the key elements people will review when deciding whether to follow you or engage with you. You should ensure that your profile picture fits with your objectives. Sticking with the cat groomer example, the profile picture could be of Mary Bloggs herself, perhaps holding a cat or an award; or it could be a picture of a beautifully groomed cat. A picture of Mary out with her friends in a bar probably wouldn't match her objectives. So be sure that your profile picture is fit for purpose.

Image sizes on Twitter

Your profile picture should be 128 × 128 pixels. It's a square. Therefore, you may need to consider how your brand fits into this space. Twitter also allows you to include a Twitter 'header image'. This should be 1500 × 500 pixels – and it can include text if you wish.

Who should you follow?

Once your profile page is complete and you're happy that it ticks all the boxes regarding your objectives, you are ready to get started on Twitter. However, let's remember **one critical thing: your objectives in using Twitter!** Who you follow and what you talk about is determined by the objective of the account.

For example, we know of one organisation, the MadeSimple Group, that has several Twitter accounts. Each account has its own specific audience and objective.

One account targets start-ups (a key client segment for the group). MadeSimple's objective is to become the thought leaders and go-to people for start-up advice – to help those starting out to set up, ask questions and get practical advice.

- **They follow:** start-ups, start-up support services, and associated businesses, their own customers and influencers in the sector.
- **They talk about:** start-up matters; starting, running and growing a business; funding; insurance; finance; accountancy; banking; office space, etc., sharing relevant topics and advice for the sector.
- **They share:** articles from their start-up blog, articles from influencers and around services and advice into the sector; Twitter updates from their other Twitter accounts, and relevant retweets.

Another account targets accounting professionals, another key client segment.

- **They follow:** accountants, accountancy networks, accountancy groups, relevant institutions, trade press, journalists, etc.
- **They talk about:** advice and topical news, the Budget, finance, company legislation, stats, facts, humour, etc.
- **They share:** articles from their professional services blog (they have relevant blogs to complement their Twitter accounts), topical news, advice in the sector, Twitter updates from their other Twitter accounts, and relevant retweets.

Each account has a different audience, therefore they have created numerous accounts so that they can be highly targeted in their approach. However, where relevant, they can also share content and showcase their expertise and diversity.

Follow in a targeted way

Any marketer will confirm that the more targeted a communication, the better chance of success.

- Be sure to grow your following in a targeted way.
- Think about who is going to be influential for you.

Going back to the cat groomer example, think about who would be potential influencers for lead generation and thought leadership. A targeted list of who to follow might look like this:

- dog groomers (people might ask dog groomers if they do cat grooming – *'I don't, but I know an award-winning expert who does')*

- cat trade press/journalists
- pet events/exhibitions
- cat owners
- people talking about cat grooming or looking for cat advice
- catteries ('*Get your cat pampered while you're away*')
- vets
- celebrities who own cats.

We could go on. But what this illustrates is that you shouldn't start to follow just anyone; you should have a clear understanding of who may be influential and looking to engage with your product and services. The question you need to ask yourself is: If I could network with just about anyone, who would that be? Who is going to be useful for me and help me amplify my message?

Remember, Twitter is a 'social' network, so when you are using the channel for business, it's fundamental that you utilise common-sense elements such as targeting. And the fact that Twitter is so 'real time' means that you can learn things very quickly.

While machine gun marketing – trying to hit as many people as possible – does often throw up some lucky hits, a targeted approach has always been a better way of using resources.

Learn about your network

As well as following in a targeted way, be sure to understand who the 'influential' people are in your network. Some will be noisier than others – they may be sharing your content more frequently, and they may be better connected.

It's important to keep growing your followers in a targeted way, but you should also focus on quality as well as quantity. The quality of people in your network is important. It's good to have a group of raving influencers who share your musings to a relevant audience every time you tweet. They are amplifying your reach and also advocating your conversations.

There's a great resource called Tweepi.com, an app that enables you to see who is active or passive in your network. It's a useful resource for keeping your Twitter network polished and effective. Also check out Klout.com. A Klout score provides you with a measure of how influential someone is on Twitter; for example, Stephen Fry has a Klout score of 89. You can even add a browser extension (Chrome, Firefox, etc.) so that you can automatically see someone's Klout score.

Remember: Twitter won't allow you to open an account and then start following thousands of people all at once – you could be a spammer. Twitter has some clever algorithms at play that allow you to grow your following based on how many people follow you back. So you want to get the ratio right. If you're doing the relevant research, you should follow no more than 25–50 targeted followers a day. Twitter won't allow you to follow too many all at once. So take your time and grow that Twitter following in a targeted and authentic way.

Following etiquette

We're often asked, 'If someone follows you, should you follow them back?' This is an interesting question because if you are doing all the right things and following people in a targeted way, if they then follow you, you've opened a conversation with a potential target.

If someone follows you, you're certainly not obliged to follow them back. You can check out their updates and see what they are tweeting about and then decide whether there's a fit. If you believe they could be useful or are well connected, then follow them. There are ways they can get your attention if they are following you for a specific reason. So if you don't follow them back immediately, that's fine.

If you find that they are a perfect fit or a key influencer, you may want to send them a message back saying something along the lines of *'Great to connect. Look forward to talking in the future.'* Or even one step further: *'I see you're also going to the XYZ event. Perhaps we should hook up?'*

We do **not** advocate autoresponders being sent to every person who follows you (for example: *'Thanks for following. Why not check out our Facebook Page and get 20% off our cat food?'*) It's not targeted, it's pushy and it's really not very human. Imagine going into an offline networking scenario and adopting that approach. Quite!

A targeted starting point

Of course, once you understand who you want to follow, you can start looking for them. The search function on Twitter enables you to search by relevant keywords, and as we saw earlier, you can also search using email addresses. Then you have the opportunity to review their Twitter stream, determine whether you have the right fit by seeing what they are talking about, and if it all stacks up, decide to follow them. Twitter also has an advanced search option, which includes search operators that enable you to drill down even further. You can also look at who they are following – or, indeed, who is following them. This is often a good way to go about finding new and relevant people to follow.

Finding the right people to follow can take a bit of time, but our advice is to put the effort in. Targeting your followers at the outset stands you in good stead for the future. After all, if you connect with key influencers and build a rapport, they have the opportunity to retweet your content to their audiences, which in turns grows awareness into a targeted audience.

Tactical retweets

While it's more effective to follow people in a targeted way, do remember that unless someone is following you back they can't actually see your tweets. A good tactic for getting people interested in you is to retweet their tweets. If they are saying something interesting, retweet their message (in effect this is a 'forward to all' function). Even if they aren't following you, and therefore can't see your tweets, they will be alerted to the fact that you have retweeted them. Every time someone mentions a Twitter @name or retweets a tweet, the person who is mentioned is notified. This may then alert them to check out who you are and if you are of interest to them, they may follow you. And, of course, if you follow people they are following, they too may retweet what you are saying, and they'll be alerted to you that way too.

Remember that the new 'retweet with comment' feature enables you to add your own comments without shortening the original tweet.

Direct @ messages

If you start a tweet directed to someone, for example: *'@michellecarvill I really enjoyed your latest blog post. Thanks for sharing and keep them coming. Would be great to connect'*, the person you are addressing is alerted that someone has mentioned them. If you are using Twitter effectively, mentions are key as these can open conversations. (And you really should be tracking your mentions on Twitter.) Even if that person is not following you, they will be alerted to your message and may feel compelled to check you out and follow you. This opens up the opportunity for them to share your tweets with their followers too.

Hot tip

One major mistake is made all the time on Twitter direct messages, and the culprit is evident right at the very beginning of a tweet. Starting a tweet with someone's username (their Twitter @ handle) is a big no-no! For example, if we tweet *'@BOBSthebook New ideas . . .'* without something in front of it, Twitter sees this as a reply and the tweet will only be seen by a limited number of people: only the sender, the person mentioned and the people who follow both you and the @handle you are sending the tweet to will see the tweet.

If that's your intention, that's fine. Perhaps you are intentionally being 'niche'. It's a way of sending a message to someone who is not following you (and who you therefore can't direct message).

But to turn a closed tweet into a regular public tweet (for all to see) you simply have to add something – any character – in front of the @. This is commonly done by adding words such as *'Hi there @ BOBSthebook . . .'* or *'Great post @BOBSthebook . . .'* Adding one or more characters before the @ means that your tweet is visible to everyone. The people you have 'mentioned' will be notified in the usual way.

If you're already pushing 140 characters, you can simply put any punctuation at the beginning. People often choose a full stop, probably because it's small, simple and almost invisible – e.g. *'.@ michellecarvill'*.

Getting followed

Getting people to follow you is good news, particularly if they have a strong fit with your objectives. Once they follow you, your tweets are visible to them. And if they like what you are tweeting about and retweet what you have to say, all their followers will see your original tweet. (This is particularly good if they have thousands of followers. If, say, you've written a blog post and your follower retweets your link, it will very quickly be sent to thousands of people who may never have found you, your blog or your website before.)

Another thing to do is register in the WeFollow directory (www.wefollow. com), using specific keywords so that you'll get picked up when people search on those keywords. It's also a good place to search for people.

Promote your Twitter @ handle

There are various places where you can promote the fact that people can follow you on Twitter, such as your email signature, your blog and your website. If you write articles and submit them to article marketing sites, your signature link can include your Twitter handle. Then there is your business card, letterhead, T-shirts, bags, point of sale materials, marketing campaigns, postcards, direct mail, appointment cards, till receipts, product packaging – depending on your objective, you can post it wherever relevant.

Replying to tweets

Once you're tweeting and seeing tweets appearing on your Twitter page from those you are following, you may want to reply to them. As discussed earlier, there are two ways to do this:

1. publicly, by using the @handle or simply hitting the Reply link in the Twitter stream
2. via direct message, either by using the direct message function or by putting a 'd' in front of the @handle, e.g. **d @michellecarvill**.

Remember: You can only send direct messages to people you are following and who are following you.

What to tweet

As mentioned earlier in this chapter, our advice is to do quite a lot of listening and looking before you embark on the actual tweeting. This will help you glean some insights into the type of content that resonates with your audience and you will be better equipped to start communicating. The planning, listening and analysing process should have been put in place and you should have a clear, focused view on what you want to achieve before you actually engage.

Remember: You are what you tweet. Be careful what you advocate as it will reflect on you and your organisation.

Rather than simply sharing just one type of content – for example, the latest post on your blog, or replicating promotional offers via tweets – it's far better to create a mix of targeted content. Content ideas could focus on:

*   an observation
*   something you're reading
*   what you're watching
*   an event you are at or will be attending
*   your own content (blog, newsletter, landing page)
*   someone else's content (another blog, video or article that resonates)
*   having a chat with someone, posing a question, sharing an answer
*   retweeting something that someone else has tweeted (and if relevant adding your own sentiment to that retweet).

What not to tweet

*   **What you're having for lunch.** Who cares? Yes, a lot of people do tweet about what they're eating or about something completely

inane which is totally off point and really isn't that compelling. Twitter does allow you to communicate your personality and humanise the business, but do keep in mind the whole point of this potentially far-reaching channel. By all means be casual, and be human. But don't bore people by sharing mundane nonsense. Remember the 'So what?' factor and avoid or minimise tweets that really don't add any value to the conversation. Ideally, keep your messaging 'on point'.

- **Anything you wouldn't say 'on the record'.** Our rule of thumb is that if you wouldn't say it to someone's face, don't say it on Twitter. (And remember: even if you delete a tweet, it can still be archived on the internet and could still be found.)
- **Malicious/defamatory communications.** Over the past few years we've seen more cases in court relating to people tweeting without thinking; and if you Google 'social media legal cases' you'll see pages of results. This has prompted a number of guides to social media and the law (see, for example, www.bbc.com/news/magazine-20782257). A recent piece of research by law firm Wiggin determined that 46% of 18- to 24-year-olds are unaware that they can be sued for defamation if they tweet an unsubstantiated rumour about someone. That compares to 17% of over-65s. Defamation law and the Malicious Communications Act are just as relevant online as they are offline – so be sure to use common sense. *'If in doubt, don't shout.'*

Plan your content and approach

The matrix below highlights a number of facets we've covered in this chapter. The matrix can help you map out the purpose of your Twitter account, who to follow, what content to create, how you will engage and what you will measure so that you can learn what's working.

There may be other elements that you need to build into your matrix; for example, if you're dealing with an international market, you need to consider the times when you need to be visible. Resources could be another element, including who is going to be responsible for the management of different accounts. You might need to break down activity on each account even further, particularly if you are running a specific promotional campaign.

Using the Twitter campaign planning template (see the diagram below) will help you apply practical objectives, specific outcomes, audience, tactics, offers and messaging, and elaborate on the metrics you are going to focus on.

Even though Twitter is probably one of the most powerful viral marketing resources currently available, campaigns are too often just pushed onto Twitter without strategic or tactical joined-up thinking. Remember

A Strategic Approach to Using Twitter

Purpose	Follow	Create	Engage	Measure
Cat Grooming Event promotion	Previous delegates, Cat owners, vets, dog groomers etc	Content around the event, interviews with speakers, # so people can ask questions pre event. Videos of experts.	Ask questions, share tips, advice. Answer questions. Showcase what's on at the event.	Number of interactions via the #. No of @mentions. Sign ups.
Lead generation	Target audience. Influencers. Those talking about my products and services.	Regular blog articles showcasing my knowledge. Case studies, testimonial videos. Ebook.	Provide tips and advice. Showcase expertise. Encourage to get free ebook.	No of ebook downloads and data capture for on marketing. No of @mentions. Site traffic.

the saying, *"Those who aim for nothing hit it with remarkable accuracy"* **and** be sure that you start with the end in mind and have your objectives covered.

Twitter Campaign

Objective:

Desired outcome - KPI: (Eg: 30 seats booked)

Target Audience:

Tactics (the how):

Any offer?:

Messaging:

Measurement:

Images and Twitter Cards

When planning your content, don't forget the visual aspect – you can share images on Twitter. In-stream photos should ideally be 220 × 440 pixels. And if you want to convey a specific message, you can run text over them too, so that they become more like advertisements. We suggest that you keep any text very simple – remember, 80% of people are looking at their Twitter stream via mobile apps, so too much text will be illegible.

Twitter Cards are another useful resource for showcasing visual 'advertisement'-style tweets, with specific calls to action and buttons that link the user off to a specific landing or web page. We'll look at Twitter Cards in more detail in Chapter 10.

Measure what matters

When it comes to measurement, you need to be sure that you are measuring what matters.

This may mean that you are measuring different things around a variety of objectives and organisational needs. For example, the team responsible for the brand are likely to be most concerned about metrics such as:

- positive mentions
- negative mentions
- general sentiment of the audience.

However, the business development team are likely to have a whole different set of metrics that they're keen to measure:

- How many people completed the lead generation form?
- How much traffic did we generate?
- Data capture.
- Competition sign-ups.
- Followers and engagement.
- Website traffic.

There are a number of resources you can use to help you better understand engagement, for example tools such as:

- Hootsuite (www.hootsuite.com), which features Hootsuite Analytics
- TweetStats (www.tweetstats)
- TweetReach (www.tweetreach).

We also love Sprout Social too (www.sproutsocial.com). And, of course, there's good old Google Analytics. You'll find that Google Analytics now includes a Social tab, so you can drill down into traffic and data specifically driven by social networks.

While you will need to determine your own metrics to measure, some typical areas of measurement to consider are:

- **Reach:** Total number of followers. Effectively, this is your raw distribution power.
- **Response rate:** Average number of @replies per tweet. The number of people who responded to each link or question. (TweetReach is good for this data.)
- **Branding and awareness:** How often people reference your company or products. Useful tools such as Google Alerts or Social Mention (www.socialmention.com) enable you to track this.
- **Tweet grade:** The overall effectiveness of your Twitter account. Calculates number of followers and their influence. HubSpot's Marketing Grader (https://marketing.grader.com) is a useful tool which covers a range of online aspects, including social media.
- **Sales funnel:** The number of visitors from Twitter who visit your website/blog and convert into leads/customers. You can find this data using Google Analytics.

Twitter #hashtags: what they are and how to use them

However long a team or person has been using Twitter, it's clear that people are often confused, and sometimes fearful, of the relatively harmless but potentially powerful hashtag. They often have questions such as *"Where do I get a hashtag from?"*, *"Who creates the hashtag for me?"* and *"What if I use a hashtag that's already been created?"*

As discussed at the start of this chapter, Twitter is a hugely versatile resource, and hashtags are a wonderful element of Twitter. In this section we'll cover:

- what a hashtag is
- how you go about creating them
- tips for leveraging them
- how to explore hashtags that are already out there.

What is a hashtag?

We're all accustomed to the hash sign (#) on keyboards or phone keypads. On Twitter, the term 'hashtag' simply refers to when a # sign has been placed in front of a word or group of words (e.g. #superbowl, #gbbo, #selfie, #havingabadday, #bigbrother, #zaynpaic, #PMQs) to 'tag' or 'group' tweets that all mention the same hashtag.

> ### Example
>
> The popular satirical BBC programme *Have I Got News for You* promotes the hashtag #hignfy. People can share their opinions using the hashtag while the show is airing. If you go to the search box on Twitter and type in the hashtag #hignfy you can see the conversations that are happening or have happened around the programme.
>
> With the growth in second and third screening (people using two or three screens at any one time, e.g. TV and laptop, tablet or smartphone), if you're watching the programme you can also watch the live buzz that's happening on Twitter. It's effectively a live conversation.
>
> The people talking and sharing about #hignfy do not have to be following each other on Twitter, but they can all be discussing the programme, asking questions, sharing opinions, etc., simply by including the hashtag #hignfy in their tweets. If you wanted to find

fans of the programme, you could search on #hignfy to see who is talking about it.

It's highly unlikely that any of the people talking about the programme would mention that they're fans in their Twitter profiles; so without hashtags how would we would know that they are fans of the programme?

A common thread

In effect, a hashtag is a way of searching for tweets that have a common topic. They are an 'anchor' to group conversations that allow you to create communities of people all interested in the same topic. The hashtag makes it easier to find them and to share information related to a particular topic.

Example

The London Olympics 2012 was deemed to be the most 'social' event in the world ever. Anyone who wanted to know or share anything about what was happening could follow the news by searching #london2012; if they were sharing news, they could include #london2012 in the tweet.

The hashtag was used by hundreds of thousands of people for different purposes: the athletes used it to share insights with fans; commentators and reporters used it to share updates; fans searched using it to keep up to date with what was happening and to communicate their praise and support for the athletes.

The diver Tom Daley gained over one million followers in the first two weeks, and sent direct replies to many of his fans.

Similarly, when we deliver social media training, particularly with Business Training Made Simple (www.businesstrainingmadesimple.co.uk), we share articles, tips, advice and offers via the hashtag #MadeSimple while we are training. At the outset of any course, we advise delegates of the # and at the end of the course, we go to Twitter search to show them the stream of information we have created during the course, and also show them tweets that already exist on the Hashtag. This allows them to see all the resources and conversations happening around the Hashtag. So it becomes a useful tool to share information and resources to a diverse audience. Previous delegates of the course often check back to the #MadeSimple hashtag as they know that we are always adding new things to it; so it becomes a useful repository for up-to-date information around the subjects we train in.

Hashtags and trending on Twitter

If enough people talk about or mention the same hashtag it can 'trend'. (You can see 'trending topics' on the left-hand side of your Twitter home page.) 'Trending' simply means that there's a huge buzz about a topic or hashtag; it's a topic that is being talked about the most on Twitter. If you click Change you can set your trends to worldwide or country-specific, and you can often drill down further into a specific city.

During the summer of 2012 Twitter introduced a 'Get tailored Trends' feature. If you click this feature, it removes location factors and focuses on things that are trending that 'matter more to you'. How they work this out focuses on who you follow and what they are talking about.

Trends   ×

| Search locations |

If you want to stop seeing tailored Trends, choose a new location now.

Recent Locations

London

Nearby Locations · Select your location

Brighton	London	Portsmouth
Bournemouth	Lille	Coventry
Leicester	Bristol	Birmingham
Nottingham		

Get tailored Trends   Done

Of course, trending on Twitter is no mean feat. With over 500 million tweets a day, your topic or hashtag really does have to get a lot of people talking about it to trend. So if it trends, that's quite an achievement.

Hashtags, search and awareness

As we've mentioned, searching for a #hashtag in Twitter Search is simple. Simply go to Twitter Search and enter your # term to find out what's happening around a topic – or to see if a # exists.

When you're searching for a particular hashtag, you may find other ones too – variations on a theme – so it may be worth investigating those other associated hashtags to see what conversation is happening around them.

And don't just search Twitter – search Google too. Hashtags make their way across into traditional searches, as does other content from the social platforms.

Promoting a hashtag

As you can see from the two campaigns highlighted below, a hashtag can dominate an advertising campaign.

The # hashtag promotion has now become a mainstream facet of advertising. It gives brands and advertisers a mechanism to anchor a community of diverse people around an online conversation by widely promoting the #. And if your audience is on Twitter, it's a great way to get people participating in your advertising campaign.

Where you do get hashtags?

Anyone can create a hashtag. There isn't a repository where you go and 'get one'. You can simply create one yourself by adding # in front of a keyword or group of words. However, it's a good idea to check out a hashtag before you start promoting it. You want to ensure that the hashtag you are about to use is either unique or isn't associated with something totally irrelevant.

For example, let's say you are running an event for veterinary surgeons – you've got 300 people coming, and so there's no way you're going to be able to have a one-to-one conversation with each of those delegates. While you can take a few questions from the floor, that doesn't provide you with the opportunity to engage with every delegate that may have a question. By promoting a hashtag for your event and showcasing this at the outset in promotional materials, you can get people connecting and talking; before, during and after the event. Let's say you want to create a brand or hashtag for the event. You go to Twitter, insert that hashtag into Search and see if it is being used elsewhere. Remember, tweets are limited to 140 characters, so you don't want to use a ridiculously long hashtag like #vetsandpetsannualevent2015 – keep it short and simple, e.g. #vetsandpets.

Tapping into relevant audiences via hashtags

To promote your event to a wider targeted audience, you may want to check out other hashtags to see if you can tap into other audiences using #hashtags that are appropriate and relevant to your forthcoming event.

For example, you might start by checking out #vets to see what that pulls in. We did this and found a lot of tweets about 'veterans' – but when we searched #veterinary, we found a number of related hashtags. These would be worth exploring and perhaps using in tweets alongside the #vetsandpets event hashtag to grow even more awareness into a targeted audience.

However, a word of warning here – **you must not**, repeat **must not**, hijack for promotional purposes totally unrelated trending or popular hashtags. The term 'mashtagging' is defined in the *Urban Dictionary* as:

Mashtag

n. A social networking status update, Tweet, or post that contains an unnecessarily large number of tags or tagged names often unrelated to the context of the post.

There have been a few incidents where brands have piggy-backed on trending topics, often highly sensitive topics, such as #Cairo and #Egypt around the time of the 2011 uprising, in a totally unrelated way and they came off really badly.

In late 2009 Habitat UK's tweets included well-known brand hashtags or trending hashtags to promote their products to a wider audience.

Since when did HabitatUK sell Apple products? The onslaught that followed their hijacking attempts was not pretty.

And as if that wasn't enough, Twitter can close your account if they think you're out to spam by using hashtags incorrectly. So beware. If enough people complain or report you to Twitter, it could be goodbye to your Twitter account.

> **Hashtags: key points**
>
> - Check whether the hashtag you want to promote is already in use. A simple search on Twitter should do it.
> - Look for other relevant hashtags and review who is talking around the topic – they may be relevant for you to talk to too.
> - **Never** jump on to trending or popular hashtags that are totally irrelevant to your promotion or conversation. It's spam, it's frowned upon and those who have done it have found that their reputation has been badly damaged.
> - If you want other relevant audiences to find your conversations, use a keyword-enabled hashtag that they can search on.
> - If you're using a bespoke hashtag for an event or campaign, be sure to promote the hashtag so that users know about it.

Twitter lists and segmenting the people you follow

Twitter lists are just what they say – lists of Twitter accounts. Used effectively, they're a great way to organise who you are following (and even who you are not following) into groups categorised by you. You can use your lists to tidy up your feed and group together groups of tweeters and their tweet streams. Lists allow you to view tweets in separate feeds and follow targeted, categorised groups of people together.

For example, if you were researching 'cat groomers' on Twitter and wanted to follow a selection of people who are tweeting and talking about cat grooming, you could find all the cat groomers on Twitter and then group them into a list. (**Note:** you don't have to follow them to put them into your list.) Having them all in one list will allow you to look only at tweets that are about cat grooming, which allows you to focus your attention and cut through the noise being made by the various other people you follow on your Twitter news feed.

In a separate list you might like to group together all your old college or university friends – that way you can simply click on their list and view all their streamed tweets together. This works especially well if you like to tweet each other a lot – you can block out all other Twitter noise and focus on the conversation going on between the people in your college list.

Another use for a Twitter list is to group all employees together. Having an employee list means that you can see the conversations the business within your business are having.

Finding new and relevant people

Lists also help you to target and find new and useful contacts. For example, when you view your lists you can see lists that you have created as well as lists of which you are a member (lists that someone else may have put you into).

Let's say you've been put into a 'UK Bloggers' list. Someone has gone to the trouble of creating a list of UK bloggers. People in that list may also be useful for you, so you can access that list and see who you would like to follow.

How to create a Twitter list

Creating a list is very simple.

1. Log in to your Twitter account.
2. Go to the List section by clicking the cog on the upper right-hand side of the top bar.
3. Click Lists. Now you can view your lists and the lists that others have put you into. You can also create a list.
4. To create a list, click Create list and then choose a name for your list.

5. Decide whether you want your list to be public or private (only you can view a private list).
6. Click Create list. And that's it.
7. Now you can add users and search for people to add to your list – you can do this from your profile page or from any following page. To add a person to a list simply click on the cog icon next to the Follow/Following button and select 'Add or remove from lists'.

Private and open lists

When you create a list you can decide whether your list will be open or private. If it's open, anyone can see that list. If it's private, only you see it. Private lists are a great way to monitor your competitors, or anyone else you would rather didn't know you are following them. You simply create a list, make it private – so only you can see it – and then add your competitors to it. This way, you are not following your competitors (if you did they would be alerted by a notification letting them know you had just followed them) – but you are still able to see exactly what they are sharing on Twitter.

Are there any limitations to lists?

As far as we can see, the rules that applied when lists came out in 2009 still apply. Lists can grow to no more than 500 people and each account can have a maximum of 20 lists. So there's plenty of scope there.

Do I want to be on other people's list?

The simple answer to this question is yes, you do. Being in other people's lists means that you will become more visible to your target audience. For example, if you are a cat groomer you want to be picked up by someone who's making lists about cat groomers. You are more likely to get followed by people looking for cat groomers and it's a verification that you've been tagged by others as a 'cat groomer' too.

Twitter is a content-rich channel and lists help you to sift through the noise and listen to targeted tweeters who are talking about what you want to hear. If you're on someone's list you are far more likely to be found by the right kind of tweeter.

Can you target tweets directly to Lists?

At the time of writing you cannot direct conversations to a list segment. This position has been the same since Twitter began, and while a few years ago there were whisperings that it might become a feature, so far it hasn't.

Given that you can segment those you follow so that you can see what a particular segment of people are talking about, it shouldn't be too difficult for the team at Twitter to find a way of enabling you to tweet into a segment. This may be a paid-for service in the future and possibly one of the ways Twitter will look to monetise their site – who knows. But given that the functionality works one way, it would certainly make an attractive proposition to be able to target conversations into segments. Let's wait and see.

Before we wrap up this chapter on Twitter, let's take a look at . . .

Useful Twitter apps

- Twilert (www.twilert.com) – set specific alerts – like Google Alert, but for Twitter.
- TweetReach (https://tweetreach.com) – useful research analysis tool.
- WhoUnfollowedMe (http://who.unfollowed.me) – see who unfollowed you.
- Buffer (www.bufferapp.com) – bookmark for tweets and optimised schedule.
- Tweetdeck (www.tweetdeck.com) – schedule multiple activities.
- Twtpoll (www.twtpoll.com) – polls/surveys.
- Twellow (www.twellow.com) – a categorised search directory.
- Tweepi (www.tweepi.com) – organise your followers.
- TweetStats (www.tweetstats.com) – activity stats.

There are literally hundreds, probably thousands, of apps and resources to help Twitter be an even more wonderful place. Those listed above are just a few of the ones we've used over the years.

Social media marketing action plan

- Think strategically – Plan, Listen and Analyse before you Engage.
- Know what your Twitter account is about and plan your content and conversation accordingly.
- Revisit your business objectives – use Twitter smartly to achieve objectives.
- Think about how you are going to blend Twitter into your marketing activities to add value and leverage.
- Get your service recovery process/escalation procedures, terms and conditions, and disclaimers in place. (See the social media guidelines in Chapter 13.)
- Use hashtags wisely.
- Leverage Twitter lists to manage your followers.
- Follow in a targeted and purposeful way.
- Remember, measurement and analysis aids continuous learning.

6 | Facebook: the new newspaper

What you will learn from this chapter:

- Facebook: the background
- Why Facebook is so important
- Facebook's visibility algorithm
- Ways to use Facebook
- Differences between the app and browser versions
- Setting up and content managing Pages
- Building your audience on Facebook
- Measuring the performance of your Page using Insights

In the 11 years that Facebook has been around, it has evolved from a simple way for college students to chat to each other into a highly sophisticated targeted advertising platform earning billions of dollars in revenue for the company. It is estimated that (at the time of writing) there are now over 1.4 billion users of this social networking site – a staggering one in seven of the world's population, or half of the world's global online population.

For thousands of people around the world, the first engagement they have with the outside world when they wake up in the morning is not TV, radio or a newspaper. Instead, it is very likely to be their Facebook news feed on their mobile or tablet device. Indeed, Facebook is aware of this. Mark Zuckerberg's long-term plan is to get the whole world connected. How does he plan to do this? Through the availability of cheap smartphones, 2/3/4G networks and of course a Facebook app.

For millions of people around the world, Facebook **is** the internet. Instead of going to a computer and surfing sites using browsers such as Explorer, Firefox, Chrome or Safari, you can stay within Facebook and have all your favourite sites, community group updates or preferred content come to you via your news feed. In effect, your personal news feed has become your own, tailored online 'newspaper'.

To explain further, let's draw on some journalistic experience and go into how a traditional newspaper is put together. Typically the news editor will start off with sheets of blank paper. First to go in will be the adverts, then off-the-shelf feature stories and finally the news. This will have come from a variety of sources including journalists, other media outlets, PR agencies, tip-offs and perhaps even phone tapping (!).

Ultimately, though, it is the news editor (perhaps the editor or maybe even the proprietor too) who decides what their target audience will want to read, based on the demographic of the readership. So the news editor of the *Star* (a UK tabloid-style newspaper) will want a mixture of sport, celebrity gossip, national news and showbiz; over at the *Financial Times* the material will be more cerebral – market trends, national and international business news, informed comment, etc. However, the very nature of newspapers means that the content is quite generic and not all of it will interest all readers. How many times have you ever read your chosen newspaper cover to cover? Probably never – you choose only to read what is of interest to you.

To summarise, then, a newspaper is a collection of advertisements and editorial content which is published daily, weekly or monthly. News is gathered from a variety of sources and content is decided upon by a news editor.

facebook : the new 'newspaper!

The news feed in Facebook, whether within a user's personal Profile or a brand's page, is very similar. When a new account is set up or a new page created, you start off with a blank canvas. Over time, this will be filled with a combination of news, features and adverts (via Facebook pay-per-click – more on this in Chapter 10).

As with a newspaper, there are a variety of news sources:

- friends
- Groups
- Pages
- people (via Subscriptions)
- Facebook ads
- apps, and, of course . . .
- **you**, as the owner of the Profile or the Page.

However, unlike a newspaper, you are in effect the editor, news editor and reporter for your news 'feed', so you get to choose exactly what you want to see.

With hundreds of millions of people getting their daily information from their personalised news feeds, it is not hard to understand why Facebook has become such a powerful force. And inevitably, even newspapers now market themselves on Facebook – via Pages, apps, pay-per-click advertising and sponsored stories – in an attempt to get their brand across via this new medium.

Check out www.facebook.com/guardiantechnology, www.facebook.com/latimes or www.facebook.com/lemonde.fr to see how traditional newspapers are using the site.

As with newspapers, though, you have a responsibility not only to provide interesting and engaging content but also to be very careful not to publish anything that could be harmful, libellous or offensive.

How and why Facebook filters content

With 1.4 billion people on the site as well as millions of Groups and Pages, there is inevitably an enormous amount of content being published on the site every day. Until a couple of years ago, anyone posting on a personal Profile or a company Page could pretty much guarantee that their friends or fans would see this content. However, since the introduction of a visibility algorithm in 2011, the social media giant has aimed to filter content posted on Profiles and Pages according to how relevant and engaging it is for audiences. The result is that now, unless you have a fan base of people who really want to engage with you or your brand, only a fraction of your audience will ever see your posts – unless you decide to push your content to them via other means and go down the advertising route.

There are two issues at play here. First, due to the huge number of users, the amount of content posted daily has reached overload, which is why Facebook has had to institute its filtering process. The second issue is monetisation. Facebook is a business that needs to turn a profit, so it has been under pressure to demonstrate new and innovative ways of making money, especially on mobile platforms.

Facebook now has an incredibly sophisticated advertising offering (much more on this in Chapter 10) and has also partnered with data-mining companies to provide brands with extremely targeted audiences. By using Facebook's Power Editor, it is even possible to reach out to more than 500 categories of user.

With Facebook, if you want to increase your reach to a specific target audience, you now have two similar routes. You can invest in reaching out to, and engaging with, fans organically (perfect for sports clubs, TV shows, pastimes and organisations with a ready-made fan base) or you can use various forms of advertising to reach selected audiences. As the majority of Pages fall into the latter category, making Facebook work involves creating interesting, engaging, relevant and regularly updated content, and then, if needs be, allocating the correct advertising budget to help position this in front of the right customer base. Remember, it is not just about getting Likes!

Facebook's visibility algorithm

Facebook's algorithm is a highly complex mathematical formula made up of 10,000 different variables. However, there are three key ingredients:

1. **Affinity:** This is based on the proximity to or how 'friendly' you are with a person or a brand on Facebook. It measures interactions – Likes, Comments, Clicks, Shares or Wall Posts – which users have with your Profile or Page. Put simply, this means that you need to engage with the fans of your Page by posting content that will be shared in some way.
2. **Weight:** This variable decides which pieces of content are more likely to appear in news feeds than others. A strong emphasis is now being put on videos, rather than photos, links or text-only updates. So this is all about posting interesting, engaging content.
3. **Recency:** Put simply, newer content is much more likely to appear than something older. The message here is to post regularly, including at evenings and weekends!

Note: You don't see your score. The only way you can monitor how well your Page is faring on Facebook is to look at your Insights – these will provide an instant snapshot of how people have been interacting with the content you post.

The key thing is not to get hung up about what your score may or may not be, and to make sure your Page ranks as highly as possible. Here are six easy tips.

1. **Post plenty of photos, videos and links.** Just as with newspapers, it is far more interesting when stories are illustrated with photos or diagrams. Also, Facebook allows you just 420 characters when updating your Page with a news story. However, if you upload a photo or video, Facebook rewards you with an unlimited word count when writing the caption.
2. **Don't be afraid to ask your fans for their opinions.** Many brands make the mistake of simply 'pumping out' information on their Facebook Pages, just as they have in the past with adverts or traditional marketing. However, social media is very different and should always be treated as a community. Where possible, take advantage of one-

to-one conversations. Facebook Pages should act like a forum where people with shared interests can have conversations. And, as in any conversation, you want to hear the opinions of others. So rather than post something about what you or your brand is doing, simply ask a question. Remember, this is 'social' media and as a brand, you are expected to want to inspire debate and conversations with your fans.

4. **Don't post too little or too much – find your pace.** Until recently, it was accepted practice that you should post no more than once a day on Facebook Pages. However, with the advent of Timeline, the more quality content you can post, the better. In fact, many successful brands are now posting hourly or more. Clearly, many companies or organisations will not have the resources to post this frequently, but it is important to try to update your Page at least once a day. Pages that are only updated weekly or less will not only rank lower on but will also not look great from an engagement perspective. However, look at what happens with your content and engagement rather than being robotic about your publishing schedule. For example, with some clients we've had, the more they post, the less engagement they have with fans. So you have to watch the engagement and learn from your audience to see what works best for you.

To assist with content publishing on Facebook, there is now the option to schedule your posts in advance using the new Page Scheduler. So if you don't want to post in the evening or at weekends, there is still a way of updating your Page with content. Simply update your status as usual, then specify when you would like it to be published – exactly as you would with Twitter or LinkedIn on a social media dashboard such as Hootsuite or Tweetdeck.

Note: It is important to bear in mind the times when your audience are most likely to be engaged with your Page. These could well be early mornings, late evenings or weekends – rarely office hours – but watch your analytics and learn when your audience engages. You can also use scheduler to backdate posts. Say, for example, you have been at an event and haven't had time to post on your Timeline; you can retrospectively add these posts to within a 15-minute time slot. Check out this great blog post which looks at scheduling in more detail: www.socialmediaexaminer.com/facebook-scheduled-posts.

5. **Use the correct tone of voice for your brand.** It is important to think about the language and tone of voice you use when engaging with your Facebook community of customers or fans. As with any other form of marketing, think about your audience. Depending on what business objective(s) you want to achieve with your Page – driving traffic to your website, building your brand, customer service, etc. – the audience may differ significantly. Using corporate language may be fine on a website but may not work on a Page, especially if it is being used for corporate and social responsibility purposes.

   And if you are using the Page as a customer services channel, you may wish to employ a similar tone of voice as you would in a call centre or face-to-face setting.

6. **Track the performance of your posts using Insights.** Using Facebook Insights gives you access to a wealth of data, comparable to that provided by Google Analytics. This can be measured over specified time periods and exported as a CSV or Excel spreadsheet. It can also be broken down into a defined geographical spread and demographic profile.
   Note: You need to have at least 30 fans of your Page to get access to Insights data.

Facebook Insights

- *Overview* gives you information on how many people have interacted with your individual posts and how the Page is performing overall.
- *Likes* lets you know where and who the people who like your Page are. It also informs you how they came to like the Page.
- *Reach* illustrates how many people you have reached through organic, paid or viral means.
- *Visits* shows the number of times the tabs on your page were viewed, as well as what the external referrers to your page were.
- *Posts* shows you how each post performed, when it was posted and what the content was.
- *People* gives you demographic information about the people who Like your Page: age, sex, location and languages all feature.

Using this data, you will quickly learn more about your audience and the sort of information they get excited about. Therefore, if you are posting

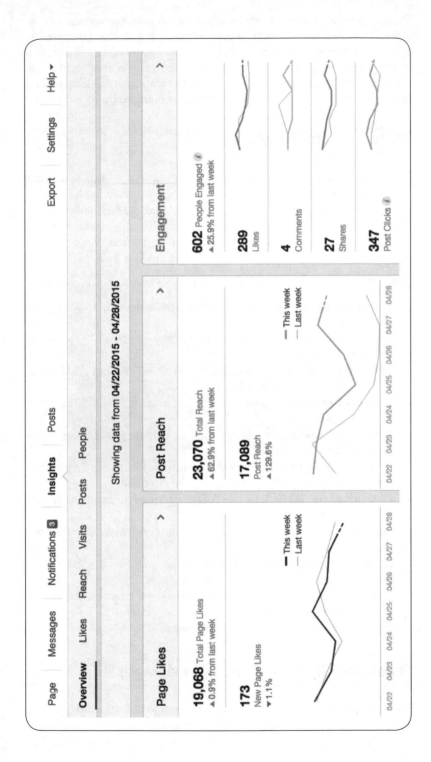

content you believe to be engaging and no one is commenting on it, chances are you need to change your engagement strategy or the quality of your updates. In conjunction with Google Analytics, Facebook Insights will give you the opportunity to hone your marketing strategy and make the necessary changes to ensure that you are achieving your objectives or hitting pre-defined key performance indicators.

Ways of using Facebook

Throughout this book we talk about how important it is to use social networks to meet specific business objectives, and Facebook is no different. It lends itself to a range of different uses, so it is vital that you plan how you are going to use it for your particular organisation. It may be that you can use Facebook in a number of different ways, so you might even consider having different Pages to reflect this.

These are the key ways we think Facebook can be used by businesses:

- **Customer support and service:** Communicate directly with your customers.
- **Lead generation:** Drive traffic to your website or Page using organic and paid-for marketing.
- **Corporate and social responsibility channel:** Reveal a different, less corporate side of your brand.
- **News distribution:** A great way to inform your client base about important news.
- **Brand awareness and establishment:** Get people talking about your products or brands.
- **Product, app, games and event promotion:** Reach out to your target audiences and engage with potential customers.
- **Gathering support for a cause:** A fantastic way for charities to educate and inform people.
- **Humanise your brand:** Become personable and showcase the people who work within your organisation.
- **Research resource:** With 1.4 billion users and Facebook Insights, you can learn about consumer behaviour.
- **Competitions:** Target your customer base with interesting and content-rich competitions to drive awareness and virality.
- **Check-in deals:** Reward customer loyalty.

Facebook Profiles, Groups and Pages

There are very important distinctions between Profiles and Pages, and many individuals and companies get these mixed up. In essence, there are three ways in which you can have a presence on Facebook: a Profile; a Group; and a Page.

Note: At the time of writing, Facebook are trialling something new, called Facebook at Work. More on this here: www.facebook.com/help/work.

Profiles

A **Profile** belongs to an individual and is their personal account. Typically this is the place where you share information with your family and friends. A Profile can be used to set up a Group or manage a Page. Ideally, it should be kept personal and not be used for business purposes.

Note: Many brands/organisations set up a Profile for their business, when what they should have created is a Page. Essentially, by using a personal Profile for business, you are a brand or organisation masquerading as a real person. This is frowned on by Facebook: **Facebook terms and conditions state that you aren't supposed to 'use your personal profile for commercial gain'.**

Subscribe feature

However, let's say that as the owner of an organisation, you're the 'voice' behind the brand. Perhaps people want to talk to you directly and find out what your organisation is doing, via you rather than via a corporate Facebook Page. Facebook Profiles can be 'subscribed' to, meaning that users can 'subscribe' to your Profile to get your news on their personal Profile news feeds. Talking about what you are doing in your business is potentially quite different from a direct sales spin.

Here's a great article from @smexaminer; it's from 2012 but is still very relevant – www.socialmediaexaminer.com/promote-your-business-with-facebook/#more-19427.

Groups

A Group is a community of people and friends who promote, share and discuss relevant topics – similar to an online forum. It can be Open (anyone can see the Group members as well as the posts), Closed (you can see the Group members but not the posts) or Secret (both members and posts are hidden to non-members). Although a useful way for people, fans or friends to communicate, a Group should not be confused with a Page. Individuals can administer the Group from their personal Profile.

Pages

A Page is a business or organisation's branded presence on Facebook. It can act as an ancillary presence to a company website or, increasingly for consumer-facing brands, it can replace the website, becoming the centre of an organisation's online marketing strategy. Pages can be branded; just as you secure a www address for your website, you can register the brand/organisation name, e.g. www.facebook.com/mybrand. Pages can be administered via a personal Profile.

In order to be the administrator of a Page, you **must** have some form of personal Profile on Facebook and you must **like** the page you want to become an administrator for.

For more information on the difference between Groups and Pages on Facebook, check out this excellent blog: www.facebook.com/blog/blog.php?post=324706977130.

Facebook policies and procedures

As we discussed in Chapter 1, about Planning, Listening and Analysing before deciding to Engage on social networks, it is important to do the correct preparation in advance of setting up a Facebook Page too. You also need to have a sensible policy in place for your staff about what they can and cannot do on the site.

We would suggest that every member of staff who has a Facebook account should set their privacy settings to maximum – i.e. only their Facebook friends can see their posts.

Also, as extra protection, all staff should ensure that their profile picture is not in any way harmful to their professional standing. Even with your privacy settings set to maximum, if you are on Facebook, your profile can be found. Even though non-friends will not be able to look at your profile, your picture will still be visible, so make sure it is suitable.

Whether we like it or not, many employers, prospective employers and potential customers now go straight to Facebook (as well as LinkedIn) to find out more about the person they are going to be dealing with. If your privacy settings are set to Public or you have an unsuitable profile picture, they may find out more than you had bargained for!

Moving into a slightly greyer area, it may be worth providing your staff with guidelines about what they should *maybe think about* when using their personal Profiles. Clearly, you **do not** control what your staff do in their private lives, but there could be times when what they post will harm your organisation.

Privacy Settings and Tools

Who can see my stuff?	Who can see your future posts?	Friends	Edit
	Review all your posts and things you're tagged in		Use Activity Log
	Limit the audience for posts you've shared with friends of friends or Public?		Limit Past Posts
Who can contact me?	Who can send you friend requests?	Everyone	Edit
	Whose messages do I want filtered into my Inbox?	Basic Filtering	Edit
Who can look me up?	Who can look you up using the email address you provided?	Everyone	Edit
	Who can look you up using the phone number you provided?	Everyone	Edit
	Do you want other search engines to link to your timeline?	Yes	Edit

> **Example**
>
> Julie, one of your junior members of staff, makes a racist remark on her Facebook Profile. Although visible only to her Facebook friends, one of Julie's friends decides not only to share the comment with his friends, but also to make the comment public. The consequences could be serious, not only for Julie but also for your brand.

We would advise setting up some simple guidelines for staff, which are just as much about protecting themselves as ensuring that your brand is not damaged.

Guidance could include the following.

- Don't write anything overtly offensive.
- Don't post anything that you wouldn't say to someone at work face-to-face – colleagues or managers alike.
- Be careful when voicing political, religious, or potentially extremist opinions.
- Beware of libel – it is a criminal offence on Facebook, as with any other form of the written word, to publish anything false that could be damaging to a person's reputation.
- Watch out for photos you may post or photos you are tagged in – nudity and drunkenness rarely look good!
- Think about your Profile. It is essentially the online personification of who you are.

App and browser versions of Facebook

Over 80% of people who use Facebook access the site via a mobile device, so it's important to know the differences between the app and browser versions of the social network.

As with any app, there is less functionality than you would get if you were viewing it on a browser. What Profile users **don't** get with the app:

- timelines for Pages
- advertisements on the right-hand side
- tabs to specific on-page applications (see below).

Essentially, everything on Facebook is now built around the news feed, so, as a rule of thumb, view your phone's screen as being the most likely 'shop window' for your Page.

Setting up and managing a Page

You have two key options if you decide you want to set up a Facebook Page.

1. If you don't have a Facebook account or if the administrators in your company or organisation are likely to change rapidly, you need to create a dummy personal Profile. This is because Facebook requires all administrators to have some form of personal presence on the site. We advise that you set up this account using a corporate email account, e.g. facebook@mycompany.co.uk. This can then be used as the login by anyone who needs to be an administrator by going to www.facebook.com.

2. If you have a Profile, you already have a Facebook account. So if you are going to be the Page 'owner', simply log into your Profile, then go to www.facebook.com/pages, where you'll see a Create Page button. Click on this and you will be taken through to this page:

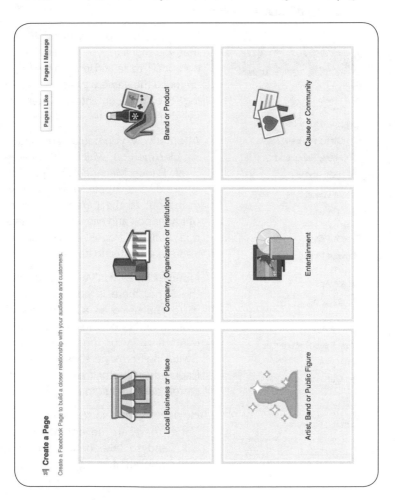

You'll see that there are six categories to choose from. Select the one most appropriate to your business or organisation, check the box saying that you agree with Facebook's terms of business (www.facebook.com/page_guidelines.php) and away you go.

Note: If you have a business that is defined by its geographical area – a butcher's shop in Tunbridge Wells or a hairdresser in Hamburg – it is best to choose the Local Business or Place option. The reason for this is that you can geo-locate (promote your location), allowing your customers to 'check in' via Facebook when they come to your premises.

Don't worry if you are unsure about how to categorise your Page – you can always change the category later using the admin settings (www.facebook.com/help/?faq=222732947737668).

When you want to administer the Page from a personal Profile, go to your personal account and in the top right-hand corner of the screen you'll see an arrow to the right of the Home button. Click on this arrow icon and a drop-down menu will appear:

When you click on any of the Pages that you manage, you will leave your personal Profile and log into the Page (in much the same way as you would log into the content management system of a website).

Alternatively, you could use a much simpler method, which is the Facebook Pages Manager app for both Android and Apple devices. This strips out all the personal aspects of Facebook and allows you to manage multiple Pages, view Insights and run advertising campaigns.

Note: Once you've logged into the Page, there is no reference at all to you being an administrator of that Page. No one will see anything related to your personal Profile. Switching from a personal Profile to a Page administrator makes you completely anonymous to everyone else.

However you wish to manage your Page, there are several steps you will need to take before you officially 'publish' it.

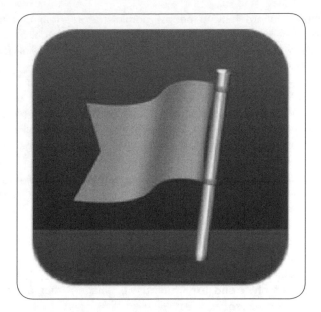

1. Ensure that you have the right number of administrators and that you have allocated them specific roles. As the creator of the Page, you may want to have one or more other appointed people to help manage it. They can have differing levels of control over the Page. Administrators must have a Facebook account, they need to have Liked your Page and they should provide you with the email address they use to access the site. You can manage administrators at any time by clicking the Admin Roles tab in the admin panel:

Everyone who works on your Page can have a different role depending on what they need to work on.

Learn more about the different roles people can have on your Page.

Craig Martindale   ×
Admin ▾
Craig can manage all aspects of the Page including sending messages and posting as the Page, creating ads, seeing which admin created a post or comment, viewing insights and assigning Page roles.

David Taylor   ×
Admin ▾
David can manage all aspects of the Page including sending messages and posting as the Page, creating ads, seeing which admin created a post or comment, viewing insights and assigning Page roles.

Julie Przn   ×
Analyst ▾
Julie can see which admin created a post or comment and view insights.

Specify an email address   ×

Editor ▾
Can edit the Page, send messages and post as the Page, create ads, see which admin created a post or comment, and view insights.

Add Another Person

Save   Cancel

When you are making people administrators, you can allocate them any of five different levels of access to the Page, from simply viewing the Insights, right up to full control. See this link for more details: www.facebook.com/help/323502271070625.

2. Go to www.facebook.com/username and register the name of the Page. You can choose either something brand-specific (e.g. www. facebook.com/SimonHowieButchers) or that is keyword-enabled (e.g. www.facebook.com/HotelsinLondon). **Note:** Unlike Twitter, once you have registered the Page, you can *only change the name once*. So make sure you get it right!

3. Make sure you have a decent 'cover' image for your Page. This should be 850 × 315 pixels in size and, like the cover of a book or old-fashioned LP record, must entice people to your Page. Facebook offers this advice on creating your cover image:

   - **Use a unique image that represents your Page.** This might be a photo of a popular menu item, album artwork or a picture of people using your product.
   - **Be creative and experiment** with images your audience responds well to.
   - **Use the cover photo to bring a strong visual impact to your Page** by extending your brand with lifestyle imagery, product images or a description of your services.
   - **Facebook now has a new Call to Action button.** This is inbuilt into your cover or sits underneath it in the app version.

   View Facebook's strict **guidelines** about cover photos here: www. facebook.com/help/276329115767498.

4. Your company or organisation's logo must fit the 180 × 180 pixel square. If it doesn't, you may need to get your logo redesigned so it can fit the space.

5. In the About section of the page, you need to put a succinct and, ideally, keyword-enabled 'boilerplate' that sums up the purpose of your business or organisation, your mission statement and an overview of what you do, complete with appropriate websites.

Example

See the Dove Page, www.facebook.com/dove/info.

At the same time, it is a good idea to list the terms and conditions for your Page. This is especially important if it is being used as a customer service/engagement channel.

6. Build up your Timeline from the date your organisation was founded up to the present. To do this, upload as many relevant photos and videos as you can, along with write-ups, as milestones. This will provide a background narrative as well as help reinforce your brand for visitors to the Page. Remember, you want your Facebook Page

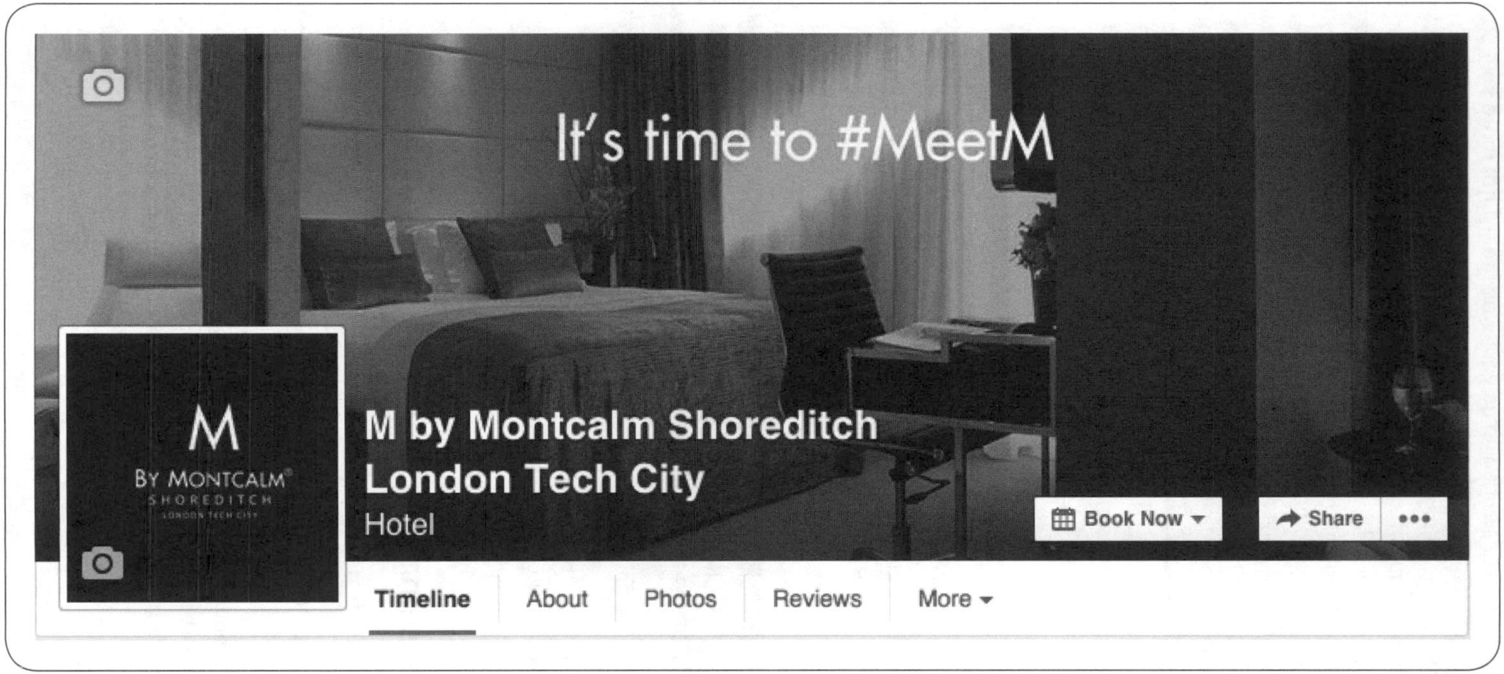

It's time to #MeetM

M by Montcalm Shoreditch
London Tech City
Hotel

BY MONTCALM®
SHOREDITCH
LONDON TECH CITY

Timeline | About | Photos | Reviews | More ▾

Book Now ▾

Share

•••

to look just as engaging as your website – if not more so – so invest time in making it look the best you can.

Note: You cannot see the Timeline in the app version of the site.

7. Think about what tabs you could have for your Page. You can see a number of Tabs below the cover, including Photos. These tabs act as 'sub pages' and can be anything from online adverts to games and even e-commerce facilities.

Note: You cannot see the tabs in the app version of the site.

8. Decide whether you want fans of your Page to be able to message you. In the Admin Settings, you can check or uncheck a box under Messages:

Messages	☑ Allow people to contact my Page privately by showing the Message button
	Save Changes Cancel

If you decide to check this, anyone who Likes your Page will see this on the right-hand side of your Page:

| 👍 Liked ▼ | ✔ Following | 💬 Message | ••• |

They will then be able to send you a private message.

Note: You cannot initiate conversations with your fans. They must contact you first.

Publishing your Page

Now you have your Page set up, you've filled your timeline with engaging content, you've added tabs and you've made sure that the right people are going to administer the site.

You're now ready to publish the Page. This is easily done. You will see a link that says Publish Your Page at the top of the screen (more here: www.facebook.com/help/?faq+=184605634921611).

Once you have clicked this link, the Page will be visible to anyone who isn't an administrator and this will herald the end of the first phase of creating a Facebook Page.

Note: Even if you don't have a specific reason to use Facebook, it is still worth creating a Page and registering the username. You can leave the Page unpublished. This means that no one else can claim your username and you can protect your brand.

Engagement tactics

The next phase involves publicising your Page and getting people to hit the all-important Like button. This button is situated underneath the cover photo on the right-hand side and it's one step in getting people to engage with the Page.

Fans can go a stage further by subscribing to all the updates of a Page. To the right of the Like button is a drop-down arrow. Click on this and you can choose to Get Notifications or Add to Lists. This is known as Story Bumping and you can read more on this here: www.socialmediaexaminer.com/story-bump.

Note: Many brands think that all they have to do is get customers/fans/clients to Like the Page. They then measure how successful it is by the number of Likes. However, Liking is just the **start** of a journey that involves getting those people to interact and engage with the Page.

During our social media training courses, we are often asked how to get people to start Liking Pages. There's really no simple answer. It is about creating a defined strategy using an array of different techniques, a few of which are listed here.

- **Printing the Page's URL** on traditional marketing materials such as advertisements, business cards, flyers and posters.

> **Example**
>
> Evian advertises on London's Underground network. They direct people to www.facebook.com/evian rather than www.evian.com.

- Put the Facebook Like button on your **website** in all the appropriate pages.
- **Word of mouth:** tell your customers about your Page.
- **Point of sale promotion:** we were in a music shop the other day and on the counter was a business card that promoted only their Facebook Page: *'Follow us on Facebook to join the conversation and get exclusive events and discounts.'* Simple!
- **Point of sale interaction:** if a customer has had a good experience or they make a comment about loving the products you sell, ask them if they have a Facebook account. If they have, offer them

a good reason to Like the Page, e.g. *'If you liked the stay in our hotel/meal in our restaurant/our shoes, Like our Facebook Page and we will have lots of special offers/interesting news/fashion tips.'*

- **Competitions:** just as in traditional marketing, these are a great way of engaging with potential customers. Again, use either traditional marketing materials or online marketing such as email campaigns and websites to entice people to your Page. However, it is important to read Facebook's promotional guidelines before setting up your competition (www.facebook.com/help/437283119636376). If you don't, Facebook can disable your Page.
- **Facebook advertising:** see Chapter 10 for details.
- **Partnerships:** as with other forms of affiliate marketing, these can be a great way to advertise your Pages. By partnering with complementary brands that have a highly visible Facebook presence, you can gain more exposure for your product or service.
- **Networking:** no company or organisation works in isolation and the same is true on Facebook. Speak to other businesses in your area and look at Liking each other's Pages. For example, a hotel could Like the Facebook Pages for local restaurants, cab companies, leisure attractions, shops and bars.

What to post on your Page

Using our newspaper analogy, your Facebook Page should be filled with content that educates, informs and entices your fan base. Ideally, you need a good selection of posts, images, videos, links, polls and questions – just as you would in a magazine or a newspaper.

Here are eight different ways of posting content to your Page.

1. **Your own content:** This could be content from your blog or news feed, a version of a press release or an opinion piece by one of your members of staff.
2. **Share someone else's content:** Including content from other Pages.
3. **Ask a question:** Remember that social media is about having continuous conversations. You want to engage with your fan base and one of the best ways to do this is by asking them for their opinions.
4. **Create a poll:** Questions are great, but they can sometimes be a little untargeted. By adding in poll options, you narrow down the answers, which will help you can do something constructive with the data. For more details, go to: http://bit.ly/1ExN8aW.
5. **Observations:** Comment on subjects that could be of interest to your fans.
6. **Recommendations:** Showcase recommendations you have been given or publicly praise members of your own team.

7. **Talk about another Page:** Mention a partner organisation's Page or post about a really engaging Page that may be of interest to your fan base. You can also put the @ symbol in front of the Page to highlight it.

8. **Respond to comments:** Facebook is about conversations. Some of them you will start; others will be started by your fans. Make sure you engage with them.

What not to post

Here are a few pointers for what you shouldn't be posting on Facebook!

1. Updates that may be defamatory or inflammatory.
2. Anything that will not help you to meet your objectives for your Facebook Page.
3. Badly put together content such as blurry images, misspelt posts and incorrect links.
4. Anything you wouldn't say publicly.
5. Tweets. Keep them on Twitter!

Posts on Facebook

There are two ways of posting. You can create an update (maximum length 420 characters) or you can post a note, which is essentially a longer version of an update (unlimited characters) with a headline.

Updates should be short and snappy ways of announcing something, drawing attention to a link or captioning a photograph. You don't have a headline, so try to make what you are writing stand out. Also remember to use a couple of your keywords. It is also possible to 'pin' your updates to the top of your timeline. You go to the appropriate post, click on the edit tab and pin it. The post will then stay at the top of your timeline for seven days. It is a little like creating a landing page on a website.

Notes are more like blogs, which you can also tag. To access Notes, go to your Page and look for the Notes tab on the left-hand side under Apps. Think of each Note as a miniature blog. It makes sense to use the normal blogging guidelines – short paragraphs, good use of keywords, simple language and no more than 400 words if possible.

Images on Facebook

Earlier in the chapter, we talked about the importance of images on Facebook and how they need to meet specific criteria. Here is a handy guide, which shows the dimensions required for all your images on the site: www.jonloomer.com/2014/01/20/facebook-image-dimensions.

We recommend that you get used to sizing your photos using free software such as www.irfanview.com or www.picresize.com so that they display properly on your timeline.

Note: As with anything online, make sure you have permission to publish images or you will be infringing copyright!

Videos on Facebook

Videos are becoming increasingly important on Facebook; Facebook even offers video advertising. So it is no surprise that they make it very simple to add videos to your timeline. You can upload them directly from your PC or mobile device. Alternatively, if you paste the URL of a You-Tube or Vimeo video it will automatically configure itself into a rectangular icon in your Timeline. Similarly, you can post your Vines or Instagram videos straight to the site from your phone via these apps (more on this in Chapter 8).

As usual, it's a good idea to have an engaging headline for your video along with some form of comment that will encourage your fans to view it. And don't forget a call to action.

Milestones

One of the key features of Timeline is Milestones. On personal Profiles these are known as life events: you can categorise your life into key personal milestones such as marriage, the birth of your children, starting a new business, etc.

With Pages, the Milestones take on a more corporate feel. These form the building blocks of your organisation's timeline. You can fill in the name of the event, the location, the day it happened, include a story and post an image to accompany it.

A great example of this is Manchester United (www.facebook.com/manchesterunited), whose timeline goes all the way back to 1878. Starting from that year, they have included a number of Milestones, all of which go a long way to building the Manchester United brand and giving a historical perspective on the football club.

Although Facebook is primarily a business-to-consumer marketing tool, this is a great example of how it can be used to build the brand of professional services firms and business-to-business-facing organisations.

World Child Cancer
Posted by David Taylor [?] · February 11 · ❀

Join the World Child Cancer family by running in this year's Royal Parks Half Marathon and helping to make a difference for children with cancer around the world.

For more info email lydia.spencer@worldchildcancer.org

▶ **Replay Video**

✎

Sign Up
www.worldchildcancer.org

16,008 people reached   ✅ **View Results**

2,718 Views
Like · Comment · Share

👍 Michael Pullen, Bethany Peters, Peter Grant and 25 others like this.

↪ 1 share

Write a comment...   📷 ☺

Instead of sticking lots of historical information on the company website, it may be better to build a content-rich and engaging timeline on Facebook. Check out IBM's timeline at www.facebook.com/pages/IBM/168597536563870.

Remember that your first Milestone **must** be the earliest event in your organisation's history.

Note: These Milestones will not appear as part of the timeline in the app version.

> **Status**   **Photo / Video**   **Offer, Event +**
>
> **Offer**
>
> **31 Event**
>
> **Milestone**

When to post

Timing can be critical in marketing and Facebook is no exception. Understanding when your audience is likely to be most engaged is vital. Remember that users can be accessing the site at any time of day or night, anywhere in the world and via a variety of different devices.

This activity can all be measured in Insights. If you know when you get the most engagement you can then schedule when you update your Page and work towards a better visibility score. It is important to analyse the optimum time for posting. It all comes back to the basic marketing rule of understanding your audience. While it is possible to schedule your posts, say, over a weekend or in the evening, you may need to be ready to respond and engage with your audience rather than leaving comments without a response.

Tip: Check Facebook Insights regularly to see when your fan base are most likely to be engaging with your Page. In the diagram below, it is clearly around 9 p.m.

Community management

By now you should be realising that managing a Facebook Page properly can be a time-consuming task, depending on what you would like it to do for you. Small companies who use their Facebook Page as the central plank of their marketing strategy may find that the part-time role they had envisaged for managing the Page turns into a full-time community management job.

If you do appoint a community manager, whether internally or by filling a new post through recruitment or outsourcing, you need to revisit the guidelines at the beginning of this chapter, clearly define the role and objectives of the job, and set out a proper strategy. Some of the questions you might need to ask yourself before going down the community management route are:

- Who are going to be the administrators of the Page and what level of access do they need?

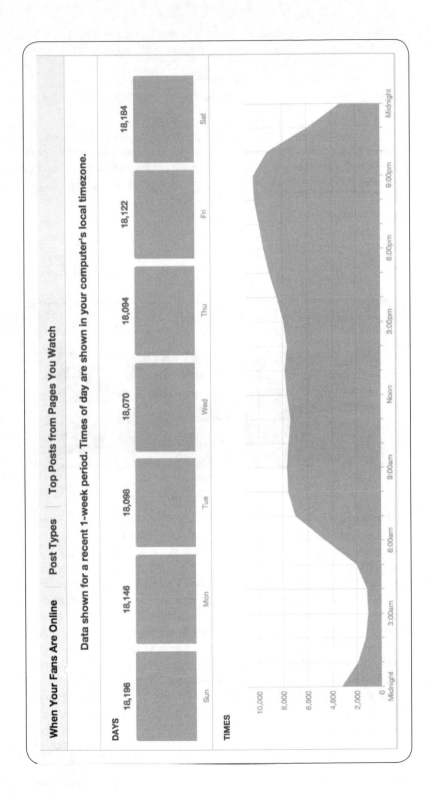

- How much time should be devoted to managing the Page?
- What are the 'lines to take' if negative comments are posted? What's the escalation plan?
- Who will monitor the Page outside office hours?
- What are the lines of authorisation when replying to people on the Page?

If you have a product or service about which you know you are likely to have a high number of complainants – local authorities, utilities companies, major brands – it is best to employ traditional brand protection techniques. The key one here would be to take those complaining off the Facebook Page and deal with them directly through a phone conversation or email.

If you are going to use your Facebook Page as a customer service/management tool, we recommend you refer to our Twitter chapter where we talk about how to engage effectively with your customers.

Case study: Devon Sun Yarns

Devon Sun Yarns (www.facebook.com/DevonSunYarns) was launched in March 2013 as a Facebook-only business selling hand-dyed luxury yarn. Initially the founder, Daisy Forster, used Facebook groups about knitting and crochet and relevant craft networking pages to gain Likes and sales. As her Page garnered sales, customers began recommending her Page and Likes grew quickly. Daisy used Facebook Groups to her advantage – as direct links to her customer base, for market research and to test new ideas. To create demand for her products she offered Groups exclusive discounts, sending her yarns to Group members at greatly reduced but still profitable prices. Daisy remains an active and genuine member of these Groups, contributing regularly and investing a lot of time in nurturing friendships in the Groups, which helps customers get to know her.

Once the Page was active, Daisy started a monthly subscription-based club. The product for the club is a 'mixed box' of Daisy's

---

picks of the month – and this activity generates lots of interest each month, with posts across all the relevant Facebook groups. These customers also come back to her Page regularly throughout the month, posting on the timeline about how they are getting on with their box contents or asking for updates about the next box. This activity really helps Page interaction (which is great for Facebook's visibility algorithm) and also encourages sales outside the subscription box members.

To begin with, to sell a new product or item Daisy would simply add a picture and details and post it, and the product would sell almost immediately. She recently changed to a monthly market night of all new stock. To boost Page interaction she sometimes promotes a small giveaway in the days before, posting regularly in the lead-up to the market night. She then pays around £5 to sponsor a post advertising the market night, and shares the post on craft networking pages as well as relevant interested people.

By gradually updating the photo album over several days with the items coming up for sale, the posts appear in Timelines several times a day, with reach growing as more comments are added. So by the time market night comes, reach is at its highest, interaction is high and customers come to buy. Daisy generally sells out within the first hour, and increased Page interaction continues for several days following the market night – due to increased activity in such a small timeframe.

Daisy is now heading into her third year of trading, with Facebook as her main selling platform throughout that time. The business has been incredibly successful, turning over a profit almost immediately and allowing her to grow the business at her own pace, without the pressure of business premises, website hosting or listing fees.

Case study takeaways:

- Use Facebook Groups to help build a valuable community online.
- Be proactive and network on Facebook with other businesses and potential customers.
- Think about creating a 'club' for Facebook users who can then be incentivised. They will also act as powerful advocates for your brand.
- Targeted advertising works even better when you have an engaged audience for your brand.

Social media marketing action plan

- Think about exactly what you want to use a Facebook Page for. If there is no specific objective, you may be wasting your time.
- Put as much energy into your Page as you would your website. Don't think of it as a gimmicky add-on – in some cases it could end up as your main online presence.
- Think carefully about who will administer your Page and what level of access you will grant to people.
- Decide who will 'community manage' it. That part-time role you envisaged may end up being almost full time for some organisations. And there's nothing worse than a Page which is rarely updated or never responds to comments.
- Be creative in getting people to Like and engage with your Page. You need to have a specific plan of action. We believe in a return to old-fashioned customer service – engaging with your customers and finding out what they think about your products or brand.
- Think about using Facebook advertising as a way to build your brand online and improve your visibility on the site. It could be a great way of driving traffic not only to your Page but also to your website.
- And finally . . . Be creative. Content is king – especially on Facebook!

7| LinkedIn

What you will learn from this chapter:

- Background to LinkedIn
- Creating the right personal profile
- Leveraging your contacts
- Ways to engage on the site
- Creating and optimising a company profile
- LinkedIn and lead generation
- Understanding LinkedIn Insights
- Using LinkedIn Apps

LinkedIn is often referred to as 'the professionals' Facebook'. It's the one social network that most people in our training groups 'get'. Admittedly, we still hear, *'Yes, I have a LinkedIn profile but I'm not sure what to do with it'*, but of the big four, it's the social network that makes its proposition very clear – We're here to do business.

Over the years, LinkedIn has grown its reputation as being the business to business (B2B) social network. A study by leading inbound marketing specialists Hubspot (www.hubspot.com) reported that LinkedIn is three times more effective for lead generation than Facebook and Twitter. That makes perfect sense as it's unlikely that you would go to LinkedIn for entertainment value.

If we were to explain Twitter, Facebook and LinkedIn very briefly, we would say something like this.

- **Twitter** is the 'buzziest' social network – a perfect mouthpiece for sharing content and information and connecting and engaging with people you have never met, and will never have the opportunity to meet. It's perfect for capturing conversations, listening in and generating reach and traction.
- **Facebook** is on a personal level about people to people conversations; on a brand level, it's about humanising a brand – the perfect vehicle for creating a community, engaging current audiences and encouraging people to share and hence market to new audiences via viral-worthy campaigns and compelling content, providing the potential to grow audience and awareness. It creates a community

of 'fans or advocates' who are willing to share and engage with your brand or business.

And LinkedIn . . . Well, LinkedIn is quite different. Unlike Twitter or Facebook, where direct self-promotion isn't really advocated, LinkedIn profiles focus on personal self-promotion. Your personal profile tells your story and goes way beyond the realms of a CV. It's a place where you can connect with business associates – colleagues, peers, alumni, prospects, clients and other business associates. You can watch their activities, see when they move roles, see who they're connected to, reach out to them and ask for recommendations and introductions. It's effectively an online 'network' in the truest traditional sense.

Where it started

LinkedIn started out mainly as a recruitment resource – a place where professionals could share their knowledge and expertise, pitch for new contracts and showcase talents to head-hunters and potential recruiters. Unlike the other big social networks, LinkedIn has a free networking service (which we will concentrate on in this chapter), but it also has a growing number of enterprise solutions.

The paid-for and enterprise options

What do they offer?

There are currently services for recruiters, sales professionals and job seekers.

LinkedIn has certainly had an impact on the recruitment profession over the years, so they have created an enterprise solution specifically for recruiters. And if you are job seeking, the plan to help you to 'land your dream job' enables you to access specific jobs that are on job boards – which are not visible in the free version. If you are a sales professional tasked with business development there's the Sales Navigator solution, specifically developed for sales and business development professionals who want to use LinkedIn in a methodical way for lead generation. Finally, the Business Plus solution is for individuals who want to upgrade from the free version to use many of the search filters and direct email functions that are locked down in the free version.

What do you get for your money?

Here are some key add-ons in the paid-for versions (but **note**: the features depend on which package you subscribe to).

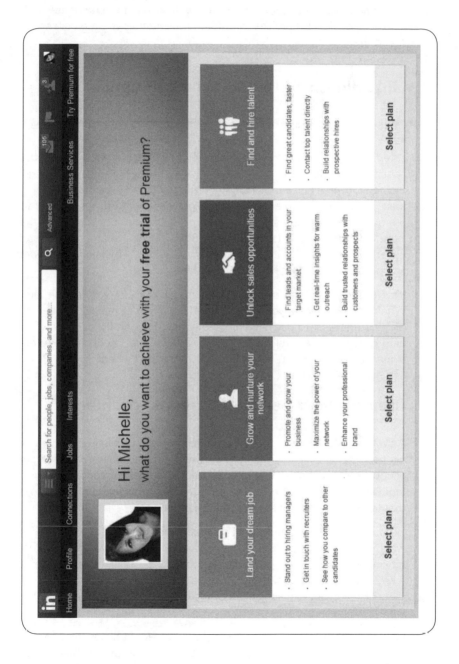

Home   Profile   Connections   Jobs   Interests   Business Services   Try Premium for free

Search for people, jobs, companies, and more...   Advanced

Hi Michelle,
what do you want to achieve with your free trial of Premium?

Land your dream job

- Stand out to hiring managers
- Get in touch with recruiters
- See how you compare to other candidates

Select plan

Grow and nurture your network

- Promote and grow your business
- Maximize the power of your network
- Enhance your professional brand

Select plan

Unlock sales opportunities

- Find leads and accounts in your target market
- Get real-time insights for warm outreach
- Build trusted relationships with customers and prospects

Select plan

Find and hire talent

- Find great candidates, faster
- Contact top talent directly
- Build relationships with prospective hires

Select plan

- See more profiles when you search.
- Add filters to your searches to make the results more targeted.
- View a full list of those who have reviewed your profile.
- Send InMails – direct emails (some with guaranteed responses).
- See people's full profiles, regardless of whether you are connected to them.

LinkedIn isn't just about recruitment

Of course, as with all of the networks in this book, LinkedIn has evolved, and continues to evolve. Businesses can now create quite sophisticated Company Profiles with associated Showcase Pages to highlight specific products and services and can use the platform to connect all their employees. LinkedIn is no longer just about individuals showcasing their talents; it's another space for organisations, large and small, to promote their people as well as their products and services, with the intention to engage, meet like-minded individuals, share opinion and expertise via LinkedIn Groups and to grow authority by sharing relevant and purposeful content on LinkedIn Pulse.

It's also becoming the go-to place to check out just who people are. Whenever we meet anyone at a networking event or business meeting, it's a natural habit to visit LinkedIn and review their profile. It's now standard practice, where relevant, to send a message to connect. Professionals are now expected to have a presence on LinkedIn.

Creating your personal LinkedIn profile

As with all of the social networks, signing up for a profile is a pretty simple process. Supply your name, email address and password and your account is open. (**Remember to document all social networking account login details somewhere, so you've got a back-up/reminder – more on that later.**) Then it's a case of creating your story.

Before you start, you may want to take a breath and consider exactly what you want to use LinkedIn for. For example, are you job hunting, looking for business development opportunities, or using your profile as a key platform to showcase your expertise and knowledge to your contacts? Remember – the objective of the channel steers the sentiment of your content.

Given that the majority of consumers now seek out products, services and talent online, being visible online is something that all businesses and individuals need to be thinking about. Having a LinkedIn personal profile is therefore useful, but if it's not 100% complete (known as All Star), it is not fully optimised for you to be found in LinkedIn searches and indeed in other search engines too. And if your profile isn't 100% complete, does that look altogether professional? We don't think so. Completing your profile to a high standard should take you no more than an hour. (We've timed it.)

Getting to 100% complete means including the following information:

- your industry and location
- your current position (with a description: be sure to add this in – it's the element that often gets missed)
- two past positions
- your education
- your skills (a minimum of three)
- a profile photo
- at least 50 connections.

Remember: LinkedIn asks for specific information, but you are completely in control of what you put into each field.

> ### Hot tip
>
> When adding your content into LinkedIn the editing features are very limited – for example, adding bullet points and emboldening text is not straightforward. We suggest that you create your profile in something like Word, and then paste it into LinkedIn. You'll find that it still loses some of the formatting, but it's a lot better than flat text.

Your LinkedIn summary

Many people forget about one of the key elements of their LinkedIn profile – their summary. This is one of the standard categories within Profiles and is essentially your personal mission statement. With up to 2,000 characters at your disposal, it's a chance for you to tell people who you are, what you've done in your entire career to date and a little personal information to add 'colour' to your personality. Remember that after your headline, this will be the first piece of text people see when reviewing your profile. In a way, if your profile is a website, then the summary is your homepage.

We find that many people really struggle to 'sell' themselves, so we recommend that you draft some text, give it to someone who knows you really well professionally and ask them to review it for you.

In your summary, you are trying to get across your personality, your professional experience, passion and key achievements – many of which can be independently validated with endorsements and recommendations.

Summary

Experienced strategic online marketer and online marketing consultant - blending and leveraging social media into effective marketing strategies. Social Media Trainer and Social Media Consultancy - having trained over 2500 people in social media marketing in the past 3 years.

Co-Author of The Business of Being Social : Harnessing Facebook, Twitter, LinkedIn and YouTube for all Businesses. (Over 68 5***** reviews on Amazon - currently the most reviewed social media book on Amazon!).

Social Media Expert ♦ Social Media Training ♦ Social Media Speaker ♦ Social Media Marketing ♦ Social Media Consultant ♦ Online Marketing Expert ♦ Online Marketing Training ♦ Online Marketing Speaker ♦ Online Marketing Consultant ♦LinkedIn Training ♦ LinkedIn Speaker ♦ LinkedIn Marketing ♦ LinkedIn Marketing Consultant ♦ Linked In Expert ♦ Twitter Training ♦ Facebook Training ♦ Twitter Expert ♦ Facebook Expert

• Experienced in developing effective marketing strategies for professional services practices - and delivering and steering the all important implementation programs.

• Running my own Digital Online Visibility Marketing Agency for the past 12 years.

• Passionate about 'Online Visibility' - leveraging websites, blogging and social media platforms.

• Director at The Made Simple Group - providers of business essentials for startups

Services at digital marketing agency Carvill Creative

• strategic marketing planning
• social media consultancy
• social media management
• social media training
• blogging
• creating an effective and integrated online presence
• social pr /social communications
• user focused website planning and design

As well as text, you can add all manner of content such as videos, images, infographics and the like. (More on this later in the chapter.)

Edit your LinkedIn URL

When you are in editing mode, you will see the Contact Info tab. When you click on this, it includes various places you can add: URLs, Twitter names, etc. And of course LinkedIn automatically creates a URL for your LinkedIn Profile.

uk.linkedin.com/in/michellecarvill/en   Contact Info

You can see the URL above, which has been edited to /michellecarvill. When you hover close to this URL, you will see a small pencil icon appear – and then you can amend it. The default URL will look like a whole string of letters and numbers – complete nonsense which doesn't mean anything to anyone. You can edit your personal LinkedIn URL at any time, and as long as the terms you want are available, you can use them. This now becomes your public URL, which you can promote and share on email footers or business cards. Be sure to add other URLs, such as your website, blog or Twitter URL too. Consider this your 'personal splashpage' where people can find out everything about you that you would like them to know.

Your LinkedIn public profile

When editing your public URL you'll notice that from your online LinkedIn profile (the profile seen by people who are connected to you via LinkedIn) the platform automatically creates a 'public profile' (as shown below). This is the profile that people see if they find you via search engines such as Google, Yahoo, etc., so when you are in edit mode, you can select which information is displayed on your public profile.

Note: Whenever you send your LinkedIn public URL link to anyone, it's your public profile they will see.

Optimise your profile with relevant keywords

Here we are again with those magic keywords – the DNA of your organisation's online visibility. After all, they are the crucial words that people will use to search for you or your services. So make sure that you pepper the content of your LinkedIn profile with relevant keywords. In particular, think about the keywords that you feature in your Professional Headline – you can change these at any time. But bear in mind why you are using LinkedIn and tailor your headline accordingly.

Using the right keywords will not only help people find you more easily when they are doing LinkedIn searches, but it also helps with Google searches too. Remember – first and foremost you are writing for human beings, not search bots, so be sure to include your keywords in a relevant and purposeful way. Aim for around 4–6% of your content to be keywords.

Maximise rich media

Around three years ago LinkedIn started to update the profile platform considerably to enable the use of rich media to enhance profiles. When you are completing or editing your profile, in most of the sections you are encouraged to include images, video, presentations, links and documents.

Public Profile

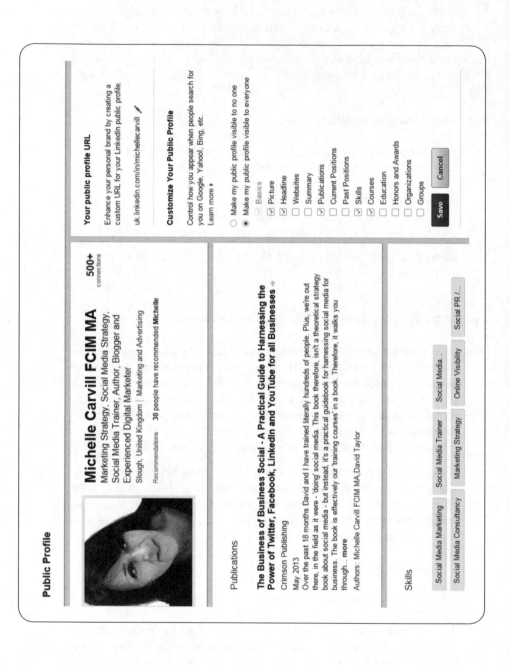

Michelle Carvill FCIM MA

Marketing Strategy, Social Media Strategy,
Social Media Trainer, Author, Blogger and
Experienced Digital Marketer

Slough, United Kingdom | Marketing and Advertising

500+
connections

Recommendations   30 people have recommended **Michelle**

Your public profile URL

Enhance your personal brand by creating a
custom URL for your LinkedIn public profile.

uk.linkedin.com/in/michellecarvill ✏

Customize Your Public Profile

Control how you appear when people search for
you on Google, Yahoo!, Bing, etc.
Learn more ▸

○ Make my public profile visible to no one
● Make my public profile visible to everyone

- ☑ Basics
- ☑ Picture
- ☑ Headline
- ☐ Websites
- ☐ Summary
- ☑ Publications
- ☐ Current Positions
- ☐ Past Positions
- ☑ Skills
- ☑ Courses
- ☐ Education
- ☐ Honors and Awards
- ☐ Organizations
- ☐ Groups

[Save]   [Cancel]

Publications

The Business of Business Social - A Practical Guide to Harnessing the Power of Twitter, Facebook, LinkedIn and YouTube for all Businesses ⬆

Crimson Publishing

May 2013

Over the past 18 months David and I have trained literally hundreds of people. Plus, we're out
there, in the field as it were - 'doing' social media. This book therefore, isn't a theoretical strategy
book about social media - but instead, it's a practical guidebook for harnessing social media for
business. The book is effectively our 'training courses' in a book. Therefore, it walks you
through... more

Authors: Michelle Carvill FCIM MA,David Taylor

Skills

Social Media Marketing   Social Media Trainer   Social Media...

Social Media Consultancy   Marketing Strategy   Online Visibility   Social PR /....

Michelle Carvill FCIM MA

Marketing Strategy, Social Media Strategy, Social Media Trainer, Author, Blogger and Experienced Digital Marketer

Slough, United Kingdom | Marketing and Advertising

Current   Made Simple Group, Carvill Creative

Previous   RAN ONE, TNSN

Education   Chartered Institute of Marketing

View profile as ▶

500+
connections

📇 Contact Info

in https://ak.linkedin.com/in/michellecarvill

Add a section to your profile – be discovered for your next career step.

Profile Strength

All-Star

Add Media: 📄 Document 📷 Photo 🔗 Link ▶ Video 📊 Presentation

This gives you the opportunity to provide showreels, product or service footage, new promotional video, design portfolios or other relevant publications. It's a great opportunity to say more with imagery than words. There's also a header image that you can include (this only comes up on desktop versions). The size LinkedIn suggests is 1400 × 425 pixels and a maximum file size of 4Mb.

You can see that you can design your profile header picture to include words that complement the profile. At the time of writing, profile header images are only applicable to personal profiles, not company profiles. LinkedIn is certainly making efforts to keep pace with the visual web – so take advantage of the features to enhance your profile.

Why perfect your LinkedIn profile?

As well as all the points we've highlighted above – making your profile look professional and enabling it to assist with social search and online visibility – LinkedIn profiles are now seen as a personal 'kitemark'.

The authors recently trained 50 partners from a division of one of the largest management consultancy/accountancy firms in the world. Whilst all partners were clearly professionals and experts in their field, their LinkedIn presence didn't tell that story. It was interesting to learn from one of the lead partners that when they were pitching for business, clients would often query why the CV of the partner or associate who had been introduced as part of the account team was so different from the LinkedIn profile they had reviewed online.

This point, one of many we have heard over the years – reaffirms that people do review LinkedIn regularly – in fact, the main activity on LinkedIn is people looking at other people's profiles, checking detail and validating trust. So make sure that you are proud of the story that's out there. If you're on the network, then consistently make the profile, your personal brand, the best it can possibly be.

Getting connected

When your profile's complete, rich with imagery and media, you can start connecting.

A great way to start is to explore which of your contacts are already LinkedIn. Doing this is pretty simple. Visit the Connections tab in the main bar and you'll see Keep in Touch (where you can view all the people you are connected with via LinkedIn), Find Alumni and Add Connections. There are two main options: you can insert contact details one by one; or you can invite your contacts via your email service by uploading a simple CSV/Excel spreadsheet list. Once you've uploaded the list, LinkedIn sees which of your contacts are already on LinkedIn and presents you with a list of contacts so that you can review and select the ones you wish to connect with on LinkedIn.

Connecting is automated – a simple click of the button and you can personalise the default message (which we also suggest you do) – and get connected to your contacts on LinkedIn.

LinkedIn's search facility

Before we move on, it's worth noting that LinkedIn has a very good search facility. Not only can you run general searches such as 'IT Manager Frankfurt', you can also specify whether you want to search All, People, Jobs, Updates, Companies, Inbox (which works as an email account between you and your contacts), Universities or Groups. So you can be pretty specific about which area you want to search in. When you search in People or Jobs, there is also an Advanced Search option to the right of the search box – and here you can filter some of the search results (although some filters are limited in the free version).

Managing your contacts via LinkedIn

The difference between LinkedIn and a normal database or customer relationship management (CRM) system is that rather than being one way (i.e. you control all the data that goes into it), the content is dynamic.

It really is a network in the truest sense of the word. Your contacts are sharing information, updating their profiles and even moving on to new careers and you can see it all happening in real time. This makes LinkedIn a very powerful and dynamic database.

Whenever we meet people in a training course, at a business meeting or in any other context – we naturally look to connect with them on LinkedIn. If someone gives us a business card, rather than leaving it to get dusty in the bottom of a bag or in a jacket pocket, we automatically go to LinkedIn, search for them and if they are on the platform, we connect. Using LinkedIn this way means that you can keep a constant database of contacts, and if they change roles you haven't lost them: their profile remains on LinkedIn.

The site also has a very powerful tool to turn your contacts into a bona fide CRM system.

When you are connected to someone on LinkedIn, underneath their photo you'll see Relationship and Contact Info. Within the Relationship tab you'll see a new menu including the following:

- **Note:** You can write a detailed note about who the person is and why you're connected.
- **Reminder:** You can set reminders for LinkedIn to email you about contacting this contact.
- **How you Met:** The date you met and who introduced you.
- **Tag:** You can tag or categorise all of your contacts, making it easier for you to search for them.

It will also show you the last interaction you had with this person on LinkedIn and when you first connected, which makes this feature incredibly handy.

Note: All this information is only visible to you!

There's another great little service LinkedIn provides, to which you can subscribe via your settings (more on settings shortly). LinkedIn Updates is an email service you can opt to receive each week advising you as to what's been happening with your contacts – who they've connected with, new roles, profile updates, etc. Should one of your contacts showcase that they've moved on into a new role, then you could even email that contact to congratulate them on their new job. And who knows where they may have moved – it could very well be to an organisation you've wanted to have discussions with for a while. And if that is the case, you now have a relevant contact.

Database management is often a big headache for organisations, but managing contacts via LinkedIn can be time-saving, long-lasting and very low maintenance.

Requesting recommendations

Asking people, contacts, colleagues, peers, clients, delegates, etc. for recommendations couldn't be easier on LinkedIn, and it turns what could be a toe-curling request into an automated process. From the desktop version of LinkedIn, simply click your photo in the top right-hand corner. Your Account and Settings tab will open). You can then simply select Privacy & Settings – and then you will see Manage your recommendations to the bottom right.

In the 'recommendation generation', where people trust what others say about products and services rather than what the brands are saying, growing recommendations grows credibility. In addition, all the extra content pads out your profile, giving you even more chance of being found in searches. And, of course, you can also use the recommendations in other marketing materials and on your website. The process is so automated that you can even (should you wish to) follow up on those who have not yet sent their recommendation.

As for the person you are asking for a recommendation, it's simple for them too. They simply have to complete their recommendation and hit Send. You can't edit their recommendation, but you do get to choose whether or not you publish it. Of course, if you think they've omitted a key element you wanted them to get across in their recommendation, there's no reason why you can't go back to them and ask them to amend their recommendation to include it.

Beyond recommendations: LinkedIn's Endorsement feature

As you will know from many comments we've made throughout this book, the social platforms are evolving all the time. New user functionalities and additional features are regularly added (which is why we are running a blog alongside this book – www.thebusinessofbeingsocial. co.uk – to keep you up to date on all updates, amends and new features.)

In late September 2012, LinkedIn introduced the Skills Endorsement feature, whereby people can 'endorse' their connections for various skills. Whereas with recommendations, someone has to take time and effort to write something about you, Endorsements enable them to simply click a button to endorse you. If they wish, they can add Skills and Reasons why they are endorsing you.

A few years later and there are mixed feelings on the net about this feature. Is it simply too easy to click Endorse – and therefore, is there a credibility issue around how meaningful it is? But it does add another element of visual content to your profile – and usually the main skills tend to be the ones that most people endorse – so it does build a picture. But importantly, and this is probably the reason LinkedIn introduced it, it encourages engagement.

If someone endorses you, you get a message advising you that your connection has just endorsed you. Of course, if you want to see what they've endorsed you for, you log into your LinkedIn account and you can see all endorsements, and you're then encouraged to endorse others. So it's an enticing mechanism to draw people into the platform.

Be human on LinkedIn

People do business with people. And while social networks provide us with clever and leveraged ways of keeping in touch with those in our networks in a more automated way, it's still important that we provide a human touch.

For example, when you are inviting people to connect with you in LinkedIn, don't simply use the default message, *'I'd like to add you to my professional LinkedIn network.'* Research has shown that people are more likely to accept and appreciate the connection if you provide some personal context – and even better if you can explain why you're contacting them and add a reason to connect. For example:

> *Great meeting you at ABC the other day – I'd like to keep in touch by connecting on LinkedIn. Thought it would be good to catch up for a coffee to carry on our discussion as I've been thinking about your proposition and have a number of ideas I'd like to share with you.*

Such a different approach – it's very human, it's authentic and it gives a reason why you want to connect. Not to mention the fact that it helps remind the person how you met.

Don't attempt to spam or directly sell on LinkedIn

Even though LinkedIn enables you to send direct emails to specific individuals, you really should consider how it's going to come across. People
will disconnect with you in a heartbeat if they think you are using LinkedIn
solely to sell your wares. Think of offline networking: you wouldn't start a
partnership or conversation by trying to sell someone something in your
opening conversation. As with all networks, online or offline, engage
with, listen to and nurture your contacts – don't spam them.

If someone is specifically discussing something you have a solution for,
by all means engage, but listen in first – don't spam.

Connections

Understanding who is connected to whom

Another key feature of LinkedIn is that you can see how people are connected. When you are searching for a person on LinkedIn, next to their
name you will see '1st', '2nd' or '3rd'.

If someone has 1st next to their name, they are directly connected to
you. If they have 2nd, someone you know knows them, and if 3rd,
someone you know knows someone they know. LinkedIn advises you
who in your network is connected to the person so that you can then
contact them and ask them to make an introduction. (Just as you would
network in the offline world.)

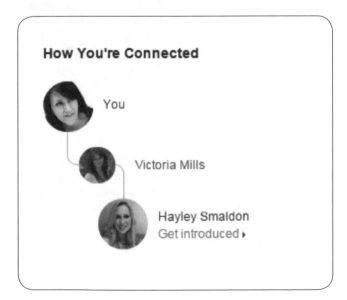

Whenever you search for a person on LinkedIn, you will see these degree of connection numbers or an 'out of your network' message, which means that you don't have any related direct connections in your network.

Using company searches to find relevant connections

If you're looking for someone with whom you don't have any connections you could also try searching for the company they work for.

Their company's LinkedIn profile (more on company profiles later in the chapter) will showcase the company's employees and it may be that other people in the company are connected to you (they could be 1st-, 2nd- or 3rd-degree connections). Therefore, you could work those connections to get introduced to the person you want to connect with.

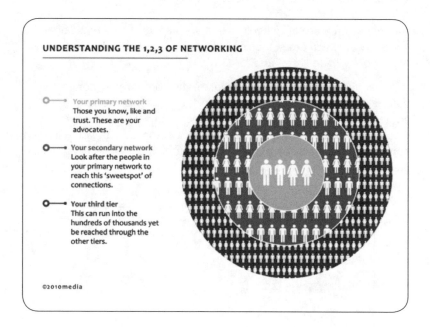

For example, let's say I'm trying to find someone who I know works at Facebook, but they are out of my network. I can search Facebook on LinkedIn and up comes the person's profile, together with insights about How You're Connected. I can then approach people I'm connected with – 1st- and 2nd-degree connections – to see if they can assist in connecting me to their colleague.

LinkedIn and business development

As mentioned earlier, LinkedIn has developed Sales Navigator (see https://business.linkedin.com/sales-solutions), an enterprise resource to assist business development and sales professionals target and manage lead activity. However, even without this tool, there is still a lot you can do to find the individuals you need to be speaking to, target them (either directly or via your connections), and then get in touch to see if you can move the opportunity forward into a meeting.

For example, if you were looking for the procurement manager at Marks & Spencer, you could go to the Marks & Spencer company page, where all employees will be listed. You can simply click on the number of employees listed and the entire list will open up. You can then use the Advanced Search feature to search 'procurement manager' and see who comes up. Then see if you have any relevant connections. If so, you can contact your connection to ask for them to put you in touch – or, indeed, you could try to contact the person direct via LinkedIn, or Google them to see if you can find any other information about them.

Another key aspect of sales and business development is listening to your clients and prospective clients. And, of course, your competitors. LinkedIn provides you with a perfect platform to keep in touch with what is happening with your clients – what they are posting, who has come on board, etc. – so that you are always informed and aware of any opportunities. Similarly, with prospective clients, you can keep your finger on the pulse and keep an eye out for any opportunities. It's interesting to see what your competitors are up to, too. It's surprising how open people are on LinkedIn – and the amount of information you can glean.

It's so much more impressive, when meeting a client or prospect, to be totally up to speed with the latest developments. So do keep in mind that LinkedIn is a valuable research resource to enable you to stay totally up to date with key clients and prospects.

Ways to engage on LinkedIn

LinkedIn Groups

There is a wide range of Groups on LinkedIn. Groups are effectively mini-networks that assist like-minded people to get involved in relevant discussions and share knowledge, advice and expertise – and, of course, to ask questions. In a Group you can add a new topic to a discussion to garner opinion or advice, answer questions from the Group members, listen in a passive way or generally interact.

If a Group doesn't already exist for the specific topic you want to network around, you can easily create one, search for relevant contacts and people and invite them to that Group.

Again, if you're not directly connected to a person you'd really like to participate in the Group, you can always see whether any of your connections are, and if so, ask them to invite relevant contacts to the Group.

To create a Group, review the Groups you're already participating in, or to get referred to Groups, simply hit the Interests tab and you'll see Groups.

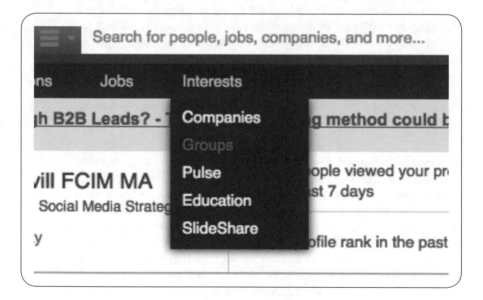

Groups can be a great place to meet like-minded people: they are in effect targeted networking groups. Our advice is to do some research into Groups to see which ones might fit your objectives.

1. Do a simple search of Groups and see which ones are relevant to you. You can search via the LinkedIn search bar or via the Find a Group option on the Groups page.

Don't see what you're looking for?

Find a group   Create a group

2. Review the types of conversation and engagement in the Group. Some people simply go on Groups to spam and sell their wares – and as we said earlier, this is never a good networking tactic.
3. Watch and listen. Then, if you think it's the right Group for you, join it. Some Groups are 'open' (you can join them automatically); others are locked, so your request may need to be approved.

One word of warning: there are Groups about Groups and you could very quickly become part of many of these online forums. It could be that there is so much noise coming from your Groups you need to tune out (see more on Settings and Privacy later to learn how you can manage the alerts from your groups). Be realistic about the number of Groups you can actively participate in. Choose those most fit for purpose and focus attention on the specific Groups and people within those Groups who meet your objectives. For example, if 'Thought Leadership' is your objective, make sure that you are growing authority in the right Groups. You may already have a blog post or info you can direct people to.

Another key thing to remember is that to have direct conversations with people you need to be connected to them. However, when you are in a Group you can liaise with other members of the Group directly.

Of course, some people join Groups to deliberately spam other members of the Group with over-'salesy' approaches, e.g. *'Hi, I see we're both members of the XYZ group so I thought you'd like to know about my latest product.'* Be careful of using Groups as a means of spamming or pushing messages at others. Groups have moderators, owners and usually rules of engagement. If a Group owner thinks you have simply joined the Group to capitalise on making contact with everyone in the Group to sell your wares, you can be blocked from the Group – and you may also be under threat of being blocked from all Groups.

Create your own hub or intranet

You'll see from the Groups tab that you have the option to create your own Group. This is a very simple process. You may want to create a Group related to a specific topic or you may want to create a private Group just for a select few. You have the option to create a members-only Group, and you could use this as a working hub or an intranet with select team.

If you are creating your own Group, be realistic about how you are going to drive engagement with the Group. You're pretty much creating a community, so you'll need to set aside time to manage a community that will need to be encouraged and cajoled to engage.

Settings and privacy

We're often asked the question by delegates and clients, 'Will everyone be able to see my connections?' The answer is – that's entirely up to you. LinkedIn has some pretty detailed privacy settings which puts you in control of both what you see and what others see about you. As you can see from the screenshot of the privacy settings on the next page, there are a number of elements to consider.

You can manage settings for your Profile, your email preferences, Group activity and your account in general. It is worth working through each of the settings so that you are comfortable with what's visible to the masses.

> **Hot tip**
>
> When you are updating your profile with new content, we suggest you turn off your activity broadcasts until you have fully completed your new profile. If you keep them on, the broadcasts will circulate to all your connections each time you make a change.

Creating a LinkedIn company profile

With LinkedIn you can have a personal profile, which focuses on you, and a company profile, which focuses on the business. Having a LinkedIn company page enables others to learn about what's happening within your business. From news updates to job opportunities, products and services, it's effectively an extension of the information people can find on your website, but it also gives you the opportunity to broadcast status updates to all those following the company.

In effect, the LinkedIn company page provides an opportunity to consolidate the many voices of the business into one centralised voice.

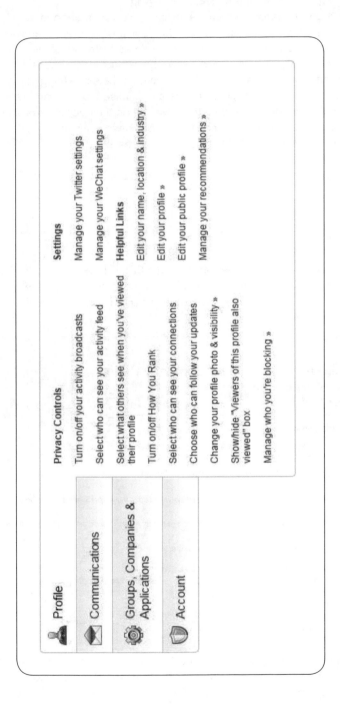

Profile

Communications

Groups, Companies & Applications

Account

Privacy Controls

Turn on/off your activity broadcasts

Select who can see your activity feed

Select what others see when you've viewed their profile

Turn on/off How You Rank

Select who can see your connections

Choose who can follow your updates

Change your profile photo & visibility »

Show/hide "Viewers of this profile also viewed" box

Manage who you're blocking »

Settings

Manage your Twitter settings

Manage your WeChat settings

Helpful Links

Edit your name, location & industry »

Edit your profile »

Edit your public profile »

Manage your recommendations »

- **Company reach:** the whole team working together to promote both themselves and the business. Win–win.
- **Product/service awareness:** creating Showcase Pages to promote in detail, with relevant keywords, your products and services, enabling you to specifically publish updates to those Showcase Pages, and allowing people to follow those Showcase Pages.
- **Brand awareness:** the whole team saying the same thing, rather than giving mixed messages. Provide an optimised 'boilerplate' (a simple sentence) for all the team to showcase on their personal profiles.
- **Business updates:** sharing regular business news and updates; acting as a consistent real-time PR resource.

We'll explore these benefits in more detail later in the chapter. First, the practicalities . . .

Adding a company profile

You'll find the Companies tab underneath the Interests tab in the top menu bar, and on that page, you'll see the option to Create a Page. There are specific requirements when adding a company profile:

 Requirements for Adding Company Pages

Who can add a Company Page?
Last Reviewed: 01/30/2015

You can add a new Company Page only if you meet all of the following requirements:

1. You must have a personal LinkedIn profile set up with your true first and last name.
2. Your profile is at least 7 days old.
3. Your profile strength must be listed as Intermediate or All Star.
4. You must have several connections on your profile.
5. You're a current company employee and your position is listed in the **Experience** section on your profile.
6. You have a company email address (e.g. john@companyname.com) added and confirmed on your LinkedIn account.
7. Your company's email domain is unique to the company.

Note: A domain can't be used more than once to create a Company Page. Because domains like gmail.com, yahoo.com or similar generic email services are not unique to one company, those domains can't be used to create a Company Page. You might consider creating a group if your company doesn't have a unique email domain.

Before you add a company profile, first check whether one has already been created. Do a simple search on Companies and check whether a company profile already exists. If there is no company profile, you can go ahead, but you must have a personal LinkedIn profile in place, and have a company domain name-related email address.

> ### Example
>
> To create a company profile for Carvill Creative, we would have to have a company-focused email address, e.g. michelle@carvillcreative.co.uk. You can't set up the profile with common email domains such as Gmail, Hotmail or Yahoo.

With your domain-related email address at the ready, to set up the profile you simply:

1. Click the Companies tab in the top menu par, then Add A Company (located to the upper right of the screen).
2. Enter company details and your work- (domain name) related email address.
3. Click Continue and simply enter all your company information. Remember to optimise with keywords where relevant. Just as people search Google, YouTube, Facebook and Twitter using keywords, they search LinkedIn too, so be sure that you have optimised your online content effectively to give yourself a good chance of being found for relevant searches.

Can anyone create a company profile?

As outlined in the guidelines from LinkedIn, you have to have a domain-related email address to create a company profile. You also need to have some form of published correlation to the company profile. This means that you must clearly indicate in your personal profile that you work for the company; to be an administrator you have to be directly related to the company. Another factor is that if you want to create a company profile, your own personal LinkedIn profile must be pretty much fully completed (Intermediate or All Star level).

Connecting employees to a company profile

When an employee states in their personal profile that they work for 'Company Name', their personal profile will automatically connect with the company profile (if it exists). If an employee is not connected, it may be that they have misspelled the company name or that they need to manually connect to the company profile. This is a very simple process: when they edit their profile, next to Current Position they click Change Company and type the full company name. The company name will appear in a drop-down box, so be sure your employee is connecting with the correct company. Once that's all done, simply click Update – et voilà.

Of course, connecting all your employees to your company profile provides a dual marketing resource for the business. Think about the power of LinkedIn and the ability to see who is connected to whom. This also rings true when bringing together employees. Take this scenario:

- A company has 10 employees.
- Each employee has their own personal LinkedIn profile.
- Each employee has 100 1st-degree connections (and of course, their connections have connections).

One account of 358 1st-degree connections actually reaches (through the 2nd- and 3rd-degree connections) a whopping 6,655,080 professionals. Let's be conservative and say that 100 1st-degree connections links to 2,000,000 professionals. With a team of just 10, even with some potential duplication of connections, you can see how amplified the reach of the company's network becomes.

The employee becomes a marketing resource for the business

When someone checks out one of your employees, not only do they get to see their profile, they also get the opportunity to link to the company profile, to find out more about what the company does. Therefore, it makes sense for companies to create a company profile and encourage the whole team to create personal profiles and connect with relevant connections.

This broadens the network – and provides more opportunity for referral and connecting those we know to help us get to those we want to know.

LinkedIn's Elevate

On the theme of utilising employees more effectively to spread the company word, and in line with the growth of effective content marketing (as outlined in Chapter 4), LinkedIn have introduced a 'content curation' service called Elevate. Elevate is currently only visible to a few organisations that have been invited to use the new platform while the service finds its feet. It is intended that by about the time this book is published (September 2015) Elevate should be rolling out to the masses.

Elevate will predominantly assist employees and organisations curate and share relevant content on their news feeds. One of the key challenges is ensuring that the content one is sharing is relevant, purposeful and compelling, and that there is enough to maintain frequency to optimise engagement. Elevate has been developed to fill this gap, using content from LinkedIn Pulse, Newsle and other content curation services to enable organisations to tailor a news stream to feed appropriate channels.

Setting administrators of the company profile

When setting up the company profile you have two options: to let all employees administer the profile; or to specify which employees are administrators.

As an administrator of a profile, when you search for the company profile you'll see a blue Edit box on the right-hand side of the screen. Only administrators will see this – which enables them to access the company profile and update it accordingly.

Optimising your LinkedIn company profile

Once you've got a company profile in place, it's simply a case of working through each area and filling it out:

- company name
- company description

- setting who the administrators will be
- company details
- location(s) – up to five
- header image – 646 × 220 pixels or larger (maximum size 2Mb)
- standard logo – 100 × 60 pixels
- square logo – 50 × 50 pixels
- company specialities.

The Company Details area is the first port of call. This is where you showcase the boilerplate of your company – how long it's been established, partners, clients, etc. It's similar to the engaging About Us section of your website. **Remember, people are more interested in what you can do for them than what you do**, so be sure to spell out the value you create.

Showcase Pages

About 18 months ago, LinkedIn removed the Services tab and replaced it with Showcase Pages.

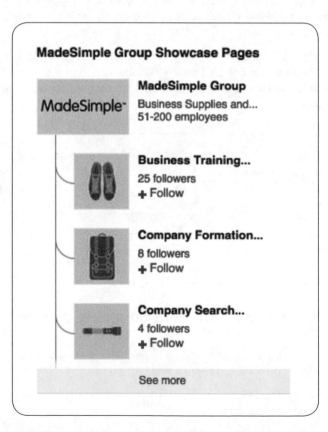

Showcase Pages are stand-alone 'landing page'-style profile pages for each service you offer, and you can include up to 10 showcase pages. Showcase Pages can be particularly useful if you are looking to drive awareness of one specific product or service area; you can post updates on the relevant Showcase Page and grow followers on a specific page, so that they only see the content for the specific Showcase Page they are following.

If you are running an advertising campaign on LinkedIn for a specific product or service, you can direct people specifically to engage with a Showcase Page rather than your company profile. On each Showcase Page information can be tailored differently for each product or service, so you can make your content highly specific, creating clearly targeted and informative pages for particular audiences.

If you get the company profile right, it can become another effective online presence for people who find you via LinkedIn. The steps to follow are:

- Create a company profile.
- Complete the profile with keyword-optimised and engaging content.
- Encourage team members to create a personal profile and make connections.
- Provide each team member with a standard 'boilerplate' which they can use when describing where they work.
- Ensure that each team member is connected to the company profile.

Analytics

As an administrator of a company page you'll be able to view various analytics providing you with useful insights into the performance of your Page.

- Updates – how your content is performing
- Reach – the reach of your content; impressions
- Engagement – shares and comments
- Follower information and demographics
- Follower trends – enabling you to assess good times to post, etc.
- Visitor insights.

You can see that there is a rich overview of information for you to keep track of. For example, if you focus activity around growing awareness of your company page and encouraging others to follow it, you can watch these insights and measure the impact of any upward trends following your campaign.

Grow your authority with LinkedIn Pulse

In February 2014 LinkedIn introduced a self-publishing platform, Pulse. Initially the platform was only available to a select group of 'influencers', but now it is open to the entire network on LinkedIn, providing the perfect vehicle for sharing content.

The Pulse link is found in the top menu, under Interests.

LinkedIn's Pulse publishing platform is similar to 'guest blogging', where you supply content to another publishing vehicle with the intention of amplifying your message to a wider audience. When you start publishing on Pulse, the posts that you publish are still shared on your LinkedIn feed, and your posts also stay on the Pulse news feed too, where they can potentially reach over 300,000 LinkedIn users. A much wider audience, then, than only those you're connected to. Pulse also enables you to follow people, search for posts and discover content that could be highly relevant for you.

Of course, not all posts that are published get featured in a prominent position on Pulse, but don't be disheartened – around 17% of the posts that do get featured are often by first-timers, not just those with hundreds of thousands of followers. Articles on the main Pulse page are sorted by the number of views: those with the most views appear on top and those with fewer views below them.

Also consider how you can promote your post outside the LinkedIn platform; share your posts on other social channels, share in emails, newsletters or other wide-reaching communication vehicles.

As you can see from the Pulse profile below, Bernard Marr has over half a million followers. You can also see that he's publishing once a day.

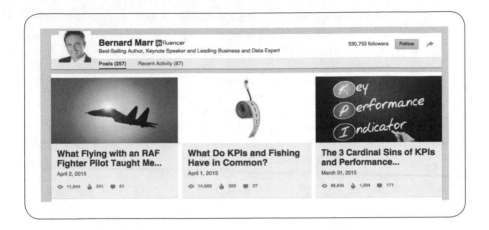

The posts that do best are those that focus on business, self development and careers. However, not all successful posts fall into those categories.

Publishing in Pulse

In your profile, when you go to create a status update, you will now see the option to publish a post.

When you click the Publish a post link, a 'blog-like' window opens and you can complete your headline, insert an image and create your article – which will automatically be published to Pulse.

The rules of publishing apply

When creating your articles to share on LinkedIn Pulse, be mindful that the rules of good publishing apply (as outlined in Chapter 4).

- **Ensure that your article is not too long:** Articles of less than 1,000 words tend to perform best on Pulse.

- **Headlines matter:** Take the time to play around with your headline. Write three or four and perhaps get opinion from others as to which is the most compelling and engaging.
- **Images matter:** It's the image and the headline that are going to grab the attention of the browser – so be sure to go for clarity, simplicity and impact. As with blogs, you can also embed both static images and videos in your Pulse article.
- **Give, give, give:** In each of the articles featured on Bernard's profile (and if you look at other successful Pulse profiles you'll see a similar theme), the headline alludes to giving gems of advice away. Do consider that time is a precious resource. Why would someone spend their time reading your content? Keep in mind that the reader is always looking to take something away from time spent reading your article – so be sure to make that clear to them via your headline. Focus on what's in it for them.
- **Call to action:** Don't forget the reason you are writing the article. Ideally, you want to grow awareness of your expertise, your products, brand, organisation. In the sign-off of your article, be sure to include a link to your website, blog or other relevant landing page, where those who are introduced to you via Pulse can continue the conversation with you one to one.

LinkedIn apps

As with most of the social networks, you'll now find a range of apps in the Apple and Google stores. LinkedIn apps include Pulse, their paid-for business development resource Sales Navigator, their paid-for Recruiter solution, and also free resources, such as Elevate and Connected. These tools for your smartphone and tablet devices enable you to keep in touch with your networks on the move.

SlideShare

Last year, LinkedIn purchased SlideShare to enable its users to directly link slide presentations into their profiles, helping to make more visual and engaging profiles. You'll find the Slideshare feature under the Interests tab in the main menu bar. There are literally hundreds of thousands of presentations on Slideshare, so you might find this a useful research resource when you are developing presentations. With the LinkedIn App you can share your presentations with your professional LinkedIn connections too.

Endeavour to update your Profile Page with content at least once a week. Every time you update your profile and show activity, you are 'visible'. Visibility + Credibility = Profitability. In simple terms, the more

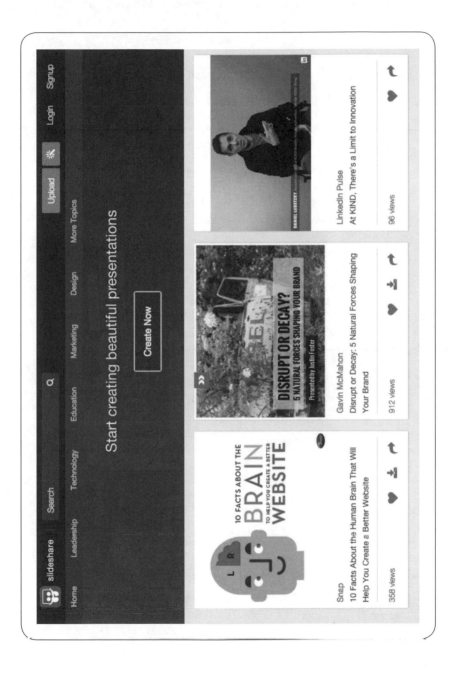

visible you are to your contacts, the more they know what you are up to, the more likely they are to contact you or think of you for a relevant reason, which may lead to a business referral. However, participation is key.

Social media marketing action plan

Clearly, LinkedIn goes beyond a place to put your CV. In this chapter we showcased the many benefits of LinkedIn. To recap:

- It's a place to connect.
- It can be used to connect the entire organisation.
- Information and expertise can be shared through Pulse or relevant Groups.
- It's a database – you'll never lose those contacts.
- You can showcase an online update of who you are and what you do.
- You can showcase your organisation, and optimise your products and services in Showcase Pages.
- Using keywords when creating your content will help you to be found in LinkedIn searches.
- Ensure that your profile is All Star – the more complete it is, the more visible you become.

---

8 | Social video: YouTube and the future of online video content

What you will learn from this chapter:

- Why video is so important
- How to fit video into your marketing strategy
- Uses for video
- Shooting videos
- Setting up and managing a YouTube channel
- Promoting your videos
- Measuring the performance of your channel

Video is now part of our daily lives. Quick, simple and easy to create, moving content is starting to replace the written word as the go-to medium in which to communicate. Why? The truth is that people increasingly have neither the time nor the inclination to read as much as they used to. YouTube, Vimeo, Instagram, Vine, BBC iPlayer, TVCatchup all offer easy-access video content, whether it's on your phone, smart TV or PC. And now we have sites like Snapchat, Meerkat and Periscope, which offer live streaming via a smartphone or tablet.

As we saw in Chapter 3, Millennials (people under 35) increasingly prefer to engage through the medium of video. In fact, the vast majority of online video consumption is from this age group (http://digiday.com/publishers/shifting-state-digital-video-consumption-5-charts/). Yet all of us now consume more video content. Cisco Systems estimates that by 2019 nearly three-quarters of the world's mobile data traffic will be video and that mobile video is expected to increase 13-fold between 2014 and 2019, accounting for 72% of total mobile data traffic by the end of the forecast period (www.cisco.com/c/en/us/solutions/collateral/service-provider/visual-networking-index-vni/white_paper_c11-520862.html).

Almost 80% of the UK's web population already watch video as part of their online activity (www.statista.com/statistics/272835/share-of-internet-users-who-watch-online-videos/). YouTube still dominates video consumption, but Facebook is now making serious inroads (www. socialmediatoday.com/content/facebook-video-vs-youtube-maximizing-results-evolving-video-landscape-0). Meanwhile, Twitter is also aiming to take a share of this audience through Twitter Video Cards (https:// blog.twitter.com/2014/introducing-promoted-video-on-twitter).

In terms of advertising, video is starting to achieve significant results. According to the Online Publishers Association, 80% of internet users recall watching a video ad on a website they visited in the past 30 days. Of those people:

- 46% took some action after viewing the ad
- 26% looked for more information about the subject of the video
- 22% visited the website named in the ad
- 15% visited the company represented in the video ad
- 12% purchased the specific product featured in the ad.

Elsewhere, according to Forbes Insight (www.forbes.com/forbesinsights/video_in_the_csuite/), 59% of senior executives would rather watch a video than read text. About 65% of those who view a video click through to visit the vendor website, 50% look for more information and 45% report that they contacted a vendor after seeing an online video ad. About 50% of those who viewed an online marketing video went on to make a purchase for their business.

And video can even improve click-through rates from email marketing, as can be seen in this article: www.emarketer.com/Article/Video-Next-Frontier-Email-Marketers/1009980#84WpKtM5xCIDTsoi.99.

In a nutshell, video is big news and should now make up an important part of any organisation's marketing and communications strategy. As with so many other aspects of the social media revolution, it has been changes in technology that have enabled video to be used so success-fully. Go back ten years, and using video within your digital marketing strategy would have been out of the reach of all but the largest organi-sations. Three key drivers have made video a viable option: first came the digitisation of film, allowing video to be made much more 'portable'; next, better internet bandwidth and speeds enabled moving images to be featured online without crashing websites or taking hours to load; and finally, mobile technology means that anyone can shoot video via their phone, edit it on the spot, then broadcast it using social media.

The result is that now, with a decent level of ingenuity, virtually any organisation can incorporate moving images into their marketing mix. Many smartphones have perfectly acceptable video cameras, and there are a host of accessories on the market that make shooting film simple. The choice of video editing programmes and apps (many of which are free) to help you make professional-looking footage also continues to grow. Such is the importance of video that some organisations are even setting aside spare rooms in their offices to create home-grown 'studios'.

YouTube

The platform that best epitomises how important video has become is YouTube, which was officially launched in November 2005 as a simple video-sharing site. Over the past ten years it has grown exponentially into a media giant. Taken over by Google in November 2006, YouTube is now the third most-visited website in the world as well as the second most-visited search engine (after Google). If Facebook has the potential to become the new newspaper, YouTube has the assets to take over from TV as the prime source of moving images. According to its own figures, over four billion videos are streamed daily, while 300 hours of fresh content is uploaded every minute by YouTube's one billion user base. In addition, there are now over one billion mobile video views – every day! The introduction of live streaming, the integration with view-on-demand sites like BBC iPlayer and 4oD, plus the ability to rent and watch full-length movies, means that YouTube has become a broadcasting giant.

In addition, the site's integration with Google+, as well as Google itself, means that many organisations can dramatically improve their online visibility by having a presence on YouTube (in the context of an overall search engine optimisation strategy) and using social extensions (www. searchenginepeople.com/blog/link-google-plus-to-adwords-for-higher-ctr.html).

Other video-sharing sites

However, YouTube is by no means the only online video-sharing site. Facebook is now placing videos centre stage with specific video advertising and enhanced visibility on the site for moving images. There are also three key apps – Instagram, Vine and Snapchat – which all allow users to make, create and edit videos on the move. Ranging from just five seconds in length to 16 seconds, these sites are now being used by brands to reach out to and engage with Millennials. We will go into Instagram and Snapchat in more detail in Chapter 9, but it is worth explaining the significance of Twitter's own video-sharing site, Vine. Launched in January 2013 as an app, users take individual images taken on their mobile device which are then 'stitched together' to make a six-second video. Many brands use this site to add a little fun to their marketing mix. It may not seem like a long time, but a surprising amount of content can be packed in to six seconds. Vines can also be used to illustrate a particular feature of a product, provide context, educate customers using moving infographics or even as an indirect lead generation tool. Business Insider lists some of the most popular brands on Vine: http://uk.businessinsider.com/most-popular-brands-on-vine-2014-10. Also owned by Twitter is Periscope. This app, which at the time of writing is only available on Apple devices, allows users to live stream content either to their Twitter followers or to other Periscope users. This offers a whole range of possibilities for brands to engage live with their target audiences.

Elsewhere, Vimeo (www.vimeo.com) actually pre-dates YouTube and is a popular site used by filmmakers and the creative industry. Viddy (www.viddy.com) and Socialcam (www.socialcam.com) are video applications built around mobile devices, while Telly.com (formerly Twitvid) is a great way of sharing videos on Twitter. In China, where YouTube is not widely available, the key video-sharing site is Youku (www.youku.com), and many other countries have their own home-grown sites. For example, India has IndianPad (www.indianpad.in), Germany has MyVideo (www.myvideo.de) and France has Wideo (www.wideo.fr). There are also sites like Animoto (www.animoto.com), where you can very simply create and manage your own videos from photographs, slides and existing videos. These can then be uploaded to one of the video-sharing sites or other social networks to reach the desired audience.

Most of these sites are compatible with Facebook, while YouTube and Vimeo can easily be integrated with websites via Wordpress or other content management systems. In the age of mobile internet, all of these sites are available as apps, ensuring that it is not only easy to make film but it is also simple to edit it and also distribute it simply using the range of social networks on offer.

Integrating video into your marketing strategy

As with any other social network, before you create a presence on YouTube or any of the other video-sharing sites, it is important to visit your business objectives. How will video help you achieve your goals and how will you go about creating a defined video content strategy?

While it may be virtually free to shoot video, and in many cases this is the desirable option, there may be occasions when you need to allocate a budget to create something a little more professional. Just as in theory, anyone can take a photograph, very few people shoot like Annie Leibovitz. The same is true with video and it can often be more cost-effective to bring in specialists. Also, is there a 'video-friendly' culture in your organisation? One of the ways you can use video is showcasing your people. If your employees would rather not appear in front of a camera or are very uncomfortable doing so, you will fail in your attempts to show the human face of your company and you may instead have to invest in an actor.

For many organisations, using video is a major step forward and one that may never have been considered before, because of the technological issues and costs associated with it. In fact, the first step could be to alter your website so that video content can be uploaded easily. Most content management systems now have easy-to-use modules. However, as with blogs, once you have committed yourself to showcasing video, you need to have a proper strategy in place to ensure that you can feed the channel regularly. If you do manage to upload videos to either your homepage or a landing page, you will be rewarded, not just by giving visitors to your site a more rounded view of your brand, but also from search engines. Google is always on the lookout for fresh content and videos rank very highly, especially when they are properly tagged; and on Facebook, videos are counted as the most valuable pieces of content.

Uses of video

Organisations may well be interested in principle in using video, but a lack of experience in using the medium may give them a fairly blinkered view on its uses – people often assume that video is better suited to creative industries. When video is used, too often there are 'talking heads' – people sitting behind a desk delivering a monologue which has neither been thought through nor properly executed.

Marketing is all about innovation and trying to do things differently. With video now being an affordable and easily accessible marketing option, it is time to try and do things a little differently.

Case study: Dollar Shave Club

A great example of this is a video posted by Dollar Shave Club on YouTube in 2012 (www.youtube.com/DollarShaveClub). At the time of writing it has had almost 19 million views. This clip will prove to you that if it is done well, video can assist a wide range of industries, professions and sectors.

In the video, which cost just $4,500 to make, the CEO of Dollar Shave Club (www.dollarshaveclub.com), an SME that ships razors from as little as a dollar a month, appeared in a 94-second clip, along with one of his employees, to advertise his products.

The result was that this small start-up with just five members of staff dramatically increased its brand awareness, signed up thousands of new customers and even attracted over $1 million of venture capital funding.

As with all other aspects of marketing, it really pays to be creative. If someone selling razor blades can get 19 million views of a video, why can't you? So here are a few ideas to get you thinking about how you could use video to achieve your business goals.

Promotional films

In the past, organisations with reasonable marketing budgets may have set aside money to shoot promotional videos. The issue was how to distribute these to potential customers. Now, videos can easily be incorporated into websites, email signatures, documents and, of course, blogs, as well as social media sites. It is rare that these are produced in house but they can be, and the cost may be less than other forms of marketing such as brochures and sponsorship.

Example

The Montcalm Hotel in London has produced a short promotional video to advertise the accommodation it offers: https://youtu.be/JsgqbzHhYul

Testimonials/interviews with customers

These days, it's not what **you** say about your products or services that matters, but what others are saying about them. Ninety-two per cent of consumers around the world say they trust earned media, such as word of mouth and recommendations from friends and family, above all other forms of advertising, and one of the best ways of building trust is to get your customers or clients to talk about the level of service they have received from you. A short 30-second clip filmed with a digital camera or smartphone will suffice. The fact that it is not professionally made will make it look that much more authentic and believable.

Example

Seaspray Hotel in Brighton is a small family-run hotel which has successfully used video on the homepage of their website to build their brand: www.youtube.com/watch?v=Ok1H_8xUPgo.

Interviews with Staff

People do business with people, so it is important to get across the human side of your business to customers. Most websites list their employees and may include photographs of them. However, film provides a 'real world' experience and reveals more of people's character. It is not just service industries where this is important, but also professional services, and the creative and educational sectors. In fact, we've yet to come across an organisation we've worked or trained with where video isn't appropriate to give a three-dimensional view of employees. Often, this may be the difference between a potential customer choosing to use you rather than your competitor.

Short 'how-to' films

How many people have struggled to put together a children's toy or flat-pack furniture? Instructions are often unclear or non-existent. However, a short video clip can often make the user experience that much simpler, as in this film about putting up an IKEA shelf: www.youtube.com/watch?v=yAzSgqe_e_A. Software demonstrations, showing how a product or service works – video provides a compelling and useful platform to convey instructions and insight.

Using humour to talk about a dry subject

As with the Dollar Shave Club video, it is often a great idea to use humour to make video clips more engaging. Done well, it can turn even the dourest subject into something that viewers will actually want to watch.

Blendtec (www.blendtec.com), manufacturers of blenders, have been very successful in promoting their products via their YouTube channel (www.youtube.com/Blendtec). With millions of video views and over 423,000 channel subscribers, their videos have acquired cult status.

Similarly, this mortgage company uses video to explain one of the driest subjects around, the mortgage application process: https://youtu.be/mosaST997I8.

Video press releases/video blogs

Journalists and bloggers, like the rest of us, are increasingly time poor and bombarded by the written word. Very often, a short video press release or blog can be the best way to attract their attention and help you to stand out from the crowd. At the same time, fresh video content added to your website will help boost your rankings on search engines.

> **Example**
>
> Here is a clip of KPMG partner Vanessa Patterson discussing involving family members in the wealth preservation process: https://youtu.be/aOcB3N-QH2A.

Thought leadership

One of the objectives of using video is to raise the profile of key members of staff or to build thought leadership in a given sector. Keynote speeches or presentations are often an excellent environment for people to shine, so they make great content for videos. Similarly, showcasing your knowledge about a specific area is a key way to build thought leadership. And video can be a powerful way of discussing and providing insight into complex matters that are difficult or dry to explain in the written word. Showreels are now part of the marketing toolkit for many firms that are eager to promote leading people in their organisation. These can be put up on those individuals' LinkedIn profiles or corporate websites to help build personal brand.

> **Example**
>
> Here is the showreel for one of the authors of this book: https://youtu.be/fpYQO2896Vw.

Podcasts/vodcasts

Sound (podcast) or video (vodcast) clips are an excellent way to get your message across or build your brand. They are listened to or watched primarily on mobile devices, and users can also subscribe to the broadcasts, enabling organisations to build a community of engaged followers.

> **Example**
>
> The global management consulting firm Hay Group (www.haygroup.com) includes a number of podcasts and vodcasts on their site as well as videos on their YouTube channel: www.youtube.com/HayGroupVideos.

Leverage video-building applications such as Animoto

There are some clever online applications that make it possible to turn slides, pictures and videos into something which looks pretty professional. Using apps such as Animoto, within just a few minutes we were able to turn a PowerPoint presentation into a short promotional video: www.youtube.com/watch?v=RemjwzND4yQ&feature=context-chv.

FAQs

If you provide products or services and host a page on your website that covers your FAQs, then you could create videos that address the main points of most queries. Often film can get the message across succinctly and clearly.

'About Us'

If you have a website, you probably have an About Us page. If you look at your web analytics, it's likely you'll see that About Us is quite a regularly visited page. Think about your own web habits: if you are researching a new provider or a product or service online, you're likely to go to the About Us page to see who the people are behind the business. Consider bringing your About Us page to life by including video that really does highlight who you are and what you do.

Sales

It is a myth that you cannot sell via social media. Remember: it's about creating the conditions to get people to know you, like you, trust you and ultimately do business with you. Video is no exception to this rule.

Many companies are now using product placement within advertising rather than directly selling. For example:

- the Katy Perry Superbowl half-time ad – https://youtu.be/DE7H-4RGdKdY
- charities that use video for direct fundraising purposes – https://youtu.be/jHuVwkcuXl0
- and this south London plumber has gone for the direct approach and has now had over 43,000 views for their promotional video – https://youtu.be/PrdWBXhPtHk.

Look at www.youtube.com/yt/advertise/en-GB to see more on advertising via YouTube, or go to Chapter 10 of this book.

Let's not forget about vloggers

We've looked at ways in which you and your business can use video in your business and briefly discussed the use of video blogs. Vlogging (blogging via video) is now a widely used phenomenon, and one where any unknown can capture the attention of the masses to the advantage of themselves and their business.

For example, take the beauty, lifestyle and fashion vlogger Zoella. Over the past five years, from humble beginnings making videos from her home, she has grown into a global brand. At just 24, she's published a best seller, purchased a home for over £1 million and sells ad space to large brands such as Christian Dior and Jo Malone for around £20,000 per month. Thanks to her regular vlogging features, her site boasts over six million visits a month. All of which goes to show that if you target the right audience with relevant and engaging content, and keep delivering engaging content, you have the opportunity to grow an audience and a strong fan base, which in turn creates other opportunities.

From a business perspective, it's worth researching and watching what successful vloggers (and there are many others) have done to grow their presence: consistent and compelling content, delivered in an engaging and appealing way to meet the needs of their audience.

Creating videos

Once you have decided that you want to use video as part of your marketing strategy and have highlighted the applications that will best meet your business needs, you need to think about actually creating the videos.

Whether you decide to shoot the video yourself or get professionals in to do it for you, it is vital that you prepare a brief. Here are some ideas of what you need to include in your brief.

- **What is the key message you want to convey?** Ideally, focus on just one or two messages. More than that and you run the risk of muddying the waters.
- **What do you want the video to achieve?** There has to be a *reason* for doing the video – brand building, thought leadership, increased sales or better customer engagement, for example.
- **Who is it aimed at?** As with all forms of marketing, think about your target audience(s). Put yourself in their shoes and try to imagine what would appeal to them.
- **What is your call to action?** As with other forms of online marketing, such as websites, AdWords and blogs, you want viewers to do something after watching the video. Do you want them to go to your website, call you, email you?
- **Who will appear in the video?** Whoever you choose to be in the clip must be a) willing and b) able to deliver a performance that will do your brand justice. Warning: This may not be the CEO.

- **What sort of budget are you going to set aside?** This goes not just for individual videos but creating a regular supply of dynamic footage.
- **Where and when are you going to shoot the video?** Do you have a suitable location?
- **How long will it be?** Anything from a six-second Vine to a two-minute corporate video is acceptable, depending on your audience and the objective of the video.

Creating a storyboard and writing a script

The next step is to prepare your storyboard. Looking rather like a set of PowerPoint slides, this will be a rough diagram giving you an idea about what you will be filming. It will contain the different scenes to be shot. Like any good story, there should be a beginning (introduction), middle (key message) and end (conclusion plus call to action).

> **Example**
>
> Here is a great video by Howcast (www.howcast.com) showing how to prepare a storyboard: http://youtu.be/65_3bq_0eSY.

Very few of us can deliver pithy, off-the-cuff performances in front of camera. Even seasoned speakers or actors need some form of basic script or cue cards in order to put on the optimum performance. So once you have a storyboard prepared, you should write some form of script. This can either be memorised or cue cards can be held up by a colleague/assistant when filming. The result will be a smooth and professional-looking video rather than a stilted and amateur one.

With your storyboard and script prepared, you are ready to film your video. Here are some handy pointers.

- Make sure that your camera is in focus and there is enough light. You may want to purchase or hire extra lighting.
- Think about investing in a clip-on microphone to ensure optimum sound quality.
- Use a tripod or other form of rest to eradicate camera shake.
- Think about the background and make sure that where you are filming is neat and tidy – and appropriate.
- Ensure that the subject of your film is dressed appropriately. If you are going to film several videos in one day they will need a change of clothes, accessories, etc.

Editing your Video

Statistics show that 33% of viewers watch only the first 30 seconds of videos, 11% lose interest and leave at the one-minute mark; altogether 60% bail out after just two minutes. So, however much footage you have, it is important to edit it down, ideally to two minutes or less – and ensure that the first 30 seconds covers your key message and is compelling to encourage users to carry on watching.

There is a range of video editing tools, many of which are free, including YouTube's own video editor (www.youtube.com/editor). There are also paid-for programmes such as iMovie (www.apple.com/ilife/imovie), Sony Vegas Movie Studio (www.sonycreativesoftware.com/moviestudiope), Microsoft's Movie Maker (www.microsoft.com/education/moviemaker) and Roxio Creator (www.roxio.com).

All these programs allow you to add sound, overlays, subtitles and special effects, all of which will enhance the final video and give it a professional feel.

There are some fabulous apps out there too. We particularly like Frameographer, which enables time lapse and stop motion movies on your iPhone (www.studioneat.com/products/frameographer).

Setting up your YouTube channel

Now you have a video or a set of videos to upload, you can think about setting up your own YouTube channel. Remember, this may be one of the key ways in which your organisation or company stays visible online, so take your time in making it look the best it can.

Here are the steps to take to get your channel set up.

1. You must first set up a Google account; this will be your login to the suite of Google accounts including YouTube, Google Analytics and Google+. Go to www.google.co.uk, click **Sign In** and then **Add Account**. You'll then be asked to fill in a form with basic details, including the username, which should be your company or trademarked name. A *yourcompanyname@gmail.com* email address will be created and this will be the login to all your Google accounts, including YouTube. At the same time, a Google+ profile will automatically be created for you. Refer to Chapter 9 for more details on this, or go to https://support.google.com/accounts/answer/27441?source=gsearch.

2. Once you have a fully functioning Google account, complete with avatar, go to www.youtube.com and click **Sign In** at the top right-hand corner of the screen. Then go into YouTube settings, click on the cog symbol and you'll see a new window, where you'll be asked to Create a Channel.

3. As with Facebook, it is a good idea either to choose a brand-specific or keyword-rich name. For example, the well known brand Marks & Spencer has www.youtube.com/marksandspencertv (brand focus); St Albans plumber Ryan Moffat has www.youtube.com/plumbersinstalbans (keyword focus).

4. Start to customise your channel. The first thing to do is to upload a background for your channel. As with your Facebook Timeline, you need to ensure that this is of sufficient quality to entice viewers. You can upload a photograph or design a custom background if you have nothing suitable. Note that this background image needs to fit the standard YouTube channel presets, so you can either engage the services of a designer or download one of the many templates available online.

5. Next, click on the **About** tab and fill in a succinct, ideally keyword-enabled 'boilerplate' that sums up the purpose of your business or organisation.

6. To showcase the videos you have on your channel, whether they are ones you have created or ones you wish to categorise into folders, go into **Playlists**. These work in very much the same way as Lists on Twitter and can be either public or private. Once you have playlists, when you view videos you can not only Like them but also add them to a specific playlist. You can also create a playlist when viewing videos, either on a PC or on a mobile device via the YouTube app. There is of course a **Favorites** list to which you can add videos. This is similar to Favoriting tweets.

7. Be social! Remember that YouTube is a social network and you want to engage with the people viewing your videos. So make sure that in your account settings you enable the Comment setting.

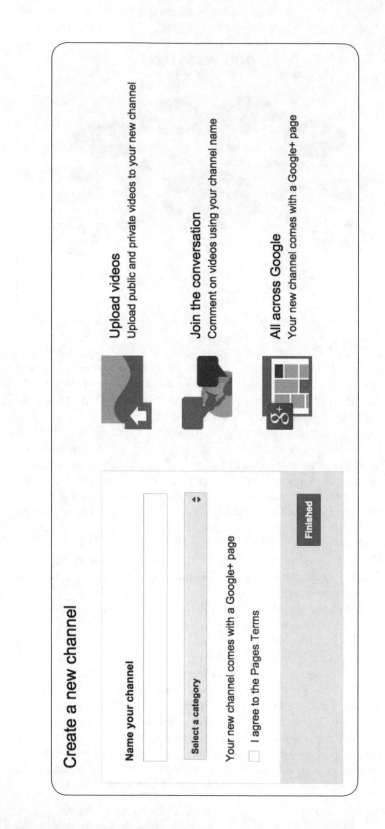

Create a new channel

Name your channel

[   ]

[Select a category   ◀▶]

Your new channel comes with a Google+ page

[ ] I agree to the Pages Terms

Finished

Upload videos
Upload public and private videos to your new channel

Join the conversation
Comment on videos using your channel name

All across Google
Your new channel comes with a Google+ page

8. Subscribe to other channels. In Facebook, when administering your Page, you can Like the Pages of partner organisations or companies you want to be associated with. The same is true of YouTube. Search for the organisations and companies whose videos you would like to feature on your channel, hit the Subscribe button and these will start to appear in your news feed.

9. Videos that you Like will appear in your news feed. Think of your channel as your own TV station. Some of the content you will produce yourself; and you will broadcast entire series (subscribing) as well as one-off programmes (Likes). Like a TV station, you want your content to be engaging, of interest to casual visitors and subscribers alike, as well as informative. Remember that there may well be occasions when your YouTube channel is where you want to drive traffic to.

10. When you click on the **Settings** tab, you will see **Creator Studio**. This takes you through to a page manager that gives you the option to see your Channel Analytics, manage your videos, manage your settings and browse the audio library in order to add music to your videos.

Uploading videos and managing your channel

You should now have a fully functioning channel as well as the means to create your own videos. Finally, you are now in a position to start uploading videos. This is a very simple process. Log on to your YouTube account and in the top right-hand corner of the page you will see the **Upload** tab.

You are then presented with three options.

1. You can upload a file straight from your PC or tablet device.
2. You can upload multiple files.
3. You can record live via webcam.

Note: There is a 15-minute limit for videos (but this can be increased) and the file size is limited to 2GB for uploads from YouTube's website or 20GB if up-to-date browser versions are used. For more information see YouTube's guidelines: http://support.google.com/youtube/bin/answer.py?hl=en&answer=71673.

Showcasing your video

However you decide to upload your video, once it is on YouTube you need to ensure that it gets maximum visibility on the site. Here are some tips.

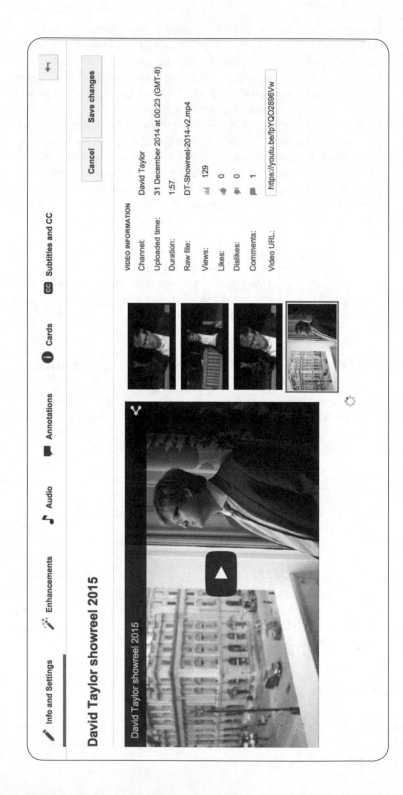

- Just as newspaper headlines are used to grab people's attention, it is important that you give your video a great title. Make it catchy and include some of your keywords. For example, Manchester family law solicitors James Maguire & Co. have their own channel (www.youtube.com/channel/UCWOWqFvMRbIJ_yvl3gAzyyg) and they use the keywords 'family law', 'solicitors' and 'Manchester' in their video title. Remember that YouTube is the second most visited search engine, so the more assistance you can give Google's search bots to drive people to you, the better.

- Underneath the title is a description box. Include the points you want to get across in the first two or three paragraphs. Again, put in a smattering of your keywords. Think of this as a short blog where there is a strong headline followed by a pithy write-up. In this example (https://youtu.be/o6UX7vJizcM), Yeo Valley have put in a full write-up. **Remember to put in your website or landing page URL if your aim is to drive people there.**

- As with metatags in your website, it is important to tag your video with as many keywords as you can as well as words/phrases which relate to your product or service. This box appears under the description and you can add as many tags as you wish to ensure you reach the widest possible audience – similar to what you would do with an AdWords campaign. For more information, check out YouTube's help page: http://support.google.com/youtube/bin/answer.py?hl=en-GB&answer=141804.

- Choose a category for your video. YouTube has 15 different categories, so select the one that is most appropriate for you. The categories include education, news and politics, travel and entertainment, etc. The category you select will appear underneath the write-up to your video.

- Choose the appropriate thumbnail for your video. Like an album cover, you want an image that best represents your video. You are given a choice of three. To apply a thumbnail, go into **Creator Studio**, then **Video Manager**. You'll see a list of all your videos. Edit the one you want and you'll see a tab saying **Customized Thumbnail.**

- Set the privacy level for your video. There are three different levels – public, unlisted and private. If you are not ready to 'publish' your video and want to make changes or additions, it is a good idea to keep it private until you are ready to go. If you aren't quite ready to promote your video but would like certain people to be able to see it, go for the unlisted option as anyone clicking on the URL will be taken to the video. And if you're happy, click Public and your first video will be live on your channel.

- Check regularly for comments. Ideally, you want people to comment on and/or share your videos. This not only increases your online visibility but also provides valuable feedback – both positive and negative. **Note:** It is a good idea to check the email notifications box in your account settings so that you will be notified when people comment on your videos or subscribe to your channel, etc. It is important that you respond promptly to either positive or negative comments, just as you would on a Facebook Page or Twitter. As with any form of online or offline media relations, you need to have in place some procedures for dealing with negative comments. It is worth noting that the more comments and shares you get, the more likely you are to appear in YouTube's search and therefore in Google's. As with all forms of online marketing, fresh, relevant content gets rewarded by higher search rankings.

- You can post on your wall, as you would on Facebook or LinkedIn. This is another way to add content but also a great way to draw attention to new videos or playlists that you think may be of interest to your channel subscribers.

Promoting your videos

While your YouTube channel provides a great online focus for all your videos, you need to think about a strategy to promote both your videos and your channel. Just as over 40% of UK websites get no traffic and many blogs remain unseen, a whole range of well-crafted and content-rich videos never see the light of day because they are not adequately promoted.

There are two key ways in which you can promote your videos: organically, via blogs, other social media sites and word of mouth; or the paid-for route of video AdWords.

One of the key drivers in the growth of video usage in marketing was film digitisation. Moving one step further, once you have uploaded a video to YouTube it will have its own customised URL. This makes it highly portable and enables you to utilise it in a wide range of media.

Organic promotion

It is important that you try to promote your new video to the widest possible audience. Depending on your audience, we recommend that you think about the best channels to use to promote your video.

For example, if you are a boutique hotel, you could employ an array of marketing devices such as posting the video on your Facebook Page and pinning it to the top of your timeline, posting regular tweets with the link to your video, incorporating it into your blog or using it within an email campaign. You may even want to look at direct mail with a link to your channel.

If you are a law firm specialising in litigation, you could think about posting the video to your LinkedIn company profile, promoting the link on

Twitter, incorporating it into press releases and perhaps even having a module on your website to highlight your latest video clips.

> **Example**
>
> Pannone Solicitors: www.youtube.com/PannoneSolicitors and www.pannone.com/media/videospodcasts.

Here are some of the ways in which you can promote your video:

- embedded within Microsoft Office applications – Outlook, Word, Excel, PowerPoint
- on your website or a specialist landing page
- email signatures
- traditional marketing – brochures, adverts, PR, fliers, posters
- email campaigns
- blogs
- Facebook Pages
- Twitter
- LinkedIn personal and company profiles, Groups and Showcase Pages
- Google+ page
- other social networks – Tumblr, Pinterest, Viddy, Vimeo.

Paid-for promotion

An increasingly viable way of promoting your video is to use Google AdWords for video. This works in very much the same way as it does on Google. The difference is that instead of users seeing an ad you have bought when searching on Google, visitors to YouTube will see a link to your video within the site. More on this in Chapter 10.

Measuring the performance of your videos

One of the mantras in marketing is 'testing and measuring'. Video is no different. You may think that the videos you are posting are great, but if you don't get anyone commenting on them or you don't use the correct promotional strategy to get them out to a wider audience, they will have less value. Using Google Analytics and YouTube's own analytics, it is possible to measure exactly how much engagement there has been with your videos as well as how much traffic has been driven via each of the different places you have promoted your video. This will give you a large amount of data, including viewer demographics, traffic sources and number of views. This can also be broken down further when linked to an AdWords campaign. In addition, you will be able to gauge the level of interaction that people have had both with your videos and also with your channel.

By accessing Google Analytics, you will also be able to measure the amount of traffic that has come to your website or specific landing page via YouTube.

There is a huge amount of data on offer, which can often become overwhelming. It is always a good idea to set four or five key performance indicators (KPIs) so that you can focus on achieving the specific business objectives you set when embarking on a video content marketing strategy for your organisation.

Social media marketing action plan

- Think about how you will use a defined video content marketing strategy to help you achieve your business goals.
- Create the right culture within your organisation before going down the video route. Filming people is a huge step forward and can be uncomfortable for many organisations.
- Be creative in how you use video. Don't just go down the tried and tested 'talking heads' route. Remember, marketing is all about innovation.
- Set aside some sort of budget. Whether you decide to shoot videos in-house or employ an outside agency, there will be some form of expenditure – even if it is purchasing a camera or smartening up one of the meeting rooms to turn it into an impromptu studio.
- Be proactive. If you are going to have a video channel – on YouTube or one of the other video sharing sites – ensure you have a strategy to keep it regularly updated with engaging content.
- Promote your videos to ensure they reach the widest possible audience. This can be done through organic or paid-for methods.
- Test and measure. Find out what works and what doesn't using Google and YouTube analytics.

---

9 | Other key social media sites

What you will learn from this chapter:

- Niche social networks
- Other key networks and how businesses are using them
- Google+: your online footprint and beyond
- Pinterest: a visual way to showcase your business
- Instagram: a visual way to engage
- Tumblr: creative content rules the day
- WhatsApp: fast, personal and highly engaged
- Snapchat: engaging in just 10 seconds
- Ello: simple, beautiful and ad free

Throughout this book, we have focused on the oldest and most common networks that are being used for business: Facebook, Twitter, YouTube and LinkedIn. However, there are hundreds of other online sites where people can communicate, interact and network.

These sites cover a wide range of interest areas, from clubbing (www. dontstayin.com) to books and reading lists (www.goodreads.com). Quora (www.quora.com) is the largest questions and answers site in the world, and Meetup (www.meetup.com) enables you to organise face-to-face network gatherings and stay connected online. There are now literally thousands of niche networks, where you can join a relevant community to discuss and network with like-minded people. There are sector networks such as www.behance.net, where designers can share ideas, work and collaborate, and www.houzz.com, the place for people to share ideas about designing their home (very popular with interior designers and those in the home and decor sector).

It is worth noting that while the 'Big Four' may be huge across much of the globe, in some parts of the world they are eclipsed by local sites. In China, there are home-grown versions of Facebook (Renren – www. renren.com), Twitter (Sina Weibo – www.weibo.com) and YouTube (Youku – www.youku.com) as well as Tencent (www.tencent.com), Douban (www.douban.com) and the mobile app Wechat.

Also, as people have become savvier with their social media channel activity, personal preferences have shifted. Networks such as Instagram and Pinterest are now as popular (and in some cases more so) and as widely used as Twitter and Facebook; and messenger services such as WhatsApp are now sending more messages per minute than Twitter. In fact, independent global messenger sites, such as WhatsApp, where groups of people can collaborate via instant messaging, have seen rapid adoption and growth globally over the past few years. Other services include QQ and Qzone, which connect groups of people all over the world.

User-generated content

The one thing all these sites have in common is user-generated content. They are also all available as mobile apps – which is important when you consider that in many parts of the world people do have smartphones but will not necessarily have access to broadband or even land lines.

When to use these sites

As we have emphasised throughout this book, it is important to focus on both your own business objectives and your target audiences. If you are a European company looking to increase your brand profile in China, it would be worth investing in a decent Renren page for your brand. Similarly, if you are looking to market your product to an Indian audience, it might be better to use Bharatstudent (www.bharatstudent. com), one of the most popular social networking sites in India, than Facebook.

Using the Plan, Listen, Analyse and Engage mantra, it is useful to ascertain exactly who your target audiences are, what channels they are using and how best to engage with them. As with all aspects of marketing, this process needs to be done constantly as social networks gain or lose popularity and users change their media consumption habits. Using data from a site like Alexa (www.alexa.com), it is possible to get traffic data, global rankings and other information on thousands of websites, including the key social networking sites.

The two key questions you should always ask yourself are: *'Will having a presence on this site benefit my business?'*; and *'Will the return on investment be worth the effort?'* Many brands have signed up to a plethora of sites and, in some cases, that may be a worthwhile strategy – with content planned and engagement high across each platform. However, for many businesses, being on seven or eight social media sites may not be that effective. In fact, if most of the sites are just 'there for show', it may even harm your brand. If you are struggling to create content for one or two channels and to keep them active, then consider whether the content you are planning to repurpose across the other six channels is relevant and appropriate. If so, great – repurpose your content to facilitate an integrated channel approach. But if not – you really have to consider why you are on those channels. For example, as we will see later in this chapter, channels such as Instagram and Pinterest are heavily reliant on visual content. If you don't have relevant and compelling content for these channels, having them in place, without relevant content, would make that channel look a little bit deserted.

It is important to understand that whatever channels you choose to use, you need to incorporate them into your overall marketing strategy. Across all channels you need to consider your tone of voice, understand your keywords, post appropriate and compelling content and listen to the conversations and engagement taking place. And, of course, it's important not to do social media activity just for the sake of it. You ideally need to monitor its effectiveness against well-thought-through key performance indicators (KPIs) that you will have set when setting up the channels. If a particular social network is not working for you, there will be two possible explanations: a) you're not using it effectively; or b) it's not the correct marketing channel for you.

A final note before we move on: virtually all social networking sites integrate with each other, thereby making it easy to share information across a range of different mediums and audiences. But don't just scattergun your content across everything. You need to think about the specific audience for each social networking site.

Google+: your online footprint and beyond

Launched in June 2011, Google+ was Google's latest foray into social networking after Google Buzz and Google Friend Connect. In just over six months, the platform amassed more than 90 million users and now has more than 300 million active users per month. As a business, Google is always looking at ways to optimise its dominance online, so Google+ was set up as a way to help Google become a better search engine by capturing more information and real-time conversations.

Integrated into the suite of services offered by Google – Gmail, maps, analytics, YouTube, Documents, Calendar – Google+ was initially focused on individual users, but in November 2011, Google rolled out business pages in the same way that Facebook has done.

Google+ allows people and businesses to create pages and develop relationships with prospects and customers on multiple levels. Individuals can add a brand to a specific Google+ circle, share a Google+ page with their network, and interact with the content posted by that company.

So, if one of your strategic business objectives is to have a higher visibility on Google, it may be that Google+ would be well worth investigating.

Setting up a business page on Google+

Let's start with the basics.

A Google+ page is your business's home on Google; it's literally Google with a plus. And as a business, you'll want to get your brand on here – because it isn't just a social network, it's part of a powerful search and social platform that integrates with key capabilities such as Google Docs, chat, hangouts, email and more. Many of us share the common misconception that Google+ is a ghost town. In reality, Google+ is home to vibrant, active communities that foster deep engagement.

What's key is learning what the Google+ features are, and taking advantage of them – but before we help you with that, you need to know how to set it up and make your Google+ business page user friendly.

It's very simple to set up a Google+ business page, but it has to be done via a personal Google+ account – if you haven't set up a personal page yet, visit https://accounts.google.com. If you already have a gmail address, you already have a Google+ account – it's just that perhaps you haven't done anything with it.

To optimise your profile, log in to Google using your gmail address and you will see the Google+ option. Fill out the relevant information – and then you're in. Once you've created your personal profile, you can then create a business page – do this by clicking on the pages icon from the left-hand navigation. Then Google will walk you through a few simple steps – picking a business category, completing a few details about your business, e.g. company name, picture, town and contact details. Alternatively, go to https://plus.google.com/pages/create to create your Page.

Once you have created your page you need to customise it. This includes a cover image (2120 pixels wide × 1192 pixels high). Yes, that is an enormous image, so you'll need a high-resolution image to fit – you don't want it to look pixelated to anyone reviewing your profile on a desktop. You'll also need to include a short description about your organisation (similar to that on Facebook or Twitter), and some contact information.

Creating content

When your page is complete, you can start posting content. This can be done in two ways. First, you can access Google+ either via your PC or mobile device and fill in the Share What's New box with an article, photo, video or link. If you have a company blog or news feed, it's a great idea to post these to your Google+ page. Remember to use a keyword-rich title plus a web link to the post on your blog or website. This will help improve your visibility on Google as well as widening the audience for your posts. As with Facebook, the more interesting and engaging content you post, the more likely it is that people will see it and the higher your visibility will be.

The other way to add content is to click the +1 that you see listed on websites or next to news articles. This will automatically share the content on your page's wall.

Setting up your Page

As with any kind of social media activity, patience is key. Don't expect to gain new followers and customers overnight. You need to promote your page as much as you can: perhaps with discreet mentions using the '+' before a name when you are sharing a post or status update on Google+ or by adding URL links to stationery and business cards; and use your existing social networks to encourage Google+ engagement (as well as making people aware that you have a Google+ presence via your website too).

Google+ is all about community, and the pages that do well are the ones that respond to shares, +1s and comments. Don't ignore reactions to your posts – if somebody likes your post and shares it, remember to go back and thank them. Keep an eye out on your +1s too; these are a popularity ranking signal for search engine optimisation (SEO) and are equivalent to the number of Likes on your Facebook Page. Add the +1 widget to your website pages and content to make it really easy for people to +1 your content.

Photos, videos and articles go really well on Google+, so if you have a blog, make sure that you update it regularly, and use your Google+ profile to promote your blog content as well as other interesting articles and content.

Take advantage of Google+ features

If you're wondering why your business needs to be on Google+, take a look at some of the Google+ features, which you won't find on any other social network.

Circle people

Like Twitter, this feature allows you to follow people, but with the added bonus of being able to put the people you follow into specific segments;

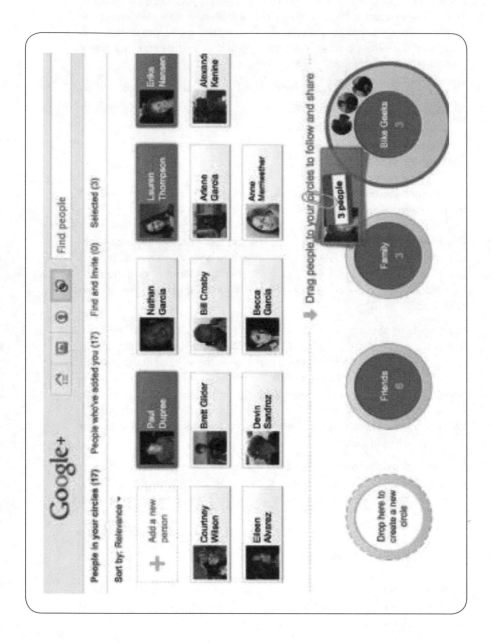

so you can group followers according to interest or any other criteria you want to assign. The people you circle will get a notification that you have done so, and are likely to follow your account back. This is a great way to closely target different interest groups, communities and conversations that matter to you. You can then communicate a message to a particular segment – really useful for targeted messaging.

Google reviews

Google reviews are important: they contribute significantly to your business's ranking in search results. When someone writes a review on Google+ they can create a simple rating using a star system. These stars have eye-catching potential as well as having been proven to increase your click-through rate. When someone writes a review, it is shared with their friends (people in their Google+ Circles), thus giving your business more visibility.

If you don't have Google+ reviews and a competitor does, they are likely to rank higher than you when customers search for your services. So, if relevant, think about ways you can encourage your customers to leave reviews on your Google+ page.

Google Hangouts

If you are looking to share knowledge or obtain feedback, Google Hangouts allows you to schedule online group events such as live Q&A sessions that enable several people to participate (think of it as a giant chatroom that you can control).

There are two different types of Hangouts: Hangouts and Hangouts on Air.

- **Hangouts** are typically used for private video chats with another person or group of people. They are not automatically recorded to YouTube and are therefore only visible to the people you invite to them – you can invite individuals or entire circles to join the Hangout. However, you are limited to a maximum of 10 people at a time on a private hangout.
- **Hangouts on Air** are publicly viewable and automatically recorded to the YouTube channel associated with your Google+ account. Your broadcast will be viewable by the public once you click Start broadcast – and the number of viewers watching your broadcast will be displayed at the top of the video call window.

Hangouts are great fun and very useful to showcase your business. Be sure not to make the same mistake we did on our first Google Hangout, when we weren't aware of the recording time delays – what you see 'live' streaming is actually slightly delayed – and so we thought it wasn't working. It's a good idea to have a test run, just to ensure you're up to speed with how the system works. Practise by doing some private ones with just a couple of people in your office.

Remember, you can record Hangouts – so you can create a great piece of content that you can then share on other platforms or via your website or blog.

Google+ influence on search rankings

Have you seen those +1s when you've been searching through Google+ pages? Shares or +1s of Google+ posts act like social recommendations that influence what searchers see in Google when they log in. When you have a Google+ page, people can +1 your page – essentially the same as a Facebook Like. Google uses the number of +1s on your page to determine how popular your business/brand is. This all helps to push your content up through the rankings.

Below is a Google+ page for Shelfstore, an online shelving manufacturer. When you type 'shelfstore' into Google, these Google+ profile pages pop up to the right-hand side of the search results. These include reviews and ratings as well as, for example, links to the website, directions and the latest Google+ posts.

Google posts are indexed

A great thing about Google+ is having your posts indexed immediately into search results. Everything you post, including all status updates,

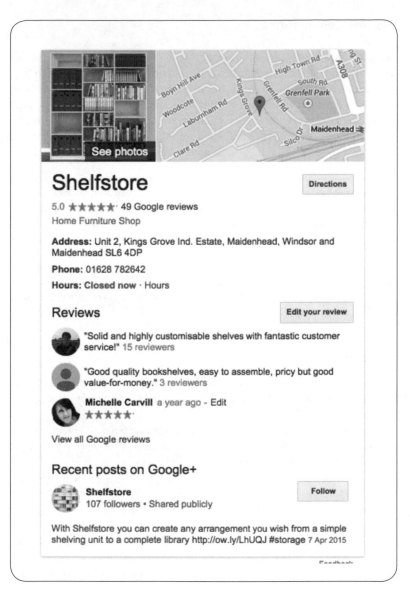

are indexed pretty much immediately into search results, which increases the possibility that your Google+ network will see your content in their search results.

Hot tip

To optimise your Google+ posts, use relevant keywords and don't forget to create tags using # before your keywords. Hashtags work on Google+ and other social networks (particularly Instagram, as we will see later) just as well as they do on Twitter.

Google+ communities

Google+ communities are in effect a way of creating your own social network. For example, you could create a customer community to provide your customers with a central place to mingle with each other and discuss your products or services. It allows you to create, or participate in, focused groups of both individuals and companies who share a particular interest – these communities can be made public or private to invited members. (See the Cadbury's Google+ page, where fans can collaborate.)

You can participate in communities using your personal profile or your business page – an option you won't find on many other social networks. This means that you can build your business's authority on a particular topic within communities as well as creating trust and getting direct feedback from customers.

Don't forget to make the most of another Google+ feature – Google+ custom URLs, which are short, easy to remember web addresses that link directly to your Google+ page.

In summary

- Setting up a Google+ page can help increase your online authority and the influence of your company or brand, and boost your search rankings.
- Hangouts enable you to run live or private webinars – which can be automatically recorded to YouTube to create compelling content which you can then share on other networks.
- Circles enable you to segment and target audiences with specific messages and/or content.
- Adding a +1 button to your website makes it easy for people to share your content.
- Post regular content – ideally once a day. Share your blogs, images or videos.
- Look for people and organisations in the search bar and put them into one of your Circles.
- Use the Ripples function – this helps you to find new and interesting people or organisations to follow based on who has been sharing information posted on Google+. It effectively helps you to tap in to the key influencers in a specific area. You can find more information here: http://support.google.com/plus/bin/answer.py?hl=en&answer=1713320.

In our view, Google+ will continue to optimise its offering. Interestingly, at the time of writing, there is talk of Google purchasing Twitter, so who knows where this will lead? There's also talk of Google+ dropping communities – which seems odd, given that they are probably one of the best aspects of the network. The key is to test and measure. If Google+ is helping you to achieve objectives and grow awareness and traction, it's worth spending time on the platform.

Pinterest: a visual way to showcase your business

Pinterest launched in March 2010 on an invitation-only basis, and went fully public a couple of years later. During 2012 Pinterest saw phenomenal growth, generating 20 million users within just a few months. However, to date, whilst Pinterest is still highly active, the user base is lower than many of the other social networks, reporting an average of 70 million users per month. Largely adopted by women (80% of the users are female), the site has seen strong adoption by brands eager to make use of the visual interface.

On Pinterest, users can share, curate, and discover new interests by posting (or 'pinning') content such as images or videos on their own or others' 'pinboards' – rather like an online noticeboard. This content can come from a variety of sources, e.g. PC, smartphone, via a Pin It button on a website or a URL.

You can see from the Ikea Pinterest account (accessible from Ikea's home page) that they break down their boards into Art, Bedrooms, Living Rooms, Kitchens, Beautiful Botanicals, product ranges, seasonal boards, etc. Also, if you take a look at any of the products on Ikea.com, you'll see that there is the option for you to pin the item; ideal for people building a 'mood board' when looking to move home or redecorate, or planning a wedding or office renovation.

Who can use Pinterest?

Pinterest is a very visual medium which lends itself very easily to creative industries such as art, design, architecture, photography, etc. Pinboards can act as online mood boards which illustrate the thought processes of the artists or designers, reflect their influences and show the creative journey. However, whatever your industry sector, if you are creating blog content and including images, don't feel that Pinterest is restricted to the creative industries. You can still share images on Pinterest that lead people directly back to your blog content.

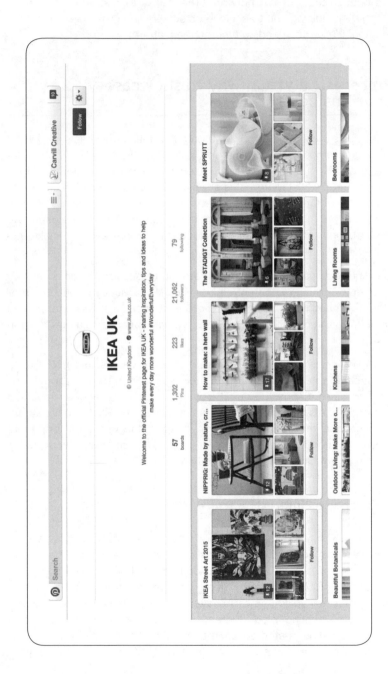

Case study: ASOS

Online department store ASOS (www.pinterest.com/asos) are successfully using the site for product and lifestyle ideas, celebrity content and competitions. They have 31 different boards, over 3,000 pins and almost half a million followers.

Rather than simply using Pinterest as a sales tool – which is discouraged and never a good idea on social media anyway – the brand is pinning ideas and giving an insight into what fashions and styles they like.

How does Pinterest work?

Once you've set up an account (more on that later in the chapter), you can start creating your own pinboards – in other words collecting images, visuals, videos, etc. and pinning them to your board. There are currently no limits to the number of pinboards you can create, so depending on your business, you might have a board for your blogs, a board for things you want to say, books your recommend, products, customers, etc. Your boards can literally be about anything you want to collect and organise.

Moving on from 'collecting and organising the things you love', how can Pinterest help you from a business perspective?

- **Encourage traffic:** One of the main and most important advantages of Pinterest is traffic! If you have any blogs that you want more people to see, Pinterest can be a great way to generate interest. You can showcase anything you want, from new products to your latest blog, but in order to get the best reaction make sure you know what it is your audience are interested in! **Key tip:** whenever possible, include links back to your website and feature landing pages within your pins, in order to drive traffic back to your website.
- **Advertise your business:** Using the Follow or Pin It button encourages your customers and fans to use and pin your products on their Pinterest boards. Again, this opens up your products and services to new audiences. If someone pins your blog post – or latest newsletter – they are in effect supporting your pin and the content that you're sharing. This is the perfect way for brands to showcase their products and services and therefore get the word out in a different way – by visually expressing (pinning) things they enjoy and sharing them with others.
- **Showcase your business's personality:** Pinterest is a great opportunity to give people an insight into your business's/brand's personality. You can make the most out of your pinboard to

showcase your employees and even life in the office – this gives your audience a great picture of what you're about. Letting people in behind the scenes also makes you appear more personable – it will encourage credibility and people will feel that they know and trust you that little bit more.

- **Build a following:** Pinterest is also a great way to build a targeted community – however, be aware that it may take more time than on other social media sites, even if you are very active. Also consider the demographics. As we stated earlier, 80% of the user base of Pinterest are women. As with anything online, 'Content Is King'. If you create compelling content and, in this case, compelling images, you'll find that people want to follow you. They'll tell their friends and colleagues about you and, in return, your following will grow.

- **Customer competitions:** Competitions are a great way to encourage engagement on any social media platform. With Pinterest you can create picture competitions. Let your fans know what the prize is and ask them to take a picture and share it to win the competition. Ask your fans to pin the pictures onto their pinboards, send you the link to their picture, and then all you have to do is come up with a means of deciding the best picture. This tactic is a great way to encourage interaction on your pinboard and interaction with your fans!

Case study: Allrecipes.com

This case study from leading recipe 'social collaboration' site, Allrecipes.com, illustrates many of the above points perfectly.

Leading up to the busy Christmas season, Allrecipes wanted to make sure that they were the first place to go for anyone planning a meal. After noticing a big surge in referral traffic from people on Pinterest, they added the Pin It button to each recipe page. They also designed a new page template where the Pin It button is above the fold, adjacent to recipe photos and videos, which made it especially easy for community members to share recipes.

Allrecipes saw dramatic results. Within three months, more than 50,000 recipes were pinned, resulting in 139 million Pinterest impressions, and clicks on Allrecipes' Pinterest content increased more than 900%. *'Since we added the Pin It button to our site, we've seen a significant increase in the volume of recipes and videos shared daily – resulting in dramatic boosts in the daily social referrals Allrecipes receives from Pinterest. This makes our content more discoverable, which grows our community.'*

Setting up your Pinterest account and boards

Given that we're focusing on using Pinterest for business, it's important to set up a specific business account. There are currently two ways to set this up: if you have already been using Pinterest on a personal basis, you can easily convert your account to a business one; or you can create a completely new account.

Changing your Pinterest page from a personal account to a business account is simple:

- Visit pinterest.com/business/convert to start. You'll need to be logged into your existing personal account.
- Fill out all the details and profile information for your business page. One advantage of converting a personal account to a business account is that business accounts display a verification badge, and enable you to add buttons and widgets to your website.
- Last but not least, you will have to agree to the Business Terms of Service agreement and privacy policy.
- Once you have filled in the form, simply click **Convert** and Pinterest will do the rest for you.

To create a new business account from scratch, you can sign up for a new business account by visiting **http://business.pinterest.com/** and clicking the button **Join as a Business**. You go through a similar process, except this time you get the chance to choose a new username.

Setting up your pinboards

As with a Facebook page, before trying to build a following, you need some content. In the case of Pinterest it is worth creating your own pinboards. For example, if you are a photographer and you specialise in weddings, corporate shots and events, you could create different pinboards for the three categories – much as you would create landing pages on a website. Alternatively, if you are an estate agent with a number of different offices, you could create pinboards to reflect the areas where you sell properties. To take another example, if you are an architect you might want to showcase not only the buildings you have designed but also the designers and architecture that have influenced you the most. You could create a board entitled My Designs, where you would upload images and links to your own work. At the same time, you could create another board entitled My Influences and pin images from other websites. You might even decide to create a board entitled Great Architects, which would highlight your contemporaries and their own designs.

Pinterest is a very visual medium, so make sure that the URLs you post or the images you upload are of a high enough quality to look good on your board.

View each pinboard as a category in which the content you share will be located. For a business, consider the key things your customers are looking for, e.g. product-based information, useful websites, technology, and so on.

- Sign in to your Pinterest account and click the **Create a Board** option in the top right-hand corner.
- When prompted, enter basic information about your board, e.g. name, category, and who can pin on this board – then click **Create Board**.
- Next you will need to name your board. The trick is to find a balance between clever and clear, so that people understand what they can find on the board, while you are also encouraging engagement. When selecting the name for your pinboard, think about what people are likely to be searching for – don't be too eclectic.
- Then you'll need to choose your Pinterest category – this is what people use to browse, so be sure to choose a category that accurately describes your board.

How to pin

A pin starts with an image or video that you choose to add to Pinterest. You can add a pin from a website using the Pin It bookmark or upload an image from your computer. Any pin on Pinterest can be repinned, and all pins link back to their source.

How to get and use the Pin It button

The Pin It button appears in the Pinterest toolbar and is a quick and easy way to pin images directly to your Pinterest boards. It lets you grab the image directly from a website and post straight to your Pinterest board without having to sign in. Here's how to enable the Pin It button.

- To download the toolbar extension, log into your Pinterest account as normal and find the **About** menu section in the upper right-hand corner of the page.
- Select the Pin It button on the second row – this will then take you to a new page.
- Scroll down and then click **Install Now** to add it to your bookmarks bar, then click the bookmarklet whenever you see an image or video you want to pin!
- The Pin It button for Chrome lets you pin things from around the web.
- You can use the Pin It button to pin almost any photo or blog you come across while surfing the internet in just a matter of seconds.

You also have the option of uploading a picture from your computer; you can pin JPG, PNG or GIF image files. You can also pin high-resolution images and videos.

Pinning on the go

One of the most popular ways to pin is through a mobile or handheld device, available for Android, smartphone or tablet. In order to get Pinterest on your mobile you need to download the app; then you can start creating pins.

- Pins can be created directly from your mobile or tablet. All you need do is click on Create Pin on the main screen of the Pinterest app.
- Alternatively, if you want to create a pin directly from the web, tap on your browser's Share button and select Create Pin.
- Next select the photo you wish to pin and choose its details and its description, along with the board you want it to be in.
- When you want to view boards and pins using the Pinterest app, all you need to do is simply tap on the pin to view its details – you are then given the option to re-pin it, like it or leave a comment.

Pinterest can be a useful resource for showcasing products in a highly visual way – and generating engagement and traffic. Keep in mind the following tips:

- **Know your audience:** This is most important as you need to know what best attracts your audience to your pinboard and what they like to share, keeping up the engagement and continually driving traffic to your page.
- **Be yourself:** It's good to pin things that express who you are and what your business is about; this is more important than the number of followers you have!
- **Be current:** Social sharing is an extremely fast-moving medium. Topics and fashions come into and go out of popularity very quickly, so make sure that the images and videos posted reflect what your business's potential customers are talking about.

Encouraging Pinterest users to pin your content

The more people who pin and share your content, the more exposure, traffic and promotion your business gets.

Now that you've done some pinning yourself and shared content belonging to other businesses, blogs and websites, you can start focusing on making sure that your own content is getting pinned, encouraging people to share your images, blogs and videos as much as possible. If people don't know that you have a presence on Pinterest, they are unlikely to share your content.

The most straightforward way to encourage people to pin your content to their own Pinterest boards is to **ensure that all your content is pinnable**. The best way to do this is to feature a Pin It button on your site (as outlined in the Ikea example above) – make sure it features next to blog posts and images that you want people to share. Bear in mind that Pinterest is about the image being shared. The images that get pinned need to be good, as your brand is reflected by the quality of the images that you have put up. Make sure photos are clearly illustrated and on brand.

Private or public?

Be aware that private pinboards are available on Pinterest. You are only allowed up to three private pinboards at any one time, whereas as you can have an unlimited number of original pinboards. Private boards will not show up anywhere on Pinterest – they can be used for adding pins that you want to be invisible within category sections. This could be useful when planning out future boards, or collections that are not due to go live for a while.

Note: If you are lucky enough to get invited to someone else's secret boards, the rules are different – feel free to accept as many invitations as you like because these do not count towards your three-board limit.

Keep in mind: As with publishing anything online or offline, it is important that you have the permission of the author/creator or you run the risk of copyright infringement.

Sharing through social media

As with blogs and videos, it is important to have a campaign in place for promoting both your boards and your pins. You can use your other social networks – Twitter, Facebook, LinkedIn and Google+ – to promote your Pinterest page. Also publicise it on other marketing channels and add the Pinterest icon to your website, so that people know you have a presence.

Finally, remember that Pinterest is a network. Try to Like as many other applicable Pinterest users to build your network and show that you are part of a community.

Ways to use Pinterest for your business

- **Use video:** As well as images, you can also pin videos, which can add an extra dimension to your boards.
- **Humanise your brand:** You could create a board for your staff to illustrate the people element of your organisation.

- **Social search:** By using hashtags in the same way as on Twitter, you can tag specific keywords which will help your online visibility.
- **Encourage others** to share your products and expand reach by including a Pin It option with your images or products to enable others to share your content on their boards. If their boards have hundreds of followers, you will expand your reach considerably, potentially increasing traffic.
- **Storyboarding and mood boarding:** If you are rebranding or renovating the office, or working on a creative project, you could use Pinterest as a mood board for your colleagues to share their ideas.

Instagram: photo sharing reinvented

Instagram is an online mobile photo- and video-sharing social networking service that provides its users with fast, simple and fun ways to share photos. Users simply snap a picture, choose from a range of pre-set filters to transform the look of the picture (no Photoshop skills are required), and then post it to their Instagram home feed. (There's also the opportunity to automatically share to Facebook, Twitter, Tumblr and other social networks.) A distinctive feature is that Instagram will only use photos in a square format – similar to old-fashioned Polaroid images.

Instagram is a relatively young platform; it was launched in October 2010. The service rapidly gained popularity, gathering over 100 million active users in around 18 months. This popularity led to the platform being acquired by Facebook in April 2012 for a whopping $1 billion. At the time of writing, Instagram has an active user base of 300 million users.

The core proposition of Instagram remains, in its own words, *'photo sharing reinvented'*.

Currently, you can only create an Instagram account by downloading the app on your iOS iPhone or Android device. While Instagram does allow you to manage certain aspects of your account via a desktop version, the majority of activity is driven by mobile.

How to set up Instagram

- Download the Instagram app from the App Store for your iPhone/iPad, or from Google Play for an Android device (see http://instagram.com).
- When the app is installed, tap the Instagram icon to open it on your device.

- Tap Register.
- Sign up for your Instagram account by entering all your details – be sure to create a username that clearly represents your business.
- Choose a profile picture by clicking on the photo icon on the top right of the screen, which gives you the option to Import from Facebook, Import from Twitter, Take photo, or Choose from your library.
- If you choose to import from Facebook or Twitter, Instagram will ask to connect to your Facebook/Twitter account so that you can choose a profile picture from either account.
- Once you have completed your information, tap Done. That's it; you're all set.

How to use Instagram

- To post on Instagram, simply click on the app icon and you'll see a camera icon in the centre at the bottom of the screen. (This requires a smartphone device with a camera such as the iPhone/iPad or an Android/tablet).
- In camera mode you have the option to edit your picture settings. Choose between always using your phone's flash, auto detecting flash, or never using flash. You can also tap to switch between the front-facing and back-facing camera.
- You can also edit an existing photo – simply tap at the bottom right of the screen to select a photo from your library.
- Once you've chosen the photo you want to work with, you can if you wish apply a filter to that photo from the choices that appear – Valencia is one of our personal favourites.
- Click Next when you have finished. Then enter a brief description of your photo in the What? text input field.
- When posting, as well as being given a choice as to which social networks you would like to post the content to (Facebook, Twitter, Tumblr, etc.), there's also the Add your Location tab. (We recommend doing this, particularly if you have a physical presence, such as a shop – more on this later.)
- Tap Done, to complete the process and post your photo. Your photo will appear in your feed and also the feed of other Instagram users who are following you.
- Hashtags are highly relevant on Instagram: in fact, many posts on Instagram have minimal text but in some cases up to 20 hashtags. Hashtags work really well on Instagram as they help users to find relevant content. Be sure to use as many relevant hashtags as possible, allowing your content to be found by those searching the platform. (More on this later.)

Photo Maps

This is an Instagram feature that many people don't use. However, from a business perspective, it can be very important, as it puts your business on the map – literally!

Photo Maps are used to showcase, via a map, where you've taken your photos, or explore where others have taken them – this also lets you rediscover previous Instagram memories (previous Instagram snaps).

You can link any photo to your map as long as you're connected to WiFi or 3/4G. Your device logs the co-ordinates of where you are (where the photo was taken) and uses that information to give you the ability to add that photo to your Photo Map. It's a great way to show-case where your business is and to see pictures of other people and places nearby.

How to use Photo Maps

When uploading a photo, turn the **Add to Photo Map** section to **on**. Instagram will send you a push notification and ask to use your current location – select OK.

Then share your photo – your selected location will appear alongside the photo and your followers will be able to see where any picture you upload was taken. This is useful for attracting attention from fans, especially if they are near your business.

Tagging

A fairly new feature allows you to tag people in the pictures you share. This is a great way to encourage engagement for your business and let others know more about you and your whereabouts!

Tap Add People, which is under your pictures caption, click on whoever you want to tag on the screen, then search for the name you want to tag. Think of it like tagging someone as you would on Facebook – you are in effect alerting them to the fact that they've been mentioned in your post, giving them the opportunity to see the post and then engage with it, sharing it with their audience.

Extending reach with hashtags

Adding hashtags to your photos allows you to find new followers and share your photos with more people. To get the most out of them, you'll want to keep a few things in mind:

- **Be specific:** Choose specific hashtags that will help you connect with others similar to your business or to target a certain group of people to get them interested in your brand/business.
- **Be Relevant:** Make it easy for other like-minded Instagrammers to find you by making sure that your tags fully describe your photo. Using very general tags might get you a few likes, but when over 700,000 people use the same tag, it's a lot more difficult for your photo to stand out and connect with the people most like you. *Tip:* Relevant tags will help you attract new followers and people who take a genuine interest in your content.

- **Be Observant:** Pay attention to the hashtags used on photos that use similar tags to you. You may discover a popular hashtag that you hadn't thought of.

Hashtags can be used in every single one of your Instagram posts and can help narrow down searches so that others who might be interested in your pictures can easily find them in one single search.

Hot tip

Make sure you hashtag your business name or brand/product name(s). This gets your brand or business name out there and makes it easier for people to search for you.

Why Instagram is good for your business

- **A picture is worth a thousand words.** Instagram gives you the opportunity to translate the passion of what you offer or do into visual images. Most people like to look at interesting images and if you can draw them in with a photo that works like an ad but isn't, it could end up being worth as much as some of the best advertising campaigns out there.

Case study: Devon Sun Yarns

Devon Sun Yarns share wonderful images of their yarns – the latest colour collections and sample boxes – together with images of the products their customers create using the yarns. They also share lifestyle content, and the production process for the creation of the hand dyed yarns. They are not overtly promoting their products – there's nothing in the content that is 'pushy or advertorial' other than the great product.

However, their activity does generate sales. What they have found via their Instagram audience is that engagement is with a slightly different audience than Facebook – and while they do generate general consumer sales, their larger 'wholesale' orders come via Instagram, which goes to prove that targeting visually compelling content to the right audience can convert, without an overt sales message.

- **Encourage customer participation.** Once you have built a reasonable number of followers, the door is wide open to encourage customers to exchange and participate in exchanges involving your business. *Tip:* Why not encourage them to share photos of themselves using your product or service, if appropriate?

- **Build a personality for your business.** You decide how you want your business to be perceived by your customers and potential customers. The right photos shared on Instagram can go a long way in building a personality for your brand and engagement.

- **Finally** – it gives your business the opportunity to have fun and get creative!

Creating compelling visual content

Instagram enables you to showcase the visual aspect of your business via images – perfect if you have a highly visual product, for example if you are a restaurateur, retailer, designer, etc. However, visual content on Instagram isn't restricted to images. In July 2012 Instagram introduced video, describing this new content feature as *'everything you love about Instagram – and it moves'*. It gives you the opportunity to create short videos (from five to 15 seconds) to promote your business, brand or product.

How to record video

- In your Instagram app you have the option to toggle between photo and video. Select video (the icon that looks like a mini video recorder).
- Press and hold the centre button (red when on video) to start recording.
- Lift your finger off the button when you want to stop recording (i.e. on for recording, off to stop).
- Tap Next to beautify your video by adding a filter.
- Then you can go on to share your video in the same way you would an image.

Enhancing your Instagram videos

A range of features make this easy-to-use mobile app pretty sophisticated.

- **Clip editing:** The greatest advantage of Instagram Video is the fact that it includes editing features. It also allows users to delete unsatisfactory past frames by clicking the delete button (marked with an X) to remove the last frame (or two).
- **Filter effects:** It wouldn't be Instagram without filtering options – 13 in all. They perform very similarly to the photo filters but have different names.
- **Image stabilisation:** Instagram also has a brand new tool – Cinema – which is a custom image stabilisation product that is designed to smooth shaky footage for a more professional, streamlined result. Impressive!
- **Cover image selection:** Instagram lets you scroll through the still of your video and select the best cover photo for it. This is a very important feature as it gives the first impression of your video and should therefore appeal to your audience.

Why is it good for business?

As we outlined in the previous chapter, video marketing has become more and more of a hot topic, and that's not surprising when approximately 46% of people say they'd be more likely to seek out information about a product or service after seeing it in an online video.

Here are some ways you might use Instagram video for your business:

- **Announcing a new product or sale:** Using videos is a great way to showcase the message you want to get across to your fans, and you can do an awful lot in 15 seconds. If a picture of your work is worth a thousand words, imagine what 15 seconds of video communicates.
- **Answering FAQs:** A simple how-to video can answer your customers' questions quickly and efficiently.
- **Your office in action:** We often hear about how brands need to showcase a more human side. Social media has blurred the lines with real-time, real-life engagement between companies and customers, creating a need for companies to be transparent and more open. Instagram videos offer a simple and creative way for brands and businesses to showcase their culture and style.

Tumblr

Tumblr was set up in 2007 and is a social network based around blogs, so it is a crossover between Twitter and Wordpress.

According to ComScore, 50% of Tumblr's visitor base are under the age of 25. Teenagers aged 12–17 are about twice as likely as the average internet user to visit Tumblr, while 18–24 year olds are nearly two and a half times as likely.

Tumblr could be an excellent way to find a wider audience for your blogs as well as create an engaged community of people who are interested in your thoughts. *Time* magazine is successfully using the site (http://timemagazine.tumblr.com) to share some of their articles. In fact, many newspapers and magazines use Tumblr to build their audience and find a wider reach for their brands: see http://gq.tumblr.com, http://life.tumblr.com and http://rollingstone.tumblr.com.

The site acts very much like a news feed with a combination of articles, images and videos which can then be Liked or reposted in much the same way as content on Facebook. And, as you can do with sponsored stories on Facebook, you can now pay for highlighted posts on Tumblr – which currently costs a few dollars.

Setting up an account

As with all social media accounts, you need to have an email address with which to sign into Tumblr. Visit www.tumblr.com and hit Sign Up to create an account. Fill in your email, make up a brand-specific or keyword-enabled username, then come up with a suitable password. You'll then be asked to connect with at least five blogs – you can simply use the search feature to find any relevant blogs you wish to follow. You will also be asked to verify your email address.

Once your account is set up, you need to configure it correctly. Hit the Settings tab and you will be able to add a cover image for your blog, and add a profile image, customise how you wish people to see/find you on Tumblr and decide whether you wish to send your posts directly to Facebook or Twitter.

Posting on Tumblr

At the top of your page (referred to as your blog) you will see this menu:

Depending on the type of content you wish to publish, you can choose from each of seven options – text, photos, quote, link, chat, audio or video. For example, if you are making a text post, simply click the Aa Text tab and you will be taken through to a window which looks much like Word Editor.

You simply add your title and text and, of course, any relevant #hashtags. You'll notice when you get started on Tumblr that posts, regardless of what they are, feature a range of #hashtags, in much the same way as Instagram. So our advice is to spend some time doing a bit of research before you dive in – and searching through Tumblr to see how others in your sector are managing posts and the level of engagement they're receiving.

The usual rules apply when writing:

- Start with an engaging and keyword-friendly headline.
- Use short, snappy paragraphs.
- Break up text with line breaks and images.
- Use inbound links.
- Make sure the text is keyword-enabled.
- Keep it short – no more than 100 words (you'll rarely see text-heavy posts on Tumblr).
- Sign off with a signature containing your applicable contact details.

Tumblr has recently brought in the option to promote your post so that it can reach a wider audience. You can either pin the post for $5 or high-light the post for $2.

There are also other ways of adding content to the site.

- Posting photos is very similar to Facebook – you upload an image, then caption it.
- It is also possible to upload videos from YouTube or Vimeo.
- Audio posts are powered by Spotify and Soundcheck.
- Quotes and links work in much the same way as in blogs.
- Chat Posts are a way to encourage conversations with other users.

Content that compels

Treat your Tumblr account as you would your website blog or Facebook Page. The more engaging, regularly updated content you can post, the better. On Tumblr the audience is probably the most discerning when it comes to 'standard content'. You'll see that from a business or brand perspective, brands work really hard on Tumblr to deliver content that stands out. The audience demographic is 'high content maintenance' – and regular content blogs are often just ignored and get low engage-ment. Visual content – particularly short videos (Vine or Instagram) and images – tends to dominate the bulk of the content shared on this platform.

Creativity in content delivery needs to be high to engage audiences on Tumblr. Here's a typical Tumblr post from PBS Food.org, which was actually a live animated GIF-style image using humour and celebrity (the

Cookie Monster) to link back to a cookie recipe on their site. This type of creativity works well for the Tumblr demographics.

Sharing on Tumblr

Building your audience on Tumblr involves sharing information and seeking out people and brands that are of relevance to your organisation. On Twitter, one of the best ways of building your community is to start following people who post interesting tweets; then start following their followers. The same is true of Tumblr.

Finding Blogs enables you to find interesting posts, while using the Explore function (www.tumblr.com/explore) enables you to select from a range of different categories as well as Tags, similar to Hashtags on Twitter.

When you find content you like, you can do three things:

1. comment or post on it
2. favorite it (hit the heart button)
3. reblog it (share that blog post on your own blog – similar to retweeting on Twitter)

Tumblr is a social network, so the more engagement you have with others in the community, the higher the profile of your brand or organisation will be.

Generally speaking, your usual social media content won't fly on Tumblr. Success on Tumblr relies on whether your content is creative, funny or artistic enough to reblog. Know your audience and give them what they want.

Ways to use Tumblr for business

- It can be a great way to engage with younger audiences who are bored with Facebook.
- It's a useful forum to find a wider audience for your blogs.
- As a research tool to find new trends and organisations.
- Thought leadership.
- As a feedback mechanism for new products.

WhatsApp: fast, personal and highly engaged

What's WhatsApp?

WhatsApp Messenger is a cross-platform mobile messaging app which allows you to exchange messages without having to pay for SMS. Instant messaging is now hugely popular around the globe and has grown significantly over the past few years. A new report from Juniper Research states that by 2018, instant messaging via mobiles will account for 75% of traffic – or 63 trillion messages! Accord to ComScore, WhatsApp is the most popular instant messaging service, followed closely by its Chinese equivalent, WeChat.

Who can use it?

Anyone with a smartphone. WhatsApp can be downloaded via the App Store and is available for iPhone, BlackBerry, Android, Windows phones and Nokia.

How is instant messaging free?

Because WhatsApp Messenger uses the same internet data plan that you use for email and web browsing, so there is no cost to message.

WhatsApp was bought by Facebook in 2014 for a whopping $19 billion. The platform is one of the buzziest around, with more than 700 million monthly active users and carries 30 billion messages per day. In January 2015, *The Telegraph* said that *'A survey of 4,000 smartphone users by On Device found that 44% of users in five countries used WhatsApp at least once a week.'*

Currently there is an annual charge of $0.99 for WhatsApp. However, this is only applicable in the USA. It is likely, given that the platform has vowed never to carry advertising, that as adoption grows and more people become dependent on the platform that this low fee is rolled out globally – or even raised to assist with monetising the platform.

Based on the stats above, we know for sure that people are using it. In fact it is now arguably one of the world's fastest-growing communication apps. The question is – how many of us are using it for business purposes?

Way to use WhatsApp for business

As a communication tool, WhatsApp ticks all the right boxes, enabling you to communicate directly with employees, clients, customers and colleagues by:

- chatting in real time
- sending multimedia
- receiving and sending voice and video messages
- transmitting messages to groups of up to 100 people.

How to get started

From your smartphone, download the app from the App Store. You can then add an avatar to set up your profile as you wish. And then it's a case of simply connecting with people in your network who are already on WhatsApp.

Two great assets of instant messaging are its ease of use and speed. It is said that it takes just 90 seconds for someone to respond to an instant message, whereas the average email response time is 90 minutes. These attractive elements mean that more and more businesses are finding it a useful way to keep in touch with groups of customers and clients.

However, it's important to remember that this platform has not been set up as a business resource. It's for this reason that direct advertising and soliciting business has been strongly prohibited and actually violates the terms of its service. There is absolutely nothing to stop you sharing blogs, images, and engaging directly with customers, though, as long as you aren't deemed to be hard selling. In this day and age, engaging directly with your customer or client is imperative. Keeping the conversation going and listening to their needs is all part of being a modern online social business. WhatsApp can assist with that – as the following story shows.

Case study: Engaging with your clients

A story in *The Telegraph* this year explained how diamond maker Rare Pink uses WhatsApp to maintain rapport with their clients. Rare Pink found WhatsApp a very personal source of communication with its customers, allowing it to stay in touch 24 hours a day and at short notice. The article gave the example of a female city trader, who was a client, and who used WhatsApp as her source of communication. The lady in question was in touch with her assigned Rare Pink consultant via WhatsApp because she was unable to make calls at work and her emails were monitored. WhatsApp allowed her to privately keep in touch with her consultant about final amendments to her ring and resulted in her spending a great deal with the brand. And because the platform allows not only text conversation, with no character limits, but also enables sharing images and video (WhatsApp sends and receives 500 million images every day, compared with Facebook's 350 million) it is a simple and quick way to share visual content, in this case the design and development of the bespoke item, and of course to get instant feedback from the client too.

Engaging with your team

WhatsApp isn't only great for client liaison, it's also a great internal communications tool that can work almost like an intranet within your business, allowing you to communicate and chat in real time with colleagues and employees. The group chat feature is arguably the most useful business aspect of WhatsApp: it allows you to chat with a group of up to 100 people at once.

To start a group chat:

- Open WhatsApp and go to the Chats screen.
- At the top of the Chats screen, tap the New Group button.
- Type in a subject or title.

- Add group participants by selecting +, or by typing the name of the contact. You can automatically add anyone from your contacts database – so you may have to add contacts first. They will receive an invitation to join the group chat.
- Tap Create to finish creating the group.

Whether you are using WhatsApp to communicate internally with colleagues or externally with clients, there are some other handy WhatsApp features that are worth knowing for business use:

- **Emailing an entire message history:**
  - o   For iOS users, go to **Settings** and choose **Email chat history.**
  - o   For Android, click on the **Menu** option in a conversation (it's on the bottom right of the screen), go to **More** and select **Email Conversation**, before entering the address of the recipient.
- **Backing up WhatsApp conversations:**
  - o   Go to the Settings menu, choose Chat preferences, and then click on the Chat history backup option.
- **Broadcasting a WhatsApp to many contacts:**
  - o   If you need to get a message out quickly to more than one person – e.g. 'Emergency meeting at 12 p.m.' – the easiest way to do this is to 'broadcast' a message in WhatsApp.
  - o   Select the Broadcast message option in the More menu and select the contacts you want to send it to. Then type your message and hit Send.

While WhatsApp doesn't promote itself as a business platform – and the founders have vowed that it won't run advertising on the channel (and when it was acquired by Facebook, Mark Zuckerberg agreed to keep the platform ad-free) – there are some useful ways businesses can utilise the service for business purposes, beyond the direct sell.

Case study: Montcalm

The team at new boutique luxury hotel M by Montcalm are using WhatsApp in two different ways, as an internal communications tool and as a customer communications tool.

The hotel's marketing team communicates with three external agencies, the hotel manager and reception staff using the site. WhatsApp messages are much simpler than emails and offer the chance for group conversations, complete with visual and video-based content.

In addition, the hotel also uses WhatsApp as a replacement for room service. We mentioned in Chapter 3 that Millennials don't enjoy using the phone, so this gives them a viable alternative.

WhatsApp chat tips and facts

- There is no limit to the number of groups you can create.
- Every group has one or more administrators. Only administrators can add or remove participants.
- Only administrators can make other participants administrators.
- If the original administrator leaves the group, a new administrator will be randomly assigned.
- Only message people you know – don't 'cold message' anyone for business purposes.

Snapchat: short-lived, personal one-to-one engagement

Launched in 2011, Snapchat is one of the newest kids on the social media block. Like Vine, WhatsApp and other purely mobile apps, Snapchat is now being adopted by marketers looking for a creative way to reach their target audience.

What is Snapchat?

Snapchat is a purely mobile application that runs on the Apple iOS and Google Android platforms. It is installed on smartphones or tablets, and users produce 'snaps' – messages that contain photographs, drawings, text and/or videos. The key attraction of Snapchat is that the content only lasts 10 seconds. By providing content with a limited lifespan, the platform combines a sense of urgency for the user together with the general engagement of social media. If they don't engage within 10 seconds – it's gone.

The platform is typically used most by 13–25-year-olds – and when it was launched was very much considered the 'rebel of the social networks'. Here was a network where people could talk directly to each other, one to one, by @tagging their contacts and sharing content with the added element that the content was largely short lived. The platform was quickly appropriated by those social adopters who were fed up with parents taking over Facebook, and who wanted more privacy, personalisation and creativity when engaging.

In the January 2015 social media statistics shared by We Are Social, Snapchat was reported to have 100 million monthly active users. With an attractive and active young demographic, over the past couple of years brands and marketers have been figuring out how to utilise the platform in a way that makes sense for a brand, yet still engages the attention of the lucrative millennial market.

The platform has also adapted and in October 2013 it rolled out Snapchat Stories, offering brands a longer conversation format than the original 10 seconds. These stories combine multiple snaps to create a replayable story that is visible to you and your followers for 24 hours. However, after the 24-hour period the content is no longer available. More recently the platform released Discover, a feature that allows brands to establish themselves in the network. The Discover feature showcases quality, snackable content from reputable publishers, including CNN, *National Geographic*, the *Daily Mail*, etc. On clicking into each publisher, users are delivered the most up-to-date photo and video content from around the world, and can click through to read or watch longer-form layouts of the stories.

Getting started on Snapchat

Setting up an account on Snapchat is very simple. You simply go to the relevant App Store, search for the app and download it. Snapchat asks for very few details – username and email address. You'll go through a short verification process – which includes giving your mobile telephone number so that verification can be done via SMS. You will then be encouraged to share your contacts and see who else is on Snapchat – and connect with them – or search for friends.

Content creation

It's worth spending some time looking at the type of content that does well on Snapchat. Instead of the polished images and beautifully crafted campaigns you might expect to see from brands on Facebook, Twitter or Instagram, Snapchat users prefer their content to be more 'organic'. Many images – even from brand campaigns – include the 'shaky handwritten' message overlay, which is ubiquitous with the speedy, 'get this message in time' Snapchat ethos.

As shown below, once you have taken your 'snap' in Snapchat, you will see a pencil icon in the top right-hand corner – this allows you to write a message over your image. It's not pretty, but brands and Snapchatters tend to use it to make their images more engaging.

There's also a T (text) button, which you can use to type a message that runs centrally through the image.

The rudimentary element of Snapchat fits with the youth market. And to date the majority of brands turning to Snapchat for business are those brands that sit in the fast-moving consumer goods (FMCG) sector, restaurants and clothing chains as well as TV and entertainment companies – ASOS, Taco Bell, McDonald's, GrubHub, NBA and Heineken, among others. The tactics they use focus on sharing promotional codes or coupons or, in some cases, showcasing exclusive behind-the-scenes footage and snippets of upcoming shows via Snapchat stories. This type of content is perfectly positioned for the youth demographic.

Growing an audience on Snapchat

Everyone agrees that Snapchat is probably the trickiest network on which to grow an audience. It's purely mobile – and given how transient the content is, there isn't the same element of 'research' available into who is sharing great content. There isn't the same etiquette of 'You follow me and I'll follow you' as there is on networks such as Instagram or Twitter. Which explains why brands work so hard at engaging users with offers and promotions, or enticing them with unique content.

The main activity is sharing content – which is largely short-lived – and therefore you @tag the people (as you would on Twitter) to alert them that you are sharing the content with them. Therefore, it's seen as a much more one-to-one, more personal platform – a less a one-to-many medium.

Another key tactic on Snapchat is to use influencer marketing: finding those who are hugely influential on Snapchat and aligning with them to engage a wider audience.

Things to consider when using Snapchat for business:

- Unique user demographics – the majority of Snapchat users are female and most users are between the ages of 13 and 25.
- It's a purely mobile application.
- Snapchat has introduced several market-friendly features, including Snapchat Stories. Here you can weave together a collection of photos and videos into stories. Brands have to be quick to adopt these stories – as with TV ads, brands can make their stories 30–60 seconds long, a comfortable and familiar format for advertisers. The benefit of Stories is that they don't disappear after a few seconds; they can be watched over and over again for a 24-hour period after the snap has been shared.
- Brands have to think carefully about how they share stories on Snapchat – they will not work if they are blatant pieces of self-promotion. The idea is to be creative, friendly and social. Use it for things like taking your audience behind the scenes of your business, showcase a new product and share your latest sales or events.
- It can be difficult to build a large audience on Snapchat.
- As you'll see if you sign up, the platform is rudimentary and a little clunky. Embrace a new wavelength of messaging: the app is supposed to be less than perfect, and that's why the youth market love it.

Ello: 'simple, beautiful and ad-free'

And last but not least, let's say hello to Ello, the network launched in 2014.

What is Ello?

Ello is an ad-free social media network with a simple and uncluttered interface. It began as a response by a small group of artists and programmers to the bombardment of advertising and personal details being used for capital gain on the other main social media networks.

When compared to the other social media platforms, it is most similar to Tumblr and Twitter. It allows a more personal element to social media engagement by allowing users to choose any sort of username they want. In contrast to Facebook, where users have to give a real name, on Ello one can be truly anonymous.

The self-explanatory drag and drop format allows you to set up a profile picture and header image with the recommended size specifications noted in the space itself. The interface is intuitive; a fluid grid layout with a lot of white space – you can tell it was created by artists and web developers. It's simple to navigate and if at any time you want to read more about how to use it you can scroll to the bottom right and click the WTF link.

Using Ello

From looking at user profiles, you get the sense that this social media network is a great space to display beautiful imagery and creativity; there's a focus on sharing images, video and written content.

A recent development to the platform is being able to embed audio/video files from external services such as YouTube, Vimeo, DailyMotion, SoundCloud and Mixcloud. These may contain ads, but you can choose to hide these in your personal settings. Features that are already familiar to social media users include Commenting, Following, Unfollowing and @Mentions.

As is the case with most of the social networks, you find friends and people to follow using the search bar; once you've found friends you wish to connect with you simply drag them into your Friends or Noise area (Friends are people you share reciprocal content with; Noise is a space where you are able to see everyone's activity at a glance).

Getting started with Ello

The platform is still in Beta, with Version 2 being rolled out just recently – in April 2015. There are approximately two millions users – and this is set to grow now that the 'invitation only' aspect has been lifted.

Signing up is simple – you enter your name, email address and then you can create a large cover image and a profile pic. Its user interface is pretty minimal: it looks like a simplified Tumblr, and behaves in the same way as Twitter.

To create an update you hover over the smiley Ello icon – and up pops a simple box. There doesn't appear to be any character limitation. You can then hit the arrow to post your update, the X to delete it or the upload icon to share images or video. To the right of the interface you will see a small F and N. F is where you see the content those you are following are sharing and then the N is the noise of others in the Ello network, giving you the opportunity to look at others' posts before you choose whether to follow them.

How businesses are using Ello

Though Ello takes an anti-commercial stance, it has no policy against business accounts. A few businesses have already embraced Ello, including Penguin Books and a fair few small retail brands such as Cheap Monday (owned by H&M) and even Ello's founder Paul Budnitz's bicycle business. However, it's fair to say that these accounts do not have a large follower count compared to some other profiles: for example, five months after opening their Ello account, Penguin had only 1,400 or so followers compared to a fan base of over 100,000 on their US Facebook account. Saying that, some of Penguin's posts have been seen by more people than their followers, so something to take away from this could be that although you might not get a high following there is still good potential for brand awareness. Here is a short quote from one of the founders of Ello, Paul Budnitz:

> In many ways, having 5,000 followers on Ello is better than 50,000 on Facebook. Reason is that Facebook will only show your posts to 1–3% of your followers unless you pay them. On Ello, everything you post goes to every one of your followers. Ello does not have ads, so we have no reason to filter!

This 'real-time' publishing is the same as on Twitter – what you publish gets shared directly into the feeds of anyone that is following you.

Content Creation and Ello

It's still too early to predict how Ello will play out, but it is clear that an important ingredient is the type of content you post. Unlike some of the other networks, Ello is taking a 'non-advertorial and non-commercial stance' – their aim is for a purer collaboration and education platform. Ello isn't an environment where you are encouraged to overtly advertise your wares and so you need to think about your tone of voice when communicating, as you could be alienating a whole audience who joined the network because they didn't want to be pitched to.

So be prepared to adapt if you want to join this network, but at the same time this is an exciting space to be more creative and inventive!

Tips and tactics for using Ello

- If you know who your target audience is, and if it's similar to Ello's 'Early Adopters', i.e. creatives and other movers and shakers, it's worth having a presence on Ello.
- Be simple – keep posts short and use imagery (a picture speaks a thousand words) and do not use 'sales speak'.
- Use large, good-quality images – the header image space is huge and highly visible.
- Create and express yourself freely, within reason (as set out in Ello's policies, for example 'Don't post other people's personal in-formation', 'Don't hate', 'Don't spam', 'Be legal' and 'Don't infringe on other people's copyright and trademarks' among many others). Adult content is regarded as NSFW (not safe for work) and you can select not to see these types of profile in your personal settings.

Will we ever be able to advertise on Ello?

As far as we know, Ello has promised that it will always be ad-free and that it will never sell the company on to someone who would use the platform to advertise. It also promises never to sell user data. But this is a young platform and things could change. At the time of writing, Ello has managed to raise another $5 million of investment in the platform. The company still has private messaging in the testing phase and is also looking at rolling out a mobile app version in the near future.

Social media marketing action plan

- Look at the array of social networking sites on offer and see whether they are likely to meet your organisation's business objectives.
- Work out a strategy for using each of the sites.
- Test and measure to see if the different channels are working for you.
- Regularly ask or poll your target audience to ascertain which social networking sites they are using.
- Never assume anything. Just because some social networks are viable for your organisation now, they may not in the future. Stay on top of what's working.
- Contact organisations in your network to find out how they have fared with specific sites; what has worked for them and what hasn't.

A final word. You **must** have free WiFi at your location. Without it, your fans or users may not be able to get online and check in. The cost is negligible and can be recouped very quickly.

10| Advertising on social networks

What you will learn from this chapter:

- Overview of social advertising
- Advertising on Twitter
- Twitter Cards
- Twitter advertising tips
- Advertising on LinkedIn
- LinkedIn Advertising tips
- Advertising on Facebook
- Facebook Advertising tips
- Advertising on other social networks

Social advertising has been around pretty much since the social networks arrived. However, initially the territory was dominated by large brands and high-end ad agencies.

Over the years, the networks have adapted their advertising platforms, opening them up to Everyman and creating turnkey systems enabling starts-ups and large agencies alike to utilise the ever increasing range of advertising options.

Leaving aside YouTube, which links into pay-per-click advertising, LinkedIn, Facebook and Twitter continue to dominate the social network advertising space – however, networks such as Pinterest, Vine, Snapchat and Instagram are stepping up and offering advertising options (though these are currently still largely adopted by the larger brands).

Social advertising is an area that has grown significantly. The latest survey of advertising trends conducted by *eMarketer* (April 2015) indicates that the amount of advertising spend on social networks will top $23 billion during 2015, a startling 33.5% increase on 2014. And growth rates show no signs of abating: 2014 saw Snapchat's first ad, video ads on Instagram, auto-play video ads on Facebook and a greater variety of Twitter Cards (more on this later in the chapter). So as these sites continue to mature, the options for advertising across an array of channels are only likely to increase.

What makes social advertising so attractive?

There are a number of smart features when it comes to social advertising. Just as it's simple to sign up to and engage on social networks, the advertising platforms on the networks are also pretty simple. You don't need to have any 'agency or enterprise' software to facilitate campaigns – you can simply set them up and let them run.

Campaigns can be scheduled

Just as you can schedule tweets and Facebook posts, so too can you schedule your advertising campaigns. This is particularly useful if you are only testing out a platform, or need to keep campaigns running while you are out of the office. Campaigns can be set up and then scheduled to start and automatically stop on a specific date or after spending a specific budget.

Targeting specific audiences

As all marketers and savvy business people know, the more targeted a campaign, the more effective it will be. Social advertising platforms do enable you to be very specific with the demographics of who you want to target; and the demographics tend to be far richer than just location and sector. You can target based on people's hobbies, likes, friends, location, age, status, keywords, etc., providing a far more granular and highly unique approach to audience targeting. Another great asset is understanding the size of the audience you are targeting. When you are selecting specific audience criteria you receive an estimate of how big that audience is as you go.

It's still pretty low cost

Even with a budget of just £5 you can participate in social advertising. At the moment social advertising isn't overly competitive, and the range of options enable you to be specific about what you want to do, who you want to target and how much you're willing to spend. The average paid-for follower or engagement often comes in at pennies, making some forms of social advertising a highly affordable way to grow audience and reach.

Content is king

As outlined in Chapter 4, content is a critical part of your marketing and, indeed, advertising tactics. Thanks to the character limitations of many social media platform posts, you have to learn to say more with less. Similarly, you need to think about the limited space you have on each ad platform. You don't have the luxury of a billboard – often you are working to promote your offering via a small image and a few words. So thinking about the content is key.

One campaign does not fit all

Just as we advise that you need to tailor your communications for each social network, so too do you need to consider the different platforms and options available across the networks for each campaign. For example, a campaign that you run on Facebook to promote an event will give you more character space than a limited update on Twitter. Campaign planning for each platform is key.

Twitter advertising

Getting started

If you are interested in getting more followers for your Twitter account, increasing exposure for your business, and promoting your tweets to a relevant audience, you could give Twitter advertising a try. Twitter ads are potentially great for any business as they allow you to connect with the people who matter and give you a powerful context in which to connect your message with what's most meaningful to your customers.

But before you set up your campaign, it's useful to know what your objectives are so that you know which option is relevant to you. The process for creating your own Twitter ad campaign is very simple. The ad choices are divided into five main categories: followers; website clicks or conversions; tweet engagements; app installs and engagements; leads on Twitter. Let's look at each campaign option in a little more detail.

Followers

Running a followers ad campaign on Twitter allows you to promote your account as one to follow, with the ultimate objective of generating new followers. For example, when you log in to your Twitter account and go to your main dashboard, to the right of your Twitter stream is the box which shows suggested users to follow based on your interests.

Followers campaigns give your Twitter profile more exposure and helps you build followers who are potentially more targeted for you and your

business – so if your goal is to achieve new followers this can be an efficient method of advertising, as you're helping more people to discover you, your brand, business or cause. Don't forget that 80% of Twitter users use the platform via their mobiles. While other ad campaigns work really well in the news feed, in just the same way as regular tweets, 'who to follow' doesn't get the same direct visibility in the main news feed. On a mobile platform, to see the 'who to follow' option you have to click into your profile – and see the Follow people tab – and then promoted accounts will be shown.

Website clicks or conversions

These ads allow you to highlight a specific message or product for which you want to get more exposure on your profile and throughout Twitter – this is great for sharing content, building awareness and building your brand or business voice and perfect for driving traffic to your website, landing page or blog.

The format of the ad is that they are regular tweets which reach a wider group of users to encourage them to explore further (by clicking off to your website or landing page). They are great for offers, sign-ups or events. Do keep in mind that people will see that these are promoted tweets: when they have been paid for they are clearly labelled Promoted.

Tweet engagements

These ads work in much the same way as website clicks or conversions, but the objective is not to take people off the platform to click through to another site to convert them, but rather to keep them on the platform and to increase the level of engagement, by serving up relevant and compelling content to your audience in a more prominent place and by potentially expanding the reach of who gets to your content. Therefore these ads should be used to promote your best content, perhaps a piece of research you've published or your latest blog post.

App installs or engagements

The focus with these ads is on getting the user to do exactly what you want them to do – and install your app.

Leads on Twitter

When you are looking to build an email contact list you can run ads that specifically focus on getting the user to share their email address with you from directly within your tweet.

How do you become a Twitter advertiser?

When you want to set up a new Twitter ad campaign, all you need to do is log in to your Twitter account via a desktop. Click on the small profile image on the top right-hand side of the toolbar to see the dropdown menu and then click on Twitter Ads. You can also type the following URL directly into your browser: ads.twitter.com.

If this is the first time you have set up a Twitter ad campaign, Twitter will first prompt you to choose your country and time zone. Once you have filled in these details, Twitter will permanently save your settings and you won't be taken back to this page again – so make sure your details are correct.

You'll also be prompted to enter the username and password for your advertising account. Use the same username and password as you do on twitter.com. Once you've signed in, click on Create New Campaign.

Twitter then gives you various campaign objective options, as outlined above (as you can see from the drop-down menu). To set these up, all you have to do is click on the link and you will be guided through the steps to set up the ad content, targeting an audience and setting a budget. You can fix the amount you're willing to pay for retweets, follows or clicks – and once that budget has been used up, your tweets will simply stop being promoted.

Quick Promote

In February 2015, Twitter introduced another quick advertising feature – not dissimilar to 'boosted posts' on Facebook – enabling you to simply

sponsor a tweet rather than run a whole ad campaign. This can be accessed via your Twitter Ads platform – when you look at the View Tweet Activity tab – or directly via your Analytics tab, which shows stats on how tweets are performing.

When you click on Analytics you will see tweet performance and you also have the option to directly promote that post. For example, let's say that you saw that one particular tweet you put out was generating a lot of engagement (recent reports from Twitter advise that 1% is a good engagement benchmark to be aiming for), you could optimise that engagement by 'boosting' or 'promoting' that tweet.

Twitter Cards

Twitter Cards are another way of getting more from the 140 Twitter characters that you usually have when sending a tweet. With Twitter Cards, you can attach rich photos, video and media experience to Tweets to drive more engagement and, ultimately, more traffic to your website. Think of it as writing a Facebook status – when you paste a link into your status, it adds a preview with title, summary, and thumbnail of the content you are referring to.

Twitter Cards are pretty easy to use once you have set them up. All you have to do is add a few lines of HTML to your web pages and the users who tweet links to your content will have a 'Twitter Card' added to that Tweet – which will be visible to all their followers.

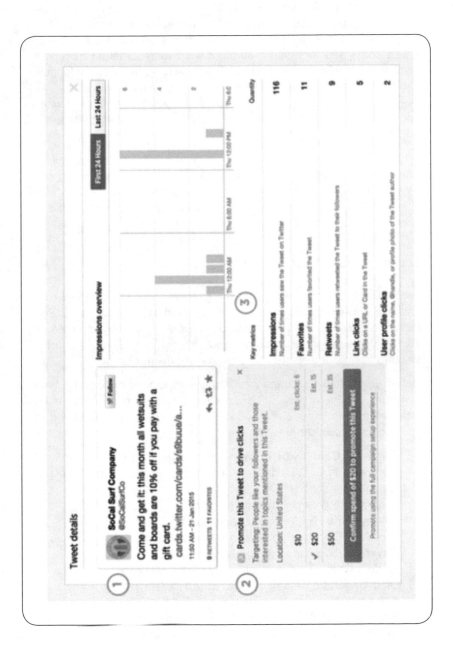

Tweet details

SoCal Surf Company
@SoCalSurfCo
Follow

Come and get it: this month all wetsuits and boards are 10% off if you pay with a gift card.

cards.twitter.com/cards/s9buuue/a...

11:50 AM - 21 Jan 2015

6 RETWEETS 11 FAVORITES

1

2 ✕ Promote this Tweet to drive clicks

Targeting: People like your followers and those interested in topics mentioned in this Tweet.

Location: United States

$10	Est. clicks: 6
✓ $20	Est. 15
$50	Est. 35

Confirm spend of $20 to promote this Tweet

Promote using the full campaign setup experience

Impressions overview

First 24 Hours | Last 24 Hours

Thu 12:00 AM — Thu 6:00 AM — Thu 12:00 PM — Thu 6d

3

Key metrics	Quantity
Impressions Number of times users saw the Tweet on Twitter	116
Favorites Number of times users favorited the Tweet	11
Retweets Number of times users retweeted the Tweet to their followers	6
Link clicks Clicks on a URL or Card in the Tweet	5
User profile clicks Clicks on the name, @handle, or profile photo of the Tweet author	2

How can they help your business?

The biggest advantage of having a Twitter Card is that it increases the number of people following your Twitter account through content attribution. Think of all those times people will tweet your links without giving you a proper shout-out. We've noticed this ourselves a number of times: some popular content curators will tweet our latest blog post without any @ reference – this is usually done to keep the tweet lengths shorter. With Twitter Cards, because your content will always be associated with that particular card, as a publisher you won't miss out when someone shares your content.

Twitter Cards not only give you control of how your content is displayed via tweets, they can also drive traffic to your site by helping you richly represent your content within Tweets across the web and on mobile devices. This gives users greater context and insight into the web links shared on Twitter, which in turn allows Twitter to send more traffic to your site or app.

Setting up your Twitter Card

Twitter Cards are powered by meta tags that you add to your website. Each URL on your site can have a unique card associated with it. Perfect, if you want to direct the audience to a specific landing page. When somebody tweets a URL with associated meta tags, Twitter will fetch the card from your website and store it in the Twitter cache.

Before you set up your meta tags you first need to choose which type of Twitter Card you require. There are eight different types that can be attached to your tweets, and you need to pick the one best suited to you and your business.

- **Summary Card (with or without a large image):** Default card that includes a title, description, thumbnail and Twitter account attribution.
- **Photo Card:** A card with a photo only.
- **Gallery Card:** Highlights a collection of four photos.
- **App Card:** Details a mobile app with direct download.
- **Player Card:** Provides video/audio/media.
- **Product Card:** Optimised for product information.
- **Lead Generation Card:** Allows you to collect people's email addresses with one click of a button.
- **Website Card:** Allows you to drive traffic directly to your website's homepage or other specific page; includes a thumbnail image representing your website.

You will see from this list that Twitter Cards are natural advertising options in Twitter. Depending on which campaign you select, the Twitter set-up process (outlined earlier) will walk you through the relevant steps.

Twitter scheduling

As a Twitter advertiser you also have the ability to schedule tweets directly from the ad platform. To do this you need to visit ads.twitter.com – and then click on the Creatives tab in the top menu. You will be able to compose a Tweet in the usual way, but this time you'll see not only the usual box to add your tweet, image, etc., but also a Scheduling tab.

Twitter advertising tips and tactics

Advertisements have always played a big role in the world of marketing, whether billboard advertising, press advertising, direct mail – or social media advertising.

Advertising is usually pretty pricey, so you need to make sure that you get it right – there's nothing worse than your latest ad going out with zero call to actions, a dreaded incorrect telephone number or glaring typo. Of course, we're only human and many of us often make mistakes – whether it's a small spelling mistake or tweeting the wrong thing at the wrong time, but it's vital to avoid mistakes, particularly on social media, where one little error can be shared with a mass audience in a matter of seconds.

Here are three advertising mistakes to avoid.

1. **Don't forget to use hashtags.** Hashtags are a great way to get the attention of your target audience, highlight exactly what you're tweeting about, and for getting your business into conversations and trending topics. Using a new ad or product image can stand out, but if you use strategically chosen hashtags in your promoted tweet, you can help your business find its target audience, reach non-followers in large numbers and help grow your influence. As mentioned in Chapter 5, just try not to go overboard with your hashtags – on Twitter, three is more than enough!

2. **Use images to your advantage.** Images on Twitter ensure that tweets take up more space on the feed and therefore help to drive engagement. It's important to include images when you're sending out a promoted tweet. Tweets that include an image receive 200% more engagement than tweets without one.

3. **Try to use a consistent voice.** It's important to consider the objective of the ad. While unique and chatty messages can make a Twitter account seem more 'human', sometimes, depending on the message you are trying to convey, being chatty or cheeky may not be appropriate and could push your platform off-message and create a backlash. Another point to consider – don't let your account sound like a robot stuck on repeat – sending out the same message again and again looks awful. The key is to find a happy middle ground where your message is clear and your voice is consistent, caring and human at the same time.

Getting started with LinkedIn advertising

If you want to grow the number of followers on your company LinkedIn page, or direct audiences to a specific piece of content, you could use LinkedIn advertising. To get started, you'll need to pull up the LinkedIn advertising platform. Simply hover over your profile picture on the top-right hand side of the menu.

Then scroll down to Advertising and click Manage. A new window will open where you can 'create a new campaign'. LinkedIn has two advertising options: creating ads or sponsored posts.

Creating an ad

This means that you are able to reach a target audience with ads featuring text, images or video. Once you've chosen the Create an Ad option, you will be taken through a process enabling you to:

- name your campaign
- include a link you want people to go to when they click on the ad
- enter a headline and description of what your ad is about (up to 75 characters)
- three options for how you want your ad to look – square, tall and long.

Having filled out all the necessary information and selected how you want your ad to look, click Next and LinkedIn will take you to the Targeting page. Now LinkedIn gives you the option to choose your targeting by location, companies and job title.

- **Location:** Here you can pick all the places/countries where you want your ad to go out – this will depend on who your target audience is.

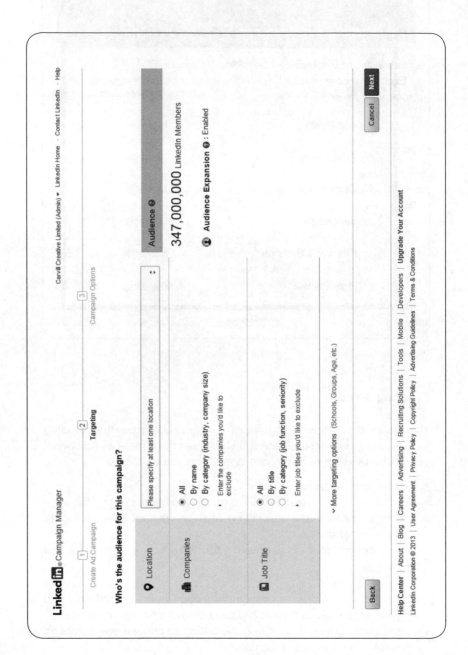

- **Companies:** Selecting all companies means your ad will go out to them all. If you only want to target specific companies, select the option By Name and you can list the relevant companies you want your ad to go out to.
- **By category:** If you are unsure of the names of the companies you want to target, or are only looking to target those from a specific industry or by company size, select this option.
- **Excluding companies:** If there are some companies you don't want to target at all you can select the option 'Enter the companies you'd like to exclude'. This is where you'd normally include your competitors.
- **Job title:** You might select All because you want your ad to go out to everyone who works in a company. Or you can be specific, and select exact job functions.
- **Seniority:** There's also a seniority option, so you can target managers, owners, partners, CEO, etc.

If you require more targeting, you can select the drop-down arrow at More Targeting Options and more granular options will appear.

Building the campaign

Once you have selected the relevant targeting, hit Next and LinkedIn will take you to the Campaign Options page. Here you will be able to enter payment details, budget and how long you want your campaign to run. Once finalised, simply hit Launch Campaign and your ad will become live.

Sponsored content

This advertising option enables you to sponsor existing or new content on your company page to reach a wider audience (similar to a boosted post on Facebook). At the Create Ad Campaign stage, instead of creating an ad you opt to Sponsor Content.

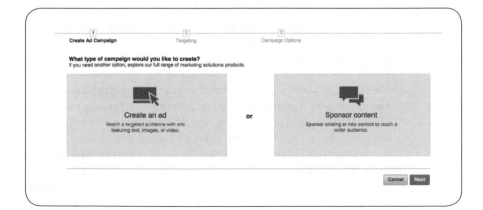

You'll be taken through the same steps as before: Targeting and Campaign Options.

The content you sponsor can be content that is shared on your main company LinkedIn page or content that is shared on a Showcase Page.

Setting an advertising budget

When creating an ad budget in a LinkedIn ad campaign you opt for cost per click (CPC), where you only pay if someone clicks on the ad. Whether creating an ad or sponsoring a piece of content, you can opt to pay cost per 1,000 impressions (CPM) each time the ad is shown.

With sponsored posts, you can set a specific budget, so that when that budget is exhausted, the ads stop, or you can set a specific end date.

Bear in mind that there is a minimum cost per click of around $3.70 – and this does fluctuate depending on budget for the campaign. (LinkedIn's ad platform will automatically provide suggestions when you're fixing a budget.) So it's worth experimenting and seeing what actual cost per conversion looks like. For some, LinkedIn ads can be very lucrative. Again, it's worth watching the analytics of the page, which will provide you with an outline of what's working both organically and paid for, so you can assess how effective your campaigns are.

How to improve engagement with your ads

It's important to know the best ways to improve the engagement on your LinkedIn company page, whether you're posting normally, creating sponsored posts or creating a normal LinkedIn ad.

To help you encourage more engagement on LinkedIn, we've put together some stats and tips that will help you to improve your posts and get the attention of your target audience.

- **Post in the mornings:** Monday to Friday. Weekday mornings are proven to engage more people on LinkedIn – so test the times of when you post and try to learn when people are engaging with your content. Again, your page analytics show the days on which people are interacting with you – so this is worth reviewing regularly.
- **Focus on post frequency:** Posting 20 status updates a month will reach 60% of your unique audience. When you're sharing ads it's important to monitor their click-through rates – it's common for this to decline if you continue to display the same ad all the time or if you are bombarding the same target audience with ads.
- **Refresh your ads often:** Don't keep pushing the same old content, and try not to post that often. We recommend one sponsored

post to one specific target audience per week. That said, you could be running a number of sponsored posts to different target audiences.

- **Include links in your posts:** Links encourage 200% more engagement. Always include clear calls to action when including links. Not only will links help to drive twice the engagement rate, but letting your audience know what they are getting from the post is highly beneficial and will encourage more engagement.
- **Use video in your posts:** Videos get a 75% higher share rate – links to YouTube play directly in the LinkedIn feed and usually result in higher engagement too.

How to post

- **Optimise the appeal of visual content:** People will engage more with rich media – images, videos, and presentations are more likely to grab someone's attention than a simple post with a link. Choose images that stand out. It seems obvious, but bright colours are proven to have an impact in capturing the attention of your audience.
- **Concise intros and snappy headlines:** Choose words that are emotive and use strong call to action phrases such as 'try', 'download', 'sign up', 'request', etc. A description with clear benefits requires a strong call to action. Also think about the use of questions – sometimes posing a question, when relevant, generates engagement.
- **Give people a reason to take notice:** Ensure that your proposition is appealing to the audience – highlight special offers, free trials, competitions, etc.

A word of caution: Before you share a post, do check that the image you want to accompany the post appears correctly. Sometimes LinkedIn's images won't show up, or they'll choose a random image from the article that isn't in context with the post. If this is the case, you can upload the correct image directly to the post, by simply clicking the paperclip sign to add an image.

Getting started with Facebook advertising

As outlined in Chapter 6, over the years Facebook has become quite a sophisticated advertising platform for brands, agencies, and business, whether large, medium, small or start-ups. Whether you are looking to create an advertising campaign to grow Likes on your business page, promote your brand to Facebook users or drive more leads to sales teams, there are options to cover all objectives. Of course, as with all campaigns, before you get started with Facebook ads, you need to consider what your objectives are.

Do you want to increase people's awareness of your brand or business? Do you want to find potential customers for your business? Or do you want to drive sales for your product and service?

Looking to increase people's awareness of your brand or business? You can choose whether to promote a post, get more page Likes, reach people near your store (local business) or direct people to view a video.

If you want to find potential customers for your business, choose whether you want to encourage clicks to your website, get people to sign up to your website, get more people to install your app or respond to your Facebook event.

And then there's a product focus too: drive people to your product or services page, get more people to purchase your product, get people to engage with your app or redeem an offer.

Depending on what your objectives are, you have a number of options to choose from. One of the most popular Facebook advertising options is the Likes campaigns – great for targeting the right people to Like your Facebook page – so we'll use this in our practical step-by-step guide (the process for setting up other campaigns is pretty much the same) and we've broken down the advertising process and demonstrated how useful Facebook ads can be in helping you to grow a targeted community.

Getting started

In order to create your Facebook ad you must be logged into and using your **personal** Facebook profile. You must also be an administrator of the Facebook Page for which you wish to create the ad. Log in as you usually would via the top right-hand side of your news feed and you will see a white box with the option to Create Advert.

Step 1: Choose the page

Choose the Facebook business page or place where you wish to advertise using the drop-down menu. For instance, if your objective is to grow Likes on the Facebook Page in question, the ad's destination should be your Facebook Business Page timeline. If you're an admin of the Page, it will appear in the drop-down menu.

What do you want to advertise?

Choose a Facebook destination
or enter a URL:

Carvill Creative

Pages and Places

Carvill Creative
Place

Step 2: What's the objective?

For the purpose of this example we are discussing how to use Facebook advertising specifically for growing your community, so we'd select Get More Page Likes from the range of options.

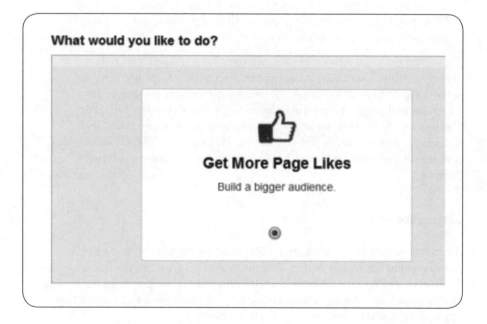

What would you like to do?

Get More Page Likes

Build a bigger audience.

Step 3: Optimise your image

This is where you choose the image for your advert. Facebook rules state that you may not have more than 20% text in your ad picture, so be wary of that. (We have tested this and they don't let ads with too much text get through their verification process.) Quite often your business logo will suffice, but it's advisable to think creatively. Pick an image that will catch your audience's attention – the ad images are small when they appear in the right-hand column, so they need to be eye-catching or include a strong call to action in order to get noticed. Images need to be 600 pixels × 225 pixels, in order to fit and appear clearly on a user's news feed **as well as** in the right-hand column of their Facebook account.

We would advise that you allow for the ad to appear in both the news feed and the right-hand column. News feed ads are getting a lot of activity at the moment and there is no harm allowing the ad to appear on both (it's a default setting, so there's no need to amend anything).

You can simply click on Upload Pictures to upload them directly from your computer, or if you've created an ad on Facebook before, you'll have the option to pick an image from the Facebook library.

Select Images

• Use up to 6 different images to create more adverts in your campaign at no extra cost. Why?.
• Recommended Image Size for News Feed: 600 pixels x 225 pixels

Upload Image

⬆ Upload Images   🗖 Browse Library

Tip

Facebook states that they will resize any image that is incorrect. When they do this the image doesn't always keep its clarity, so it's much better to upload the images yourself to the correct size.

Step 4: Ad content

As mentioned earlier in the chapter, your ad headline and text are as important as the image you choose to accompany them. What you say in this small space will determine whether people are interested enough to click on your ad.

Make sure your headline is snappy and eye-catching, and keep your text concise but informative. It's worth looking at a few ads and seeing how others have laid them out to get some inspiration.

Step 5: Choosing your targeted audience

The more often your ad is displayed to the right users – the people who are likely to be interested in your product or service – the better your ad will perform. You can target via the following criteria:

- **Location:** You can narrow down your location to country, country region and town/city. You can't proceed with your ad until at least one country has been selected. If you choose a town or city as well you can include other cities that appear between a 10- and 50-mile radius. However, if you choose more than one country you will not be able to pick towns/cities as well.
- **Age/gender:** Think carefully and realistically about the age group you wish to target and whether your ad needs to be targeted to males and females. You can create much more of a niche audience and avoid wasting budget if you know the age group of the audience you wish to target.
- **Precise interests:** This is where you will see your audience dwindle in size – depending on the categories and precise interests you enter.

Remember, the beauty of Facebook ads is that you can pinpoint your exact audience, making sure that the right people see your ad. The targeting is very precise and should be used as effectively as possible. Aim to get your audience down to a low number (at least below a million) by entering precise interests and categories that you believe they would associate themselves with on Facebook. Simply type in the keywords that are most relevant, and Facebook will automatically show you options and the estimated size of the audience.

Facebook will help you target people based on their interests by looking at things such as the Pages they have liked, their interest and activities. A topic marked with a hashtag includes related interests. For example, #social media includes people who are interested in 'digital marketing', 'inbound marketing' and other topics related to social media. The more interests you add, the more related interests Facebook will suggest.

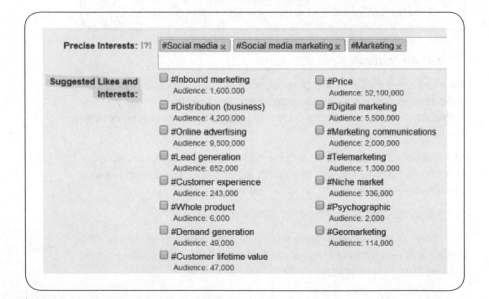

- **Broad categories:** Use this targeting option to reach groups of people who share similar interests and traits, such as activities related to key terms, e.g. 'marketing'. This information is pulled from what people have included in their personal timelines and will help you to reach your ideal audience. For example, if you were a baby clothing company looking to build your community on Facebook, you might find the category that allows you to target 'expecting parents' very useful.

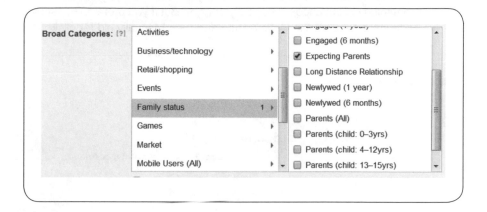

Step 6: Targeting connections

In the steps above we've targeted our ad by interests, age and location. Facebook also allows you to target your ad to people based on who you are connected to on Facebook. For example, you can target people who are connected to your Facebook business page or specific apps, and you can even target their friends. As you can see below, all you have to do is enter your organisation's name and it should appear in the box.

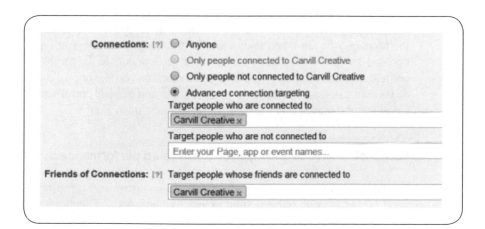

Step 7: Advanced targeting options

Advanced targeting is great for narrowing your audience down even further. Click on the See Advanced Targeting option in order to target people by relationship status, languages, education and workplace.

Step 8: Advertising budget

Facebook will automatically charge you on CPM pricing (cost per 1,000 times your ad is displayed) rather than CPC (cost per click – you only pay when someone clicks your ad). If you prefer CPM, you needn't do anything except choose your daily budget. But if you prefer CPC, select Optimise for Clicks in Optimisation and then Manually bid for clicks.

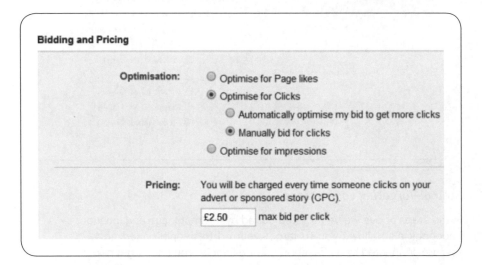

Finally: review your ad

Have one last look over your selected options – review your targeting, budget, text and image. If you're happy, click Place Order.

Facebook takes a few hours to review the ad and once it's approved, it automatically goes live. Just remember to keep an eye on the results in the Manage Ads area, and take a look at the budget daily. If your Facebook ad isn't performing well you can make adjustments to the targeting, content or image. You can tweak the ad as much as you like once it's live, so be sure to keep a beady eye on its progress and general performance – don't waste money on an advert that isn't performing well.

Facebook analytics and tips for positive ad performance

To access ad analytics, click on the drop-down arrow at the top right-hand corner of your screen. Then select Manage Ads – Facebook will then take you to view all of your campaigns.

To see how well your ad is doing, all you have to do is click on the ad you want to check on and depending on which type of ad you have created, it should tell you the number of website clicks or likes you have received, the total reach (number of impressions), the frequency, average number of times your ad was seen by each person, the amount you've spent during your selected time period (or so far) and the average cost per website click or page Like.

Facebook will also provide a graph showing the number of clicks you've had over a period of time. You can choose the period you want to see, whether it's in the last week, the last 14 days, the last 28 days, this month, this quarter or the lifetime history of your campaigns.

To find out even more about your ad, click on the ad, which will then show in a table at the bottom of your page. This will tell you the number of clicks you have had, your click-through rate and your relevance score. The relevance score is important: it's a score based on how well your ad is performing among your selected audience. A higher score indicates that more people are engaging with your ad (clicks, likes and comments). The relevant score is a score out of 10 – so a 9/10 score is telling you that your ad is hitting the right audience and doing well on the engagement front.

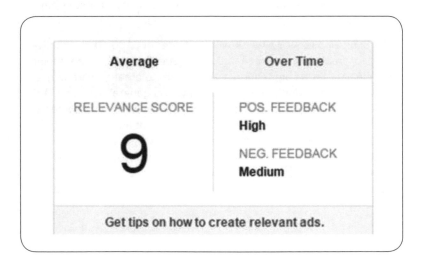

From a low level of activity in December 2013, at the time of writing their Facebook page has almost 20,000 Likes, there is a good deal of interaction from fans and Facebook is now one of the key referrers of direct traffic to their website.

The company's marketing team has used a small amount of page advertising to increase the amount of Likes, which has resulted in their fan base growing by around 1,000 per month. At the same time, most posts have been boosted to ensure that they reach the widest possible audience. Given the large number of Likes, this means their total reach is magnified further.

Facebook has gone from being a form of marketing 'window dressing' for the company to being one of the most important referrers of traffic to their website. It has also massively boosted awareness of the brand.

Case study: Norbord Europe - 'Use Wood Wisely'

This case study demonstrates an engagement and awareness campaign via a sponsored post testing a small budget.

The campaign ran for a week with a budget of £100. The objective was to create engagement around a specific post, encouraging people to enter a competition and generally to create awareness of the Use Wood Wisely brand. The campaign generated over 1,000 likes on the post, 165 shares and 2,664 post engagements. Although the campaign was set for engagement and not directly for page Likes, indirectly, traffic to the Use Wood Wisely site increased, and there were a number of new Likes generated the week the post was sponsored.

Use Wood Wisely shared their album.
Posted by Victoria Mills [?] · 13 February · Edited · 🌐

Where is the world's most magnificent forest? Vote for your favourite to win and enter our prize draw to win £100 voucher with Forest Holidays - simply click like on your favourite forest and then private message us your details. http://bit.ly/17s15sL

Use Wood Wisely added 10 new photos to the album: Click Like on Your Favourite Forest to Enter Into Our Prize Draw.

In celebration of the planet's most magnificent forests, simply click 'LIKE' on your favourite forest. Everyone who enters will be entered in a prize draw to win £100 voucher with 'Forest Holidays' - remember to private message us your email and name as well.

47,891 people reached   ✔ **View Results**

Unlike · Comment · Share

👍 Use Wood Wisely, Maria Szczepaniak Houston, Liz Negus   Most Relevant ▾
Steele, Daphne Patricia Hunt and 1,001 others like this.

Other social media channels

In this chapter we've covered in detail a practical approach to advertising on Twitter, Facebook and LinkedIn, still the most popular advertising channels used by businesses, brands and agencies. But of course, as mentioned earlier, advertising is growing rapidly on other channels, such as Pinterest, Snapchat and Instagram. In fact, as recently reported in *Adweek*, Instagram is working on features that would make the service a better marketing platform for e-commerce businesses looking to directly take people from images to product pages where they can buy directly.

As platforms look for ways to monetise in order to continue innovating, growing and supporting their followers and communities, it's highly likely that the range of advertising options will continue to grow too. We'll keep you updated on new options and other updates in this book's blog, www.thebusinessofbeingsocial.co.uk.

Social media marketing action plan

- Before you start, do your research. Understand the specific demographics each platform enables and how targeted your campaigns can be. Look at what's working for others.
- Be strategic. Social advertising offers you the opportunity to run campaigns that focus on generating traffic, direct sales, gaining followers, driving engagement or generally boosting online visibility and awareness – be sure you are clear about your objective, then design the ad and the call to action for optimum impact.
- Think about your content – remember, images and words need to compel, even with limited space.
- Target your audience with relevant campaigns and messaging. You can be very targeted on social media, so take advantage of the granular targeting options.
- Keep reviewing what's working. Scheduling campaigns is a great feature, but do be sure that you are also measuring effectiveness rather than just letting things run and run.

---

11 | Listening and analysis

What you will learn from this chapter:

- Why listening is so important
- What you should be listening for
- Understanding your audience and influencers
- Techniques and tools for listening
- Analysis – taking those business insights and turning them into purposeful action

The importance of listening can't be underestimated whether you're in the real world or online. If someone is talking to you and you don't answer, at best you're unaware of the conversation – at worst, you're being ignorant.

You may have been told by a stern aunt or a schoolteacher, 'You've got two eyes, two ears and just one mouth – kindly use them in accordance.'

This statement also applies directly to all social media activity – listening is simply vital for marketing and communications strategies. In fact, many businesses now only use social media for business intelligence, monitoring competitors or Research & Development. Latest research suggests that almost half of users on Twitter now don't tweet at all. Marketing itself has been defined as:

'fundamentally about understanding and anticipating the needs of the consumer so that organisations can create products and services to meet those needs, profitably.'

What's important to note are the two words **understanding** and **anticipating**. Both of these can be achieved only through effective listening and being close enough to consumers to understand and anticipate their needs.

In the past, listening would have focused on customer surveys, market research methods and consumer trends. Now we have social platforms where millions of people are sharing millions of conversations. This 'real-time' buzz and chatter is happening around the world 24/7 and across a range of social platforms. We live in an 'always on' society and with so much 'noise' being made across the social platforms, the challenge is to know how to cut through the noise to find the conversations that are relevant for you.

People to people

Listening is a very basic human function – it's one of the key senses that enable us to survive. And in business, listening aids survival too.

Think about listening from a people-to-people perspective and take the art of listening into the real networking world for a moment. Let's say you meet someone at a networking event. You walk up to them and, before you even ask their name, or what they do, or why they are here and how they're finding the event, you start talking at them. You don't let them get a word in, you just keep talking. If they ask a question, you ignore it and carry on talking and sharing your news. At best, they'll smile before they walk away, thinking you're a conceited egomaniac!

Listening is one part of conversing. If social networking is about continuous conversations, you can't just shout at your audience all the time. To strike an effective balance, you need to be continuously listening too. When we talk about focused listening versus unfocused publishing, we mean that if you have listened to customer need, you will be prepared to publish meaningful content. Instead of simply sharing what you think your customers want to hear, listen in and find out what matters to them. Then create content and solutions based around that need.

Social story

A technical devices company was very keen to create regular videos as part of their content mix. Because they often had to create product demonstrations they already had in-house resources which they could use to create video on an ongoing basis.

They set about creating a suite of videos, all based on things they thought would be useful to their audience. While the videos were very well put together, the level of engagement from their customers was disappointing. That's when they reached out for some advice.

They were encouraged to do some focused listening as to what was happening in their space, reviewing what their competitors were doing, looking at feedback on customer forums and listening in to real-time conversations on both Facebook and Twitter.

What they discovered was that there were a number of clear 'pain points' around a couple of the products. Recurring themes related to upgrade features and practical elements such as transferring data from one device to another. Armed with this information, the company created a suite of videos that focused on those very challenges.

Focused listening resulted in creating content which was highly engaging – not only for their customers, but for others having similar issues with competitor services using the same devices. The traction to the videos was significant and far surpassed their usual web traffic levels.

This confirms that in many cases, it's powerful to respond to a shared need rather than pushing out content that isn't targeted. Targeted content really does show who's been listening.

If you listen to the challenges of your audiences and potential audiences, you will be able to provide solutions. You can then target those solutions direct to the people asking questions or looking for solutions. And of course, if a few vocal people have an issue around a particular area, it's likely that you are also meeting the needs of those quieter, less vocal audiences too.

What should you be listening for?

Depending on what you are listening for (which should relate back to your objectives), the listening may take hours, days, weeks or even months – but it needs to happen. Listening in helps you to gain some really useful insights:

- what's important to the people you want to connect with
- what's being said in your sector
- what the influencers are talking about
- when they are visible
- what they are looking for
- what problems or challenges they have
- what solutions they are looking for
- what your competitors are talking about
- what people are engaging with
- when they are engaging
- what's working
- what the issues are
- what they are saying about you, your brand, your products.

Listening is so important that a whole new industry has been created around it. A growing number of marketing agencies, social media agencies, advertising agencies, as well as PR agencies, now offer 'social listening' services. Simply type the words 'social media listening' into

Google and you'll find a huge and growing number of tools and services, some of which we have mentioned in this book.

Uncovering insights

When you listen (which is effectively like real-time research), you want to make sure that you are actively learning in order to glean useful insights to increase your knowledge about your market and audiences. Applying the tried and tested fact-finding questions – who, what, why, when, where – can provide some valuable insights, as the box below shows.

Who?

- Who are they?
- What is their demographic profile?

Discover if their gender, age, location aligns with your typical customer profile.

What?

- What did they engage with?
- What did they share and with whom?

Learn about what's working and create more targeted content to drive engagement.

When?

- At what time of day are they engaging?
- On mobile/desktop/tablets?

Understand how times of engagement (weekends, weekdays, working hours, out-of-hours) influence platforms used, and vice versa.

Where?

- Where did they come from? Twitter, Facebook, LinkedIn, Google+, YouTube, blog?
- What's driving them to your site?
- Which platforms are they on?
- Can you see any patterns?

You can start to build a picture of which channels your audiences are using, and what's driving what.

Why?

- Why are they engaging?
- What made them engage?

Understanding this gives you ideas for improving engagement tactics, such as offers, free guides, downloads, referrals from other sites.

Business intelligence

Data is one thing, but interpreting it is another. The who, what, when, where and why example box demonstrates that even with basic analysis you can glean a significant amount of information. What's important is that the information is then turned into business insights which help to drive strategy and tactics.

Tune in to your influencers

Just as Pareto analysis delivers the 80/20 rule – 20% of customers deliver 80% of profits – there is similar analysis at play in social media and online. In 2012, Meteor Solutions collected data from more than 20 brand marketer clients. Their research identified that on average, approximately 1% of a site's audience generated 20% of all its traffic, through sharing the brand's content or sharing site links with others. These influencers are clearly key to amplification and it was shown that their influence also drove a higher share of conversion.

Once you have identified who your influencers are, it is clear that there will be benefits from developing relationships with them. Directly engaging with them and sharing exclusive opportunities, special offers – perhaps even unique content – will be beneficial, as these influencers will be far more powerful in creating a buzz than you are.

Of course, the challenge is to befriend these influencers in a very human way. Using social media isn't about direct selling, as we've said throughout this book, it's about getting people to know you, like you, trust you – building share of mind so that they ultimately do business with you. If you focus attention on 'pushing' sales messages at these valuable influencers, you run the risk of being too promotional – and losing your biggest fans.

Advocacy is probably the most powerful form of promotion. Once you've found your influencers, develop a programme (strategy/tactics) to nurture and develop this valuable channel in the most authentic and engaging way possible. The more raving fans you can create for your business, the more advocates you will have out there in the market place amplifying your marketing for you. If people are saying great things about you, your products, your services – and sharing links and information – you need to know who they are, thank them, get to know them and build relationships to keep them happy and busy.

Listening for relevant conversations

A great way to start listening to what's being said is to track relevant keywords. Even without a formal social media dashboard (see Chapter 9) in place, you can track important keywords online and set alerts, so that you are notified of any mentions as they happen. Google Alerts and Social Mention are very useful, but there is a range of other services such as TweetBeep or Twilert.

Google Alerts

A simple tool like Google Alerts (www.google.com/alerts) will enable you to track what is being said about your brand, services or products. You can set alerts about absolutely anything, and whenever those words are mentioned online, you will receive an alert. You might, for example, want to track competitors or a key influencer.

Google Alerts sweep content that has been indexed by Google. Tweets and Facebook updates get into these alerts too. You can decide when to receive your alerts: you can have them sent to you in real time as they happen, once a day or once a week.

Social Mention (www.socialmention.com)

This service is similar to Google Alerts but specifically designed for the social networks. You can choose what you wish to track – for example your name, brand or product mentions (on Twitter, Facebook, YouTube and other social platforms) – and again, you can set the frequency with which you receive alerts. If you are using a social dashboard you will also have options to track keywords and sentiment.

Whichever platform you choose to use, you need to be clear about what you are tracking and why. There are a number of ways of tracking key-words and key phrases:

1. **Finding new followers:** Let's say you want to follow people who are talking and sharing about social media, professional services marketing and user experience. You can track these keywords to help you tune in to relevant conversations.

2. **Tracking competitor activity:** Watching what's happening in their 'keyword' space and being alerted to any relevant followers, influencers and conversations.
3. **Brand reputation:** Tracking your own brand/product names.
4. **Tracking direct response key phrases.** By this we mean key phrases that not only house the keyword but also include a direct response element such as 'looking for help with'/'can anyone help with'. You can string these key phrases together with keywords to help target relevant conversations. This is quite useful when leveraging social platforms for lead generation.

As always, you should be very clear about what you are looking to achieve – this will determine what you look out for.

Other useful tools to help you see conversations, who is saying what and influencer reach include the following applications (we've already mentioned some of these in previous chapters):

- Klout (www.klout.com)
- Kred (www.kred.com)
- Peer Index (www.peerindex.com)
- Sprout Social (www.sproutsocial.com)
- Tweetreach (www.tweetreach.com)
- Tweepi (www.tweepi.com).

These applications (and others) enable you to track engagement and sentiment, and view influencer reach, but if you are focusing on specific objectives, you may prefer to determine your own set of analysis criteria to monitor and measure.

Some areas you might wish to include in your analysis criteria are:

- members and number of active profiles
- posts – frequency and density
- comments and brand mentions (including sentiment – positive or negative)
- inbound links/traffic
- tags, votes, bookmarks.

And for value awareness and influence:

- brand loyalty/affinity
- media placements
- share of conversation
- sentiment of posts
- interaction with content.

Determining your objectives is key to understanding what you need to be listening for. However, not only do you need to be clear about what signals you need to listen out for, you should ideally keep listening in a continuous and concerted way. Conversations on social media are continuous, so you need to develop processes and systems for listening and learning in a continuous way too.

Plan to listen: developing a social media listening strategy

Let's take a step-by-step look at a simple, practical approach.

1 Determine where your audience is

Once you start listening you will very quickly start to gauge which platforms your audiences are participating in. For example, if you are a professional services firm, you'll be listening out for who is talking about what on which platform:

- Are people talking about 'professional services' on Twitter, Facebook, LinkedIn or Google+?
- What type of people are talking about your sector?
- Are there any influencers who stand out and that you need to be connecting with?

Listening in is illuminating. Listen often and regularly, then analyse who is talking. You will quickly build up a pattern and learn which platforms are 'noisier' and what part each social network plays in your sector. Use the what, when, who, where, when model to build metrics that help you learn about your audience.

2 Identify your influencers

Listening in is key to understanding who the influencers are in your space. Influencers can be highly valuable to a business. The more you understand who they are, the easier it will be to find more of them. The more influencers you have, the more reach and amplification opportunity you create.

Influencers can include your clients, journalists, bloggers, thought leaders, politicians, authors and industry commentators. In fact, many companies are now instituting specific influencer relations strategies which combine elements of PR, lobbying and public affairs.

Watch who is sharing your information, sharing links and driving audiences to find out about you. Many of the services we've mentioned in this chapter (particularly Kred and Peer Index) provide you with analytics about just how influential your influencers' sharing activity is. Know your influencers – perhaps categorise them as A, B, C and D – and build a programme to nurture your As and Bs as well as moving your Cs and Ds to As and Bs.

3 Understand the data

In many ways, this is an age of data overload. There are so many facts and figures available, it can be a struggle to make sense of the chaos of information you receive. It may initially seem a daunting task, but it's worth understanding what the data is telling you. Data speaks and you need to create a process to help you mine the gems you need out of the mass of information. You could use customer demographics, purchase patterns, online transactions driven by social interaction – you decide. Once you understand the metrics that are important for your business, you can listen more insightfully to the wealth of data available via social media networks.

4 Know your keywords

To tune in to relevant conversations, you need to start somewhere. This is where keywords are useful – you can start to listen in to the words that are relevant to your business and track conversations in real time. We explained keywords in some detail in Chapter 4. As we said, keywords are the DNA of your online visibility, so be sure you know what yours are. Track conversations around those keywords, set alerts in Google Alerts and Social Mention, or in your social dashboard (see Chapter 9), so that you are informed and can build insights around keywords that matter to your business.

5 Create listening criteria

Even when you're using targeted resources to help you tailor your 'social listening' effectively, because conversation is continuous there's an awful lot to listen out for. So set yourself some robust listening criteria based on what is relevant for your business and your specific objectives. Your criteria might include:

- how many times you were mentioned
- sentiment – positive or negative
- by which audience
- on which platform
- in what context.

And, of course, while we've focused primarily on gleaning information from the social networks don't forget that you may also be able to gather rich information from industry forums or specialist blogs. Be mindful that your 'listening' might need to extend beyond what's happening on social networks. This is why it's often good to include a blend of automated listening tools such as Google Alerts and Social Mention. While the latter focuses on social networks, Google Alerts will pick up 'online' activity generally.

We've explored a number of platforms that enable you to use your eyes and ears online, but whichever platforms you decide to choose, and even if you choose not to participate on any of the social platforms, you can still be listening and gleaning insights from all the chatter that's happening online.

The key message to remember is – to be informed, be sure you're listening!

Social media marketing action plan

- Measurement and analysis aids continuous learning.
- Create listening criteria that are relevant to your objectives.
- Explore the tools for listening and choose the right one(s) for you.
- Identify your influencers and build a programme to nurture them and grow more of them.
- Determine the who, what, when, where and why of your audience.
- Plan to listen.

12| Daily management of social media

What you will learn from this chapter:

- The range of multiple account management platforms
- Set-up and daily management via Hootsuite
- Creating streams of information
- Scheduling
- Shrinking links
- Measurement of social media marketing activity

You will be aware by now that embracing social media platforms requires a significant commitment.

Often, when we're training or consulting, people realise the magnitude of managing the channels on offer and ask the question, '*Is there a simple way to manage multiple accounts?*' Fortunately, the answer to that question is a very loud **yes**. Welcome to social media dashboards.

Social platform dashboards have been around for as long as many of the social networks, so it's staggering to find out that roughly 80% of the businesses and practitioners we train (some with very established social media presences) do not use or are unaware of social media dashboards. This means that many people managing business Twitter, Facebook or LinkedIn accounts are literally logging in and out of each separate social media network each time they want to share an update. For example, the basic Twitter platform, while it's been enhanced significantly over the years to make it far more user friendly, still has its limitations. For example, let's say we wanted to schedule a tweet for tomorrow, an hour from now, next week or next month. Unless you are using a complementary application (e.g. Buffer, which sits within Twitter. com – refer back to Chapter 5) you can't do this on Twitter. As soon as you set up the tweet you have to send it.

Social dashboards

There are various social media dashboards. Some of them are totally free to use while others offer a free starter service with enterprise versions. Just a few of the many are Tweetdeck, Sprout Social (free trial option), CoTweet, Social Oomph and NetVibes. Then there are more advanced enterprise-only solutions such as Radian6 (now part of Sales Force Marketing Cloud), Meltwater and Sysomos in which the dashboard is specifically tailored as a management, listening and reporting platform. In fact, google 'social media dashboards' – and you'll see quite a selection. (Note: many of the free versions also have sophisticated enterprise versions – the enterprise versions we mention here don't have free versions.)

Both of us have experimented with Tweetdeck, Twhirl, CoTweet and we've had dealings with Radian6, but the one we both favour and have stuck with throughout our personal Twitter journeys has been Hootsuite.

In this chapter we'll showcase the workings of Hootsuite as a social media dashboard, but there are many other social measurement, monitoring and listening tools to automate activity. It's entirely up to you to decide which one best fits your tastes and needs.

Hootsuite

This book is concerned with the practical side of social media, so we thought it only right to showcase the platform that we believe to be the most practical and user friendly. Hootsuite (www.hootsuite.com) has various levels of enterprise solutions – from very basic to more sophisticated options – but the free version is a great starting point to get to grips with what you can expect from a social media dashboard.

In this chapter we'll look at setting up your account and scheduling communications. We'll also touch on listening in and managing social conversations.

Getting started

Step 1: Setting up your account

Visit www.hootsuite.com and set up your account. This is really very simple – you need a username and unique email address for each account, and that's pretty much it.

Step 2: Bringing in your social network accounts

Connecting the dashboard with any social networks you have already created is, again, relatively simple. On the left-hand side of the dashboard you'll see a range of icons. The first is the Owl icon. When you click on the Owl you will see an account overview. In the area 'My Social

Networks' the various social networks you are already streaming into the dashboard are outlined. You can add new social network accounts into the stream via 'Add a Social Network'.

When you click the 'Add a Social Network' box, you are presented with a menu asking which social network you wish to pull through to the dashboard. Select the medium (Twitter, Facebook, LinkedIn, etc.) and verify your username, email address and password for the account you wish to pull through.

The free version of Hootsuite enables you to bring in up to five social media accounts. If you want to bring in unlimited social accounts, you will have to opt for the Pro Version and pay a fee of $9.99 a month.

Should you have requirements outside of their Free or Pro version, you can tailor a solution. And that steps into Enterprise territory.

Step 3: Creating streams for your social network

You can manage how you view the information coming in from each social media account. Even with the many changes and updates (and there are likely to be more) to the Twitter.com platform, to see @ messages and direct messages plus lists, you still have to click on various links in Twitter.com to be taken to those specific information feeds. One of the major assets of Hootsuite (and indeed other plat-forms) is that all the information that is usually hidden behind tabs and links within Twitter.com can be laid out in a 'single view' social media dashboard.

Organising your Streams

You will see from the image below that you can pull in data for your streams from various channels. In the Networks tab you can choose the network – for example you can see that we have selected the @michellecarvill Twitter account – and then you can select whether @mentions, retweets etc. You'll also see an Apps tab too – and this enables you to bring in content from various apps.

And, of course, you can manage the order of the information feeds, giving you control over how that 'single view' dashboard is arranged.

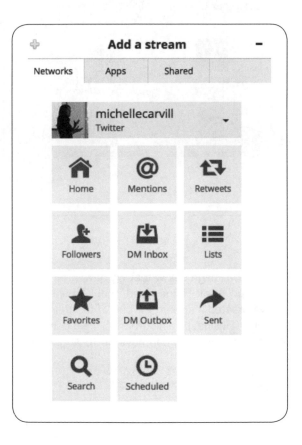

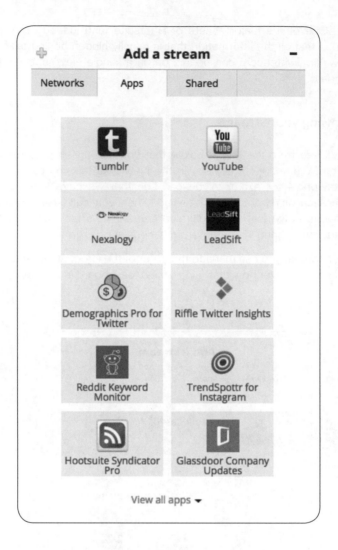

You can see from the image below that we have arranged the @michellecarvill Twitter account as Home Feed, then @mentions and then for this demo we've created a stream for one of the training organisations we both train with – BusinessTrainingMadeSimple.com – their Twitter @ handle is @GetTrainedUK. You can have up to 10 streams in any one account.

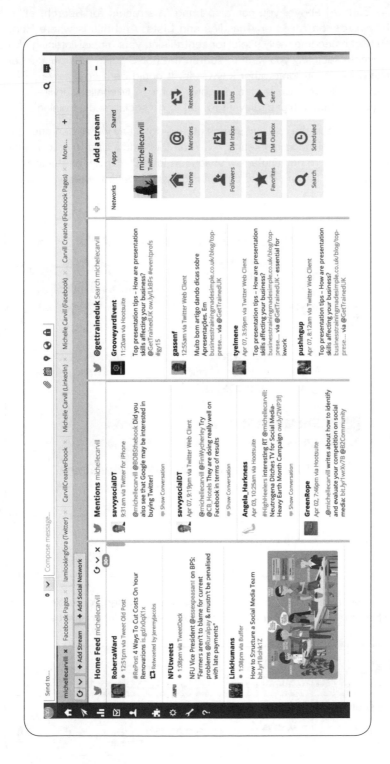

As outlined above, you can also bring in streams for **Search**, either **Keywords**, hashtags or @handles and **Lists**. And this is where Hootsuite can become really useful for centralising your 'social listening'. For example, let's say you want to **search** the noise going on around a certain hashtag or some other keywords. It could be a company name – e.g. Carvill Creative – or a person's name – Michelle Carvill – or a keyword/phrase that's relevant to you, e.g. 'social media training'.

You can insert the relevant search query – let's say we've searched the words 'social media marketing' – we can then add a filter (by clicking the little downward pointing arrow style icon [see the arrow on the image]) such as UK, helping you to cut out irrelevant location noise.

> **social media marketin...** 🧑 ↻ ∨ ✕
>
> | Search ⇕ | uk ✕ | ✕ |
>
> **Bizitalk**
> 1:13pm via Sprout Social
>
> Propel Your Brand | Graphic Design | Digital Marketing | Social Media |mediaraft.co.uk @MediaraftUK #bizitalk
>
> **SocMediaStream**
> 12:19pm via Sprout Social
>
> QUICK! There is ONE LAST ticket remaining on our #FREE #content #marketing workshop for #SME's @TheLandingMCUK bit.ly/1Dk18Vw
>
> ↻ Retweeted by TheLandingMCUK

You can also attach your specific location too when you click the Add Stream tab in the main top menu of your Hootsuite dashboard (as below).

And then click the Search tab – you will see a compass style arrow head. When you click this you can see that you can Append your location to localise search results.

Add Stream   ×

Twitter
Facebook
Google+
LinkedIn
WordPress

Shared with team:

Apps

Stream   Search   Keyword   Lists

Select a profile:

Click to select a social network

Append your location to this query to find local results

Enter search query:

Show examples

Add Stream

Similarly, you can set up **keywords**. While you can't geolocate these, you can track multiple instances. The Keyword tab allows you to track up to three keywords. Adding and removing keywords is simple, so you can test results very quickly. If the keywords you are using don't deliver

Add Stream   ×

Twitter
Facebook
Google+
LinkedIn
WordPress

Shared with team:

Apps

Stream   Search   Keyword   Lists

Select Profile:

Click to select a social network

○ Use existing list

○ Create a new list

Enter a name for a list

Enter description (optional)

● Public list   ○ Private list

Add Stream

the results you were hoping for, remove and optimise until you get the insights you require.

You can also add **lists** to your stream. This can be really useful in monitoring List activity. (See Chapter 5 for more on Twitter lists.) Twitter lists effectively enable you to segment Twitter users or put people, such as your competitors, into lists, so that you can watch conversations without having to follow them. You can see on the previous page that you simply select your profile, select the relevant list and then create a stream – the list will appear as a stream of data on your dashboard. You can then watch what's going on in that list, alongside your social media management.

In Hootsuite you also have the option to create a new list, so you can create lists directly via this platform too.

Step 4: Using Hootsuite to schedule your social media activity

On your dashboard is a mechanism to share information directly via Hootsuite. To compose a message, simply click the top left-hand corner of your dashboard. Click on 'Compose message' and write your message. You can add a URL link and/or an image and then over on the right-hand side of the message box you'll see the range of accounts that you have pulled through, so you can select which accounts are relevant to share that 'message' from.

For example, if you want to send the message to the Michelle Carvill Twitter account, the Carvill Creative Twitter account and post it to the Michelle Carvill LinkedIn Profile too (should the message be relevant to hit all three networks), you can simply create one message and send it to all three networks simply by checking the boxes showing these accounts.

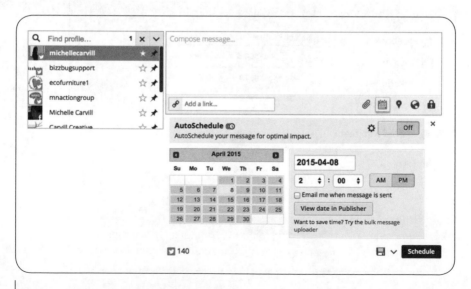

Scheduling activity

If you don't want to send your messages immediately, you can schedule any number of messages to be sent at a later date.

To do this, click the calendar button (which works in the same way conventional online calendars work) and choose your date. There are no limitations on the date – you could schedule something weeks, months or even years ahead! This feature is useful for aligning social activity around a marketing campaign: you can plan your messages and schedule them to fit in with other activities so that there is a concerted and planned push across multiple media.

Once activity is scheduled, you can review and, if relevant, approve any pending messages. Any typos or messages that are irrelevant can easily be amended, rescheduled or removed.

If you are using the Enterprise Version – and have a number of team members all using the same platform – it may be that someone needs to approve the messages before they are deployed. And Hootsuite offers a 'Require Approval' feature too.

You'll also see an AutoSchedule option in the scheduling area. If you switch this feature to On, Hootsuite will endeavour to determine the optimum time to send your messages. This is based on historical activity of the account and when people are engaging with you.

The other great feature is that if you schedule to send one message to numerous accounts, the AutoSchedule feature will automatically stagger the messages, so that your message doesn't hit all accounts/channels at the same time.

Sharing updates to LinkedIn or Facebook via Hootsuite

When sharing an update to either Facebook or LinkedIn via Hootsuite, you still get to say a bit more. These platforms don't have the same 140-character restrictions as Twitter and you'll notice that when you make an update and include LinkedIn or Facebook accounts you still get to say more.

Our advice is always to be as targeted as possible to each audience. People on your Facebook Page will expect a certain dialogue, Twitter is much faster and more fluid, while it's worth remembering that your LinkedIn connections are mainly your professional network, so you may use a totally different tone of voice on that platform.

Be mindful that not all updates will be appropriate for all platforms: one message doesn't fit all. You can still use Hootsuite to manage your Facebook posts or LinkedIn updates, but you can tailor them individually.

Also note that in Facebook your post will show as coming from Hootsuite, so people on Facebook will know that you are using a tool to post to Facebook. Our preference is to post directly to Facebook – using the scheduler on Facebook – particularly as posting directly on Facebook will ensure that your images render correctly – and your audience know that you're directly participating via the channel they are engaging with you on.

Shrinking links and Ow.ly

Twitter and other platforms often limit the amount of information you can include in a status update. Twitter is famous for its 140-character limit. However, there is an easy way of cramming in more information.

For example, let's say you want to include a link to a blog post or article you have found. This is the link: www.carvillcreative.co.uk/blog/how-to-watch-your-competitors-on-twitter-without-them-knowing. It comes in at a whopping 100 characters, which doesn't leave you with very much space to add a compelling headline or your viewpoint. If you paste that link into the link box and hit 'shrink' (all automated for you via Hootsuite), the 100-character link is shortened to just 18 characters: http://ow.ly/e64Km.

There are other URL shrinking tools such as www.bitly.com and http://tinyurl.com, but these are stand-alone websites that aren't built into dashboards, as Ow.ly is on Hootsuite.

Understanding your social media account activity

Measuring activity around your social media accounts is important and can provide some interesting insights. For example, the content that people are engaging with, which posts are getting shared the most, etc. Hootsuite has an Analytics tab – some report services are free while some are paid for.

For example, as we've just discussed the Ow.ly URL shortener, you can see that there are template reports which you can review via Hootsuite. These reports provide you with information around your activity. You can set date ranges and which profile you wish to review.

You can also bring in other analytics to keep all your data in one centralised dashboard. Google Analytics can be brought into Hootsuite, as can Facebook Insights.

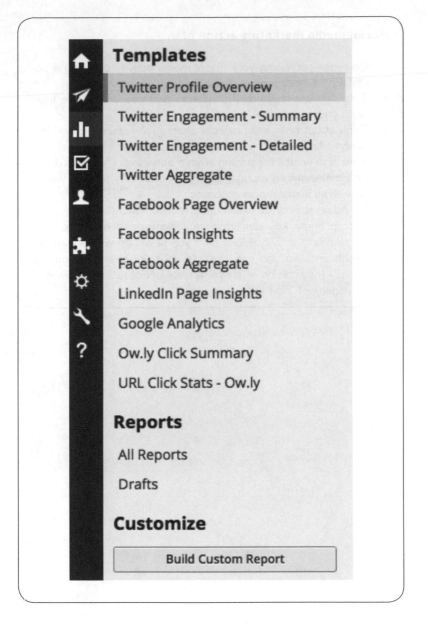

Social dashboards on the move

As we are now in the mobile internet age, it is equally important to be able to manage all your social media channels on the move.

Fortunately, Hootsuite and most of the other dashboards, are available as apps with much of the same functionality as the desktop versions.

This means that as long as you have a mobile signal or WiFi, you can still post, manage, respond and engage via multiple channels.

Social media marketing action plan

- Consider optimising your social media activity by using a social media management dashboard.
- Test different dashboard platforms and see which one best suits your needs.
- Think about both the practical sharing of messages and the analytic functions.
- Tune in to what's happening in your networks. Use your dashboard streams to monitor conversations, lists and keywords as well as social media accounts.
- Schedule activity for maximum effectiveness.
- Set up some key performance indicators to measure your social media activity. Make sure you have app versions of the dashboards so you can manage your social activity on the move – they can be as simple as number of retweets, level of engagement, new followers, etc.

13 | Pulling it all together

> What you will learn from this chapter:
>
> - Understanding how to grow your business
> - Putting together business and marketing strategies
> - Creating a social media 'culture' in your organisation
> - Making sure your website is up to the job
> - Understanding the importance of a content pipeline
> - Finding out about community management
> - Keeping up to date with developments in marketing

Throughout this book, we've kept up the mantra Plan, Listen and Analyse **before** you Engage, then Measure.

- Plan your objectives.
- Do your research.
- Understand what it all means and what you need to get in place.

Before you . . .

- Dive in and Engage.
- And measure performance against your original business objectives.

Be prepared!

As we've highlighted throughout this book, often the planning seems a bit back to front. Because the social channels are relatively simple (and free) to set up and get started on, many organisations rush to get on board with social media, without really thinking the whole game plan through.

Social media activity isn't about doing it for its own sake. It's fundamentally about delivering on your business objectives. It's taking a step back and thinking about the bigger picture.

From a business objectives perspective, an organisation's objectives will be highly specific. However, fundamentally, most businesses are keen to continue to grow. And therefore, there are just four basic principles that sit at the core of most business growth strategies.

1. **Keep customers coming back for more.** Increasing the frequency of purchases; getting customers to keep coming back to you. This could relate to the customer experience, or the fact that the product or service you sell offers a reason for them to keep coming back to you.

2. **Increase average spend – get the customers to buy more.** A great example of this is the classic McDonalds training mantra, '*Would you like fries with that?*' Consistently getting your customers to buy more from you when they do buy. Amazon do this so well with their 'people who bought this also bought . . .', then bundling offers.

3. **Increase the number of customers.** Getting new customers, then – of course – retaining them, increasing frequency of purchase and increasing average spend.

4. **Increase the effectiveness of each process in the business.** Creating effective systems and processes to create significant business efficiencies.

When you look at business objectives with a top-line focus, rather than broken down into specifics, you can see that social media activity lends itself very well to delivering on these key growth objectives.

Let's take each point in turn and see how social networking activity ties in with it.

1 Keep customers coming back for more

Via social media you can have continuous one-to-one and one-to-many conversations. The fact that customers can engage, share ideas, discuss issues directly with the brand or organisation builds a relationship. You can develop a direct dialogue with your audiences – growing loyalty and rapport, giving them a good reason to keep coming back to you.

2 Increase average spend. Get customers to buy more from you

We've already talked about the 'recommendation generation'. People trust what others have to say more than they trust brands and advertising. When customers are on your website and are researching or looking to make buying decisions, if they see social signals from their friends or other people highly recommending or praising a complementary product or service, they are more likely to trust their views than your promotional messages. If they've made a purchase from you and they see rave reviews for a complementary product or service, they may be more inclined to add that product or service to their basket too.

3 Increase the number of customers

The net can be thrown very wide across social networks. The opportunity for fans to spread the message to other fans is vast. The virality of the platforms means that information and offers can be shared at the touch of a button. Whether campaigns are driven by incentive or by the sheer delight of a service engagement, the reach potential is significant. Furthermore, with the advent of social advertising, it is now even easier to reach out to entirely new target audiences.

4 Increase the effectiveness of each process in the business

As we have shown in this book, social media cannot be viewed in isolation from the rest of your marketing strategy. There are also few parts of your organisation that may not be touched in some way by social media – customer relations, sales, marketing, internal communications, HR, recruitment and even the way your business is structured and resourced. We have stressed the importance of having a proper strategy. Any organisation has goals and must look at the various routes to achieve those goals. Without these it is impossible to grow as a business.

One of the key impacts of social media is that all organisations now need to have a proper, defined marketing strategy. Making assumptions about your target audiences and carrying on doing the same types of marketing is foolhardy and could result in disappointment or even business failure.

What we have demonstrated over the preceding chapters is the breadth and sheer creativity of marketing tools required to communicate in the twenty-first century. Any business now needs to use a number of marketing methods – traditional, web-based and social – to achieve its business goals.

We would advise that you adopt a complementary model, where these are used in combination with each other.

Creating a defined marketing strategy

Going right back to our Plan, Listen, Analyse, Engage, Measure model, instead of just focusing on the social media element you need to look at your entire marketing spectrum.

Clearly, your website will be at the heart of your online marketing strategy. It is your most visible online presence (that you own) and is the glue that binds together all your marketing activities.

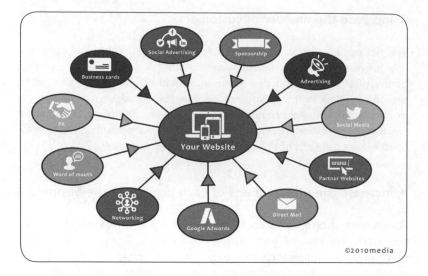

©2010media

Today's websites look very different from those of just five years ago. Responsive (i.e. they work on all devices – mobile, tablets, PCs, smart TVs), socially-enabled and packed full of great content, in effect they are starting to look more like social networks. Which is not really a surprise as customers are getting used to the way that information is delivered to them – simple newsfeeds, swipeable menus and plenty of interaction.

Once you're happy with your website, you then need to decide how all the other tools will work in conjunction with it.

Putting together your strategy

In order to do this properly, there are a number of questions you need to answer as an organisation. We recommend that the management team, senior directors or even the C-suite take time out to make sure they focus clearly on these questions. Some of them are fundamental marketing objectives, but we have added a number of new ones that reflect the changing media environment. (Refer back to Chapter 3 for more advice on strategy.)

- **What are your objectives?** What are you trying to achieve with your marketing?
- **What are your tactics?** What marketing tools will you use to achieve these objectives?
- **What are your key messages?** They should be simple and succinct.

- **Who are your target audience(s)?** Think carefully about the precise demographic you are targeting.
- **Where will you find them?** Don't make assumptions about how they consume social media.
- **Where do you send people?** To a website, landing page, social media site?
- **What's your unique selling point?** You may not have one, but try to focus on one or two. Most of the time it is you and your staff who are unique!
- **What are your keywords?** These are critical to online visibility.
- **How do you get your audience to share?** An integral part of social media campaigns.
- **How do you incentivise your audience?** Give them a reason to like your product or service.
- **How are you going to participate?** It is all about continuous conversations.
- **What are your competitors doing?** Can you do any better?
- **Are you resourced effectively?** Who will assist with marketing? In house or consultancy?
- **What's your compelling content?** Remember, content is king!
- **Does it fit with what your audience want?** Test and measure to see if this is the case.

Once you have looked at all this in detail, you can then start to look at the various channels and marketing tools available to you before putting together your strategy.

Make sure your website is up to the job

We recommend that you take a hard and objective look at your website. Technology is progressing incredibly quickly, and with the advent of mobile internet, around half your audience will be accessing your site from a wide range of smartphones or tablets. So is your website really up to the job? Here's a simple 12-point plan for what your website must be and do.

1. **Easy to read, interesting and pertinent to your target market(s):** This may involve having specific landing pages to focus on these target markets.
2. **Reflect the character and personalities of your company and staff:** People buy from people and very often your only real unique selling point will be those who work for you.
3. **Search engine friendly:** Websites have two audiences: humans and search 'bots'. It is important that your site can be found by the search engines so the humans can read it.

4. **On or close to the first page of search engines for key search terms:** A large proportion of UK websites get no traffic because they don't have a proper SEO and keyword strategy.

5. **Easy to update/have a simple content management system:** You should have control over your website and be able to update it without having to pay costly management fees.

6. **Have a regularly updated and visible news page and/or video feed:** Google is always looking for fresh, keyword-rich content particularly since the introduction of the Hummingbird algorithm in 2013. A news feed or video feed will provide this and reward you with a better position on search engines as well as a heightened awareness of your brand.

7. **Be responsive:** Your site should be built primarily to be seen on mobile devices as well as PCs. It should also look good, no matter what browser you use, whether it's Explorer, Chrome, Firefox or Safari. On 21 April 2015, Google rolled out their mobile-friendly update, boosting the ranking of mobile-friendly pages on mobile search results. So having a mobile-friendly site is now officially important for online visibility.

8. **Have Google Analytics embedded into all pages of your site:** This simple and free tool from Google will tell you how your website is performing as well as indicating what effect social media and other marketing activities are having on your web traffic. Do remember to check the analytics regularly and try to set some key performance indicators to track performance.

9. **Include a strong call to action:** As with any other form of marketing, you should encourage visitors to your site to do something – call, email, visit Facebook or sign up to a newsletter. Ideally this should be in the top right-hand corner of your site.

10. **Fast loading:** With so much choice around, people expect immediate results online. Ensure that you don't lose out on valuable visibility because your site isn't fast enough for searches.

11. **Something you are really proud of:** This is your key shop window. If you're not proud of it, what message are you conveying to your target audiences?

12. **Socially-enabled:** Provides plenty of opportunity for your customers to share information on your website via a range of different social networks

Get your website right, and all your other marketing activities will work better. Get it wrong, and all the time you spend on social media may be in vain. After all, if you are driving people back to a website that doesn't deliver, rather than your activity failing, it's the fundamental call to action that isn't working.

Establish a content strategy

In Chapter 4 we spoke about having a specific content creation strategy. Now that you have an overall marketing strategy and a willingness to engage on social media, it is important to work on the content pipeline.

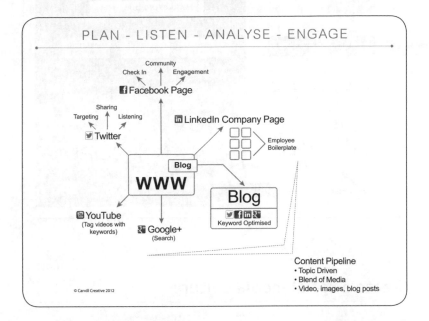

Depending on the number of social media accounts, websites or blogs you manage, there may be a large demand for good, keyword-rich, engaging content and your job is to ensure that there is a steady supply. It's no good having great intentions and setting up a blog or social media accounts only to run out of steam after a few weeks and give up. Think back to the Content Reservoir in Chapter 3. Remember, social media is all about **continuous** conversations.

You will need regular access to information from within your organisation, high-quality images, videos, ideas for news stories, testimonials and well-written blogs. Where is this going to come from and how are you going to ensure the supply is constant? You may even want to create an 'internal newsroom'.

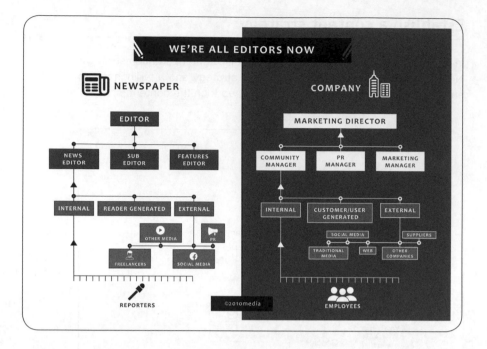

Create a social media culture

Once you have a strategy, have earmarked the social media channels that you will be using to meet your specific business objectives and have identified a viable pipeline for content, it is important that you create the correct culture within your organisation as well as setting down your policies and procedures for engaging on social media. You need to establish:

- terms and conditions for your website and social channels
- HR policy for staff using the internet and social media sites
- guidelines for those adding content to your website, blogs and social media sites
- disclaimers.

IBM's Social Computing Guidelines (www.ibm.com/blogs/zz/en/guidelines.html) are seen as a touchstone for how an organisation should embrace social media. Kodak also has an excellent document (www.kodak.com/US/images/en/corp/aboutKodak/onlineToday/Social_Media_9_8.pdf) outlining its terms of engagement with social media.

We have pulled together our own core principles, which you could adapt to suit your organisation's needs.

1. **What you say is permanent and always accessible. You cannot delete an ill-judged status update or post.** It is virtually impossible to remove something from the internet, so exercise caution when expressing an opinion. Any internet post is visible to a huge mix of colleagues, clients, suppliers, competitors, journalists, etc. and even the most obscure topics will be found, so ensure your social activity stays within the Social Media Guidelines.

2. **Be honest about who you are. Don't pretend to be anybody else.** You must always be honest about who you are – but avoid revealing any personal information. If you are talking about [Company Name], identify yourself as a [Company Name] employee in the content of your post or comment. This is the ethical thing to do, and there may be personal liability under UK law if you don't.

3. **In personal accounts, where relevant, all employees must make it clear that the opinions expressed are their own (and not those of the firm).** Readers *must* know that the opinions expressed are yours rather than [Company Name]'s. You must include a disclaimer notice on every social media profile, e.g. 'Opinions expressed here are my own and do not represent the opinions of [Company Name].' Don't use [Company Name] logos or trademarks unless you have approval to do so.

4. **Be respectful in all communications. Consider how you would like to be treated.** Remember, you have no authority to speak on behalf of [Company Name] (unless this has been explicitly granted), so do not portray yourself as a [Company Name] spokesperson. Despite these caveats, you will be perceived to be the voice of [Company Name], so your actions and behaviours must be appropriate at all times.

5. **Only share information that is in the public domain – never share confidential or sensitive information. Take a common sense approach!** It's clear that certain subjects should not be discussed on social media. If you would not discuss an issue with your friends, why do this openly on the internet? Certain issues should be kept confidential: avoid speculating on future products or services, do not disclose sensitive practice or personal information, and stay within topics that are in the public domain. Be aware of intellectual property issues and avoid discussing financial matters. Rule of thumb: Would you be happy for this information to go out as a press release?

6. **Do not engage in discussions with clients or partners around specific work-in-progress issues.** Where relevant, when you do make a reference, link back to the source. Don't publish anything that might allow inferences to be drawn that could embarrass or damage a client.

7. **Mind your manners and treat everybody with respect.** Treat everybody as you would wish to be treated yourself. Never post materials that could be offensive, abusive, threatening or inappropriate. If a

discussion escalates into a path you don't wish to go down, simply withdraw from the conversation. Respect the fact that others may have different opinions. Don't get into an argument or battle of opinions online. Don't pick fights, and be sure to be the first to correct your own mistakes.

Protect others and never share their personal information, comments or opinions (unless you have their permission). Be careful when introducing someone to an online conversation as this could affect your relationship and may even create legal or confidentiality concerns. Respect your audience. Don't use ethnic slurs, personal insults, obscenity, or engage in any conduct that would not be acceptable in [Company Name]'s workplace. You should also show proper consideration for others' privacy and for topics that may be considered objectionable or inflammatory – such as politics and religion.

8. **Understand when an official response may be necessary.** Some topics or issues may require a formal response from [Company Name]. In that case, quickly raise the issue with your line manager or relevant team member so that it can be effectively dealt with before it gets out of hand. If you have any doubts, speak in the first instance with [Named Contact, Tel. _____].

9. **Critical considerations.** Inappropriate comments (e.g. derogatory, offensive, bullying or discriminatory comments towards employees, ex-employees, staff of clients, [Company Name] managers or team, or any comment that potentially or actually brings the firm into disrepute), whether placed on social media sites during working hours or outside working hours, are a disciplinary offence. Furthermore, depending on the circumstances, a single incident can result in dismissal on grounds of gross misconduct for a first offence. Further details of the disciplinary procedures can be found in the Employee Handbook.

Any breach of these guidelines could be considered a disciplinary issue by [Company Name]. See [Company Name] Handbook for details.

Specific guidelines for social media platforms

Twitter

Twitter corporate: If you are working on one of [Company Name]'s corporate Twitter accounts, you will be acting as the community manager of that account. Therefore, you will be the 'voice' of that account for [Company Name]. This is not a personal account, nor will the person tasked with managing that specific account be named.

Twitter personal: If you have a personal Twitter account and use Twitter for personal use, unless it is agreed that the Twitter personal account will be used as part of [Company Name's] social media strategy the company asks that you ensure a disclaimer notice is added to your account to indemnify any relationship between [Company Name] and that personal account, e.g. 'This is the personal Twitter account of _____. Opinions expressed here are my own.'

Facebook

Facebook corporate: If you are working as the community manager on [Company Name's] corporate Facebook Page, you will be acting as the community manager of that account. Therefore, you will be the 'voice' of that account for [Company Name]. This is not a personal account, nor will the person tasked with managing that specific account be named (unless a specific decision is taken to feature the admin in the About section of the page).

Facebook personal: If you have a personal Facebook account and use Facebook for personal use, the company asks that you ensure that a distinct line is drawn between 'work and play' – for example, the company does not encourage members of staff 'befriending' clients on Facebook. For example, 'My Facebook account is personal and so I do not accept clients or associates from my place of work as friends.'

LinkedIn

LinkedIn personal: [Company Name] advocates that all employees have an up-to-date and an All Star LinkedIn Profile. Where the employee inserts details of being employed by [Company Name] we ask that any references to [Company Name] are made as follows:

First paragraph under Current Experience: [Insert Keyword Optimised 'Boiler Plate' for Company Name].

Second paragraph: Describe current role at [Company Name].

LinkedIn corporate: As above for Facebook corporate.

Get talking!

As explained earlier in the chapter, social media touch many parts of organisations. We recommend that when putting together a marketing strategy for the business, time should also be devoted to creating a co-ordinated approach to communications, internally and externally.

In larger organisations, the management team or heads of departments should have regular meetings to discuss any issues that may have an impact on the business and end up in the social domain. Supply problems, staffing disputes, quality control, customer service and supplier complaints could all end up going public. The sooner you have policies in place to deal with these issues, the better placed you will be to prevent them harming your reputation or your brand.

Alternatively, in a smaller organisation you could have a simple weekly huddle to discuss what's happening in customer services, sales, marketing and product development.

Extract information to share

These meetings could also be useful forums to garner information that could be used as content on your social media sites. You may even consider getting together a group of people in the organisation who can act as your social media committee. Their job would be to ensure a steady supply of information and to ward off potential issues before they arise.

This committee's job could also be to instil in all staff the importance of the business being an open organisation and the value that social media could bring. In effect they would be social media champions.

Responsibility for social media

Whatever the size of your organisation, there needs to be a strict delineation of who is responsible for being your representative on social media. Whether you are a one-man-band or a multinational company, you need to have lines of reporting.

Remember that whoever has responsibility is essentially representing the company online, in the same way that a press office or PR agency would represent them to the traditional media. So they need to be well informed, articulate, able to cope under pressure, creative, good listeners, able to synthesise data and information quickly, and be entirely trustworthy. Fundamentally, they've got to know your business or brand.

If you were thinking about getting an intern or a school leaver to be your 'community manager', think again – as you can see, this is quite a skilled and responsible job. You wouldn't let someone who is a trainee mechanic service your Porsche, so don't hand over such a focused form of marketing to someone who isn't trained.

In fact, depending on your business objectives and how you wish to use social media, you may well require more than one person. Many large organisations now employ entire teams of community managers to handle different social media accounts.

You may decide to keep all your community management in house, or you may decide to outsource it to an external agency. Each approach has its merits, but one thing to bear in mind is that social media is quite personal and, unlike PR, you cannot delegate it entirely to other people to manage. You still need to be proactive, engaged and interested in what is happening, and feed news to your social media managers (be they in-house or external) so they can create relevant content. Even if you've got experts managing the implementation as an extension of your team or brand, it's important that you play a part – and this can be quite time consuming.

Social media community management is a large employment growth area. The role of these staff is solely to manage your social media accounts and devote the necessary time to them in order to deliver on your strategic objectives.

You may consider hiring someone to perform this function, in which case you need to think about the qualities involved. It is vital that your organisation is open to being proactive on social media or, no matter who you have to manage your accounts, they will not have the necessary buy-in to be able to do their job properly. This also applies to any organisation that has outsourced their marketing or PR to an outside agency. Ask yourself: 'Do they have the necessary skills to manage your social media accounts – are they a true extension of my team?'

A typical day of social media activity

Here's a very quick guide to how to go about effective daily social management for general awareness. This schedule is by no means prescriptive and you can work the timings around your organisation's specific requirements.

Clearly, your activity will focus on the objective of specific social media accounts. For example, if your Twitter account is for customer support you'd refine it in line with customer support requirements. Similarly, if Facebook is being used to generate sales leads, mould it to these needs.

Note: Anyone who is managing social media accounts MUST have a suitable mobile device with all applicable apps. Marketing is now something no longer confined to the office so community managers need to be able to work anywhere and in fact at any time, if needs be!

This schedule relates to a 'general' awareness, daily PR focus. For each account:

8.30 a.m. – 9.00 a.m. (Or possibly earlier, if you can do this via your mobile device during your commute to work.) Review account activity: check for mentions, direct messages and what your followers are talking about – respond, thank, retweet, engage and react accordingly. How long this takes will depend on your level of 'engagement' and on how many accounts you have. So you may have to revise your timescales here a little.

9.00 a.m. – 10.00 a.m. Scout all relevant trade press, review your Google Alerts, keyword tracking in Hootsuite, Twitter search and relevant blogs and portals that you subscribe to, and review any up-to-date and relevant news. Speak to the marketing/sales team or, if relevant, the senior management team and ensure you're up to date on any marketing activities, business news and promotions that can also be shared on your account(s).

9.00 a.m. – 11.00 a.m. At the same time as researching, schedule your day's content into Hootsuite (or other social dashboard), blog or Facebook Page. Don't schedule all these updates to follow one another so that you block up your audiences' feeds: spread them out, usually at hourly intervals – and if it's big news, don't be afraid to repeat the message on Twitter, but be sure to give it a different 'spin'. With a well thought through social media strategy, you'll also have some key influencers or target audiences to engage with. Each day you should set some time to ensure you are locating, targeting and engaging with relevant connections – to grow your networks in a targeted and purposeful way. Remember, on platforms such as Twitter, you can't simply follow hundreds of people at a time – you first have to engender engagement and get others to follow you to work in line with the follower to followed ratio. Focused activity, little and often is our advice.

11.00 a.m. – 11.15 a.m. Check accounts and alerts to review any activity, mentions, retweets, etc., and any engagement.

11.15 a.m. – 1 p.m. Content creation. This activity and the timescale related to it will vary according to how many blogs you're writing and what content (if any) you are creating. You may have determined to create at least one blog post a day – if so, this is your time to create.

Throughout the afternoon . . . Keep watching those alerts, mentions and engagement.

The busiest time is changing . . .

The times when people are most active on social media are changing. At one time, most activity happened in the afternoon and engagement levels were generally higher. With the emergence of smartphones and social apps activity is shifting. Early morning (commuter time), between 6.30 a.m. and 8.30 a.m., is now a busy period for social activity. Lunchtimes are also busy; then there is another spike at the end of the day – 6.00 p.m. to around 7.30 p.m. So be mindful of this when scheduling your updates and looking at engagement. Most Facebook posts get engagement between 11.00 a.m. and 4.00 p.m. and after working hours. So test, measure and learn what's working on the timing front for your organisation. Facebook insights, Hootsuite and LinkedIn analytics will provide you with plenty of information to help you understand when the best time to post is.

Finally, remember that each account is an important communication channel and you are acting as 'brand custodian'. It's not just about pushing messages out but more about sharing the personality of the brand as well as engaging and communicating with your audiences.

Staying ahead of the curve with your marketing

The world is changing, technology is constantly evolving and the world's consumption of the media is in a constant state of flux. It is vital that you stay vigilant and keep on top of these changes so that you can make sure that your company is equipped to adapt.

Marketing methods come and go, and so will social media sites. While Facebook may have over 1.4 billion users now, it may fall out of favour and a new network take its place, much as happened to MySpace in the mid-2000s.

One of the cornerstones of marketing is the need to test and measure. Keep reviewing your sales figures, the analytics from your website and the return from your social media channels. See if you can spot any emerging trends or areas in which you need to improve.

Once you have a social media marketing strategy, keep updating and adapting it to the changing times. You may need to overhaul it completely every year, depending on what is happening to your customer base.

At the time of writing, it is impossible to predict what may happen in the coming years. We may see a time when the main channels start charging subscriptions, or we could end up seeing the social networks moving into the marketing verticals or becoming more geographically based (e.g. Twitter.co.uk, Facebook.fr).

There will also always be entrepreneurs and innovators coming up with new ways of communicating, so expect more social networks, more mobile-based applications and better ways of tracking customer movements. With the progression of 4G technology as well as near field communication (NFC), brands and organisations have never had so many ways of engaging with a potentially global audience.

The trick is to harness the technology and understand how to use it correctly. Many companies will also have to change dramatically their approach not only to communications but the way they do business. Becoming a social and easily digital adaptive organisation is no easy feat and it may involve a high amount of resistance. However, the world is changing fast and cheetahs will outrun the sloths.

The other thing to keep in mind is that whilst these channels have been around for a number of years now, we're not yet into decades. From a business strategy perspective, these channels are relatively new and learned best practices and models are fertile territory.

Effectively, we're all learning together.

To end

Developments in social media are moving at such a rapid rate that by the time this book is published, some of it will, alas, already be out of date!

However, fear not – we will keep you constantly updated via the blog we've created to run alongside this book (www.thebusinessofbeingsocial.co.uk) via Twitter (@BOBSthebook) and via our own Twitter accounts @michellecarvill and @savvysocialDT

Join us on the journey and we hope you'll gain as much from social media as we have. As we said earlier – let's learn together.

Social media marketing action plan

- Institute a full review into your business to establish your strategic goals.
- Create a fully integrated marketing strategy, including social media, to achieve these goals.
- Make sure your website is up to the job and mobile friendly.
- Work towards creating a social media culture in your organisation.
- Ensure you have a decent content pipeline.
- Test and measure – everything.
- Stay informed and never assume that things will stay the same – business agility is key.

Social media glossary

Twitter

@username: The name you choose to represent yourself on Twitter, this is shown at the beginning of all your tweets and starts with the @ sign.

Direct message: A private message to somebody who is following you on Twitter. A direct message can only be sent to somebody who is following you. You can do this by putting d (not DM) in front of their Twitter name, e.g. d @michellecarvill. Using social dashboards such as Hootsuite enables you to send a direct message as one of the standard message features.

Follower: Someone on Twitter who is interested in watching/listening and 'following' what you tweet. They 'follow' your tweets from their account and automatically see your Twitter updates.

Following: When you follow someone else on Twitter. You automatically see their Twitter updates.

Handle: The @username is also sometimes referred to as your Twitter 'handle' (an old CB radio term).

Hashtag (#): The # can be used to categorise your tweet to a particular topic. Then someone searching for the topic will see your tweet. For example, if I were to tweet about this glossary I could hashtag the tweet #twittertips. (For more on hashtags, see www.carvillcreative.co.uk/blog/demystifying-the-hashtag-and-how-to-leverage-on-twitter.)

Klout: Your Klout score demonstrates how your influence is measured on Twitter. It starts at zero and the more people who tweet you, share your tweets on and retweet you etc., the higher your score becomes. Klout is deemed by some as an unfair measure of reach and engagement on Twitter as it measures only basic sharing – fluctuations in Klout scores are often not focused on too heavily.

Locking your profile: You can lock your Twitter profile so that only people you allow to follow you will see your Twitter updates.

Mentions: This is how you can tell if somebody has directly tweeted you, by writing @your username in front of their tweet. You can pick up their message under your 'Mentions'. (Mentions are recorded in a number of Twitter management platforms.)

Microblog: Tweeting is sometimes referred to as microblogging – you are effectively writing a 140-character mini-blog.

Retweet (RT): A retweet is used to repeat a specific tweet. It can be used to reiterate what somebody else has said in agreement or to show all your followers a tweet that you are replying to.

Social dashboard: A dashboard where you bring in all your Twitter feeds into one central place so that you can manage multiple accounts more effectively. Common dashboards include www.hootsuite.com, www.tweetdeck.com and www.cotweet.com.

Tactical retweets: Retweeting the tweet of somebody you want to notice you and follow you back or retweet your tweets.

Targeted followers: Targeting the people who listen to your tweets for a purpose and following people you want to follow you back.

Tiny URL: This is the name of one website that shortens your URL so that you don't take up too many of your 140 characters with a link (http://tinyurl.com). There are others, including bit.ly.com. Twitter management platforms such as Tweetdeck, Hootsuite and CoTweet either have their own URL-shortening programs or use the more common ones.

Trends: Popular subjects that are being tweeted about; categorised by the hashtag (#). For example, this glossary would appear in the trend #twittertips because that's the subject we have categorised (hashtagged) it to in our tweet.

Tweet: A message (maximum length 140 characters) sent via Twitter.

Tweeter: Somebody who uses Twitter.

Twitter cards: You can add rich content to your tweets which are then designed to maximise traffic through to your website.

Twitter chat: When a group of users on Twitter connect and converse not by following one another, but by following a # around a conversation, e.g. #blogchat or #usguys. These are ongoing conversations, often held at a specific date and time each week or month.

Twitter lists: You can sort your followers into segments by creating lists so that you can better organise your Twitter thread. See here for how to create and manage Twitter lists: www.carvillcreative.co.uk/blog/twitter-lists---what-they-are-and-how-to-use-them-effectively.

Facebook

Algorithm: A scientific formula developed by Facebook to govern what is displayed (and how high) on the news feed.

Boost: A way of targeting your content to a specific audience using Facebook advertising.

Business timeline/business page: A business timeline is not a profile. This is a way to promote a business or brand (not an individual) on Facebook through your personal profile. You cannot become friends with a business timeline, you can only Like it.

Cover photo: A large photo (850 × 315 pixels) that stretches across the top of your timeline, like a banner, just above your profile picture. Cover photos will remain public, even if all the rest of your photos are private. Be aware that there are some strict guidelines on the cover photo for your business timeline (see www.facebook.com/page-guidelines.php).

Facebook personal timeline: Your timeline represents you personally and not as a business. It is your own personal profile, in which people can see a 'timeline' of your activity, photos and wall posts since you joined Facebook. It is a way to share information about yourself with others in order to socialise and network.

Friends lists/smart lists/close friends: A way of organising your 'friends' into lists giving you options as to who sees what.

Friends: Other people on Facebook who want to link themselves to your profile and follow your activity.

Group: Usually created by brands, companies, organisations and individuals to drum up support or to promote something. You can Like a group and/or become a member of that group.

Insights: Analytics that show how a user's Facebook Page is performing. Shows interaction, users and reach.

Like: If you Like something on Facebook it means that you approve of whatever is being represented, promoted, shown or discussed. You can Like videos, statuses, business pages, people, photos, groups and discussions.

Network: A group of people who have joined together on Facebook who have something in common, usually a business, school or university network.

Notifications: Facebook notifies you with optional messages that let you know if any activity has occurred on your Facebook.

Page Manager: This app allows you to control your Page from your mobile device.

Page Timeline: Appears in browser versions of Facebook and shows key milestones since your company or organisation was founded.

Poke: If you poke somebody on Facebook you are interacting with them, you are virtually 'poking' them It's as simple as that.

Profile picture: A small picture (200 pixels wide) that appears on your personal or business timeline. It will appear on the site to represent you whenever you comment, post or Like anything on Facebook. Your profile picture on a business timeline is most likely to be your logo or company branding, whereas on your personal timeline it will probably be a picture of you.

Status update: This is described by Facebook as the way you can 'give positive feedback and connect with the things you care about'. Status updates contain information that you want to share with people connected to your Timeline – personal or business-related. The status may contain a picture, link or video.

Story bumping: Allows fans of your Page to subscribe to your updates.

Stream: This is where all activity is logged instantaneously from your friends' personal profiles, business pages and groups you have liked. It is a way of keeping up to date with everything that is going on in Facebook.

Tagging: Being mentioned in a status update or identified in a picture. You are notified when you have been tagged.

Wall: This appears in your Facebook timeline. It's a space that allows other people on Facebook to post messages to you that everybody can see.

LinkedIn

1st-degree connections: Direct connections with people who you know on a personal level.

2nd-degree connections: Connections to your 1st-degree connections.

3rd-degree connections: Connections to your 2nd-degree connections.

Company profile: A company profile is connected to the employees/people related to it. Company profiles can be populated with products and service information.

Connections: Similar to friends on Facebook, 'connections' is the term used when you link yourself to other people you wish to be associated with on LinkedIn.

Endorsements: These are a simpler way of recommending your connections by endorsing them either for the skills they have on their profile or skills you think they have.

Groups: Groups on LinkedIn allow professionals to advance their careers by sharing expertise, experience and knowledge on a specific subject. You can search groups and join relevant groups or create your own groups.

InMail: This is a message that can be sent to people that you are not connected to in the paid-for version of LinkedIn.

Introduction: Messages that allow members to contact you or be contacted through a shared or mutual connection.

Invitation: An invitation sent to an existing member of LinkedIn to join a network.

Networks: A group of LinkedIn users who can contact you. They can be up to three connections away.

Profile: Your personal profile, in which you can showcase your expertise, skills and recommendations. It's your personal brand.

Pulse: LinkedIn's own news service which includes articles from thought leaders, those in selected industries and of course your own content.

Recommendations: This is when somebody is recommended on LinkedIn. Users usually ask business partners, colleagues or service providers or clients to 'recommend them'. They are effectively online referrals/testimonials.

Relationship: The tab underneath your connection's profile picture. Allows you to use LinkedIn as a CRM tool.

Showcase Pages: These are like 'microsites' off the main Company Page. They can have their own followers and content as well as working with social advertising.

Summary: This is similar to your elevator pitch. Up to 2,000 characters in length, with the option of adding rich content such as slides and videos, this is a way to tell users who you are, what you have done in your career and what makes you different as a professional.